The Storied Landscape
of Iroquoia

BORDERLANDS AND TRANSCULTURAL STUDIES

Series Editors:

Pekka Hämäläinen
Paul Spickard

CHAD L. ANDERSON

The Storied Landscape of Iroquoia

History, Conquest, and Memory in the Native Northeast

University of Nebraska Press | Lincoln

Library of Congress Cataloging-in-Publication Data
Names: Anderson, Chad (Chad L.), author.
Title: The storied landscape of Iroquoia: history, conquest, and memory in the Native northeast / Chad Anderson.
Other titles: Borderlands and transcultural studies.
Description: Lincoln: University of Nebraska Press, [2020] |
Series: Borderlands and transcultural studies |
Includes bibliographical references and index.
Identifiers: LCCN 2019035379
ISBN 9781496218650 (hardback)
ISBN 9781496221247 (epub)
ISBN 9781496221254 (mobi)
ISBN 9781496221261 (pdf)
Subjects: LCSH: Six Nations—History—18th century.
| Iroquois Indians—New York (State)—History—18th century. | Iroquois Indians—Colonization—New York (State)—History—18th century.
Classification: LCC E99.17 A637 2020 |
DDC 974.7004/9755—dc23
LC record available at https://lccn.loc.gov/2019035379

Set in Sabon Next LT Pro by Mikala R. Kolander.

For my parents, Leonard and Vicki
And for Brandie and Elizabeth

| Contents

List of Figures | ix

Acknowledgments | xi

Introduction: Reading the Early American Landscape | 1

1. Visions of the Great Island | 17

2. Predators of the Vanishing Landscape | 47

3. The Many Deaths of John Montour and the Mystery of the Painted Post | 75

4. The Decline and Fall of the Romans of the West | 113

5. The Burned-Over District | 155

Conclusion: Storied Monuments | 179

Notes | 199

Bibliography | 227

Index | 255

| Figures

1. Detail of John Mitchell, *A Map of the British and French Dominions in North America* (1755) | 2

2. Detail of Lewis Evans, *A General Map of the Middle British Colonies in North America* (1755) | 5

3. Guy Johnson, *The Country of the Six Nations* (1771) | 8

4. David Cusick, "Stonish Giants" | 36

5. [Benjamin C. Vanduzee], "First Sketch of the Pioneer" | 65

6. [Benjamin C. Vanduzee], "Second Sketch of the Pioneer" | 65

7. [Benjamin C. Vanduzee], "Third Sketch of the Pioneer" | 66

8. [Benjamin C. Vanduzee], "Fourth Sketch of the Pioneer" | 66

9. Benson John Lossing, "Queen Esther's Rock" | 91

10. Simeon De Witt, *Map of the State of New York* (1802) | 127

| Acknowledgments

My journey in writing this book has taken me from the sun-drenched landscapes of Northern California, Davis, and then Sacramento, to the slightly less sunny (but still pleasant) hills of Oneonta. Along the way I have met generous people who have offered their time, knowledge, and encouragement which made completing this work possible. This research began when I was a graduate student at UC Davis and had the good fortune to have Alan Taylor as a dissertation adviser. Ari Kelman has been a constant source of sage advice and encouragement. At an important moment for my academic career and research, Ellen Hartigan-O'Connor offered excellent suggestions and helped guide my work. Funding from the Department of History and a fellowship from the UC Davis Humanities Institute greatly helped to provide the time to conduct research.

Davis during my graduate school years was a special time and place, full of energy. I arrived to find a cohort of exceptionally talented scholars, who have become invaluable friends and colleagues, especially Jakub Beneš, Jordan Lauhon, Bob Reinhardt, and Paul Richter. Miles Powell charted the Cache Creek backcountry and has also spent hours reading my writing. In this storied landscape a trail of rewarding memories connects the seminar rooms of Davis to Napa Valley, Point Reyes, Plainfield, Donner Summit, and Yosemite. You might need the right guide to see it, but the tales are there.

A book of this scope necessarily relies heavily on the thoughtful work of many other scholars, and I am grateful for the work done by those listed throughout the endnotes. I first encountered the Montours in James Merrell's excellent scholarship, and he graciously agreed to read my attempt to solve another Montour mystery and encouraged me to make a stronger argument.

At Hartwick College I would like to thank my colleagues in the History Department for their support of my career over the past three years as I completed this book: Kyle Burke, Cherilyn Lacy, Edythe Quinn, Mieko Nishida, and Peter Wallace. I would also like to thank Shelley Wallace for her help in the archives and preparing images.

At the University of Nebraska Press I have been extremely fortunate to have Matt Bokovoy as an editor. Preparing this manuscript for publication has benefited from the expert work of Ann Baker, Heather Stauffer, Andrea Shahan, and my copyeditor, Elaine Otto. I would also like to thank Pekka Hämäläinen for his support of my work in this excellent series. Finally, I am also grateful for the thoughtful comments provided by Robert Jarvenpa and an anonymous reviewer.

Friends of many times and places have listened to my ideas over the many years it took to complete this book: Sam Alexandroni, Luke and Nisha Anderson, Rosana Avila, Keith and Amanda Banks, Kevin Brewer, Steve Cote, Conor and Katelyn Foley, J. V. Loperfido and Kim Lamon-Loperfido, Charlie Mastny, Mike Murphy, Jeff and Katie Perez, Nathaniel Shriver, Justin Teske, and Bryan and Katherine Ott.

Finally, this book simply would not have been possible without the support of my family. As anyone who has recently attempted a career in academia knows, it can be rewarding, but the path is not always easy. My parents, Leonard and Vicki, have always supported my academic goals, even as this dream took me from Minnesota to California. Brandie and Bruno accompanied me on my second time traveling Interstate 80 across the country. In Cooperstown we welcomed Elizabeth to our family. I am thankful for our past and future adventures together, wherever that road may lead.

The Storied Landscape
of Iroquoia

| Introduction

Reading the Early American Landscape

This is a book about the heart of North America during the eighteenth and early nineteenth centuries, specifically the homelands of the Haudenosaunee (Iroquois Six Nations), with a particular focus on the region's built and natural landscape and the important places that one would encounter there. If you want to locate and possibly understand such a region, a good way to start is with a map—a visual interpretation of that landscape. Ideally this map would be created by those with expert knowledge of the terrain, namely, the Haudenosaunee. Unfortunately, although Native Americans were instrumental in the creation of Europeans' geographic knowledge and sometimes specific maps, Europeans often fully or partially erased this authorship as they recorded their guides' words and printed the maps. Therefore, as we chart a journey to a past land, we must consistently read against the designs of outsiders who had their own interpretations and dreams about the continent's future, whether drawn on maps or described in travel narratives. One such outsider was British cartographer John Mitchell, who resided on the other side of the Atlantic Ocean, far outside of Native North America. During the mid-eighteenth century, no map of North America attracted more attention than his *Map of the British and French Dominions in North America*. Mitchell completed his work after the Seven Years' War—a contest to define

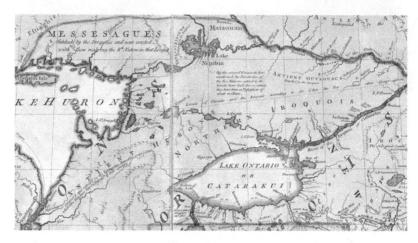

Fig. 1. Detail from John Mitchell, *A Map of the British and French Dominions in North America* (1755). Library of Congress, Geography and Maps Division.

much of the continent's future—had already begun. One of the great achievements in eighteenth-century cartography, Mitchell's map was bold. At the height of the most extensive war the world had yet seen, Mitchell drew British colonial borders clear across the North American continent, through lands actually controlled by Native Americans and also claimed by Britain's chief rival, France. Mitchell's map can be dismissed as an outrageous attempt to lie about the reach of the British empire in North America. Yet this exaggeration points to the essential lesson about studying the extent of Native North America: things are not always what they seem to be (fig. 1).[1]

Upon closer inspection, it becomes clear that Mitchell's map has a more complicated story to tell about North America's history, and that story always involved Native Americans and their built environment. More than two hundred Native American settlements appeared on Mitchell's map, and the cartographer could spin just about any Indian village into an ally of the British empire, thereby stretching that empire across the continent. Bordering on the absurd, his confidence actually exposed the tenuous claim of the British to North America. Mitchell's distortions revealed an essential truth: after 150 years, the English and their descendants had actually done very little to change most of the

North American built landscape, even as Eurasian diseases, plants, and animals wrought profound changes upon the continent's ecology and peoples. Despite Mitchell's fantastic borders, across most of North America, Native Americans continued to define the nature of settlement and to shape the lands around those villages, as his map clearly indicated. As such, what appears at first glance to be a symbol of European control, the ability to represent the geography of North America, reflects much of the power of American Indians or, in the language of historians, their "agency."[2]

Although hundreds of Native American villages appeared on his map, Mitchell's paragraphs of explanations often point back to one group in particular: the Haudenosaunee, a confederacy of culturally related but distinct Indian peoples that include the Mohawk, Oneida, Onondaga, Cayuga, Seneca, and Tuscarora (who joined in 1722). Haudenosaunee means "people of the longhouse," in reference to their traditional form of housing, which is how the Six Nations refer to themselves today, but they are also frequently known as the Iroquois. As ancient occupiers of the land, the Haudenosaunee had formed their confederacy by 1500, shortly before their contact with Europeans. For centuries, they had lived in substantial villages, ranging in size from a few homes to hundreds of individuals in what is now central and western New York State. Their villages were largely supported by nearby fields of corn, beans, and squash. A complex series of trails connected these villages and the waterways of eastern North America. Throughout the period of European colonization, the Haudenosaunee remained the dominant power in their homelands and important diplomatic players in the struggle for the continent.[3]

In their own languages, the Five Nations' names reflected a strong attachment to their homelands. The Seneca call themselves Notowa'ka, or Great Hill People. The Cayuga have a few names related to places, including Kayohkno'nq?, variously translated as "People at the Landing," or "Where the Boats Were Taken Out," in reference to a landing spot for canoes on Cayuga Lake. Today the Cayuga Nation goes by People of the Great Swamp. The Onondaga share a similar name with the Seneca, calling themselves Onota?keka?, which means People on the Hill. The Onondaga and Seneca names reflected the tendency of the early Haudenosaunee to settle on fortified hilltops. The Oneida are Onyota'a:ka, or People of the Standing Stone, after a sacred stone (or stones) that represented their identity as a people. In 1796 two American travelers, Jeremy Belknap and Jedidiah Morse, saw one of these stones near Kanonwalohale (Oneida Castle). An elderly man named Silversmith explained to the pair of travelers that this stone "follows the nation in their removals." When the Oneida established a village, they likely chose a stone to symbolize their people. Lastly, the Mohawk are Kanyuʔkeha:ka, or People of the Flint. Anthropologists and historians often refer to these Haudenosaunee homelands as Iroquoia.[4]

Occupying a strategic position between New France and Britain's coastal colonies, these homelands constituted an especially favorable geographic position for an Indian confederacy in eighteenth-century North America. The great historian of Haudenosaunee diplomacy, Francis Jennings, noted that a "division by watersheds" defined Iroquoia. In the east, during the mid-1620s, the Mohawk fought against a neighboring people, the Mahican, and gained control of a north-south corridor between Albany and Montreal. This valuable route consisted of two waterways, one leading to the Dutch (and then to the English) and the other to New France (see fig. 2). First, the Hudson River flows south through Albany to New York City. Just north of where the Hudson turns toward Albany, Lake George provides a northerly route between the Adirondack and Green Mountains, eventually flowing into Lake Champlain, which flows into the Richelieu River and takes a traveler to the St. Lawrence. A second key route, the eastward flowing Mohawk River, led west from the Hudson Valley and into the Haudenosaunee's heartlands. This eastward flowing river led to the "Oneida Carrying Place," a portage between the Mohawk and Wood Creek, which eventually took travelers to Oneida Lake and Lake Ontario beyond it. Finally, the Haudenosaunee had important outlets to the south and west. To the south of the Mohawk River valley, the Allegheny Plateau dominates the southern margins of Iroquoia. Cutting through this plateau, an equally impressive number of streams drain into the Susquehanna River. Originating in Otsego

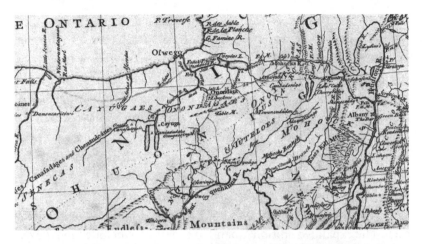

Fig. 2. Detail from Lewis Evans, *A General Map of the Middle British Colonies in North America* (1755). Library of Congress, Geography and Maps Division.

Lake, the Susquehanna provided a southern gateway all the way to the Chesapeake Bay. And it was not far from the western boundaries of the Susquehanna watershed to the Allegheny River, which joins with the Monongahela River at present-day Pittsburgh and flows into the Ohio River, the gateway to lands coveted by Europeans from the colonial period to the early American republic. Consequently, even after British victory in the Seven Years' War and its conquest of New France, the Haudenosaunee remained a potentially important connection (or barrier) to other Indian nations and lands in America's interior, especially in the Ohio and Great Lakes regions.[5]

At the height of the Seven Years' War, Iroquoia was arguably the most important component to the imperial geography of eastern North America. Although rooted in specific homelands, Haudenosaunee influence and territorial claims stretched far beyond the boundaries of what is now New York State. The Haudenosaunee's actions helped convince Mitchell that through seventeenth-century wars and eighteenth-century diplomatic positioning, they had established an Indian empire in eastern North America, a notion he was eager to accept. Beginning in the 1670s, the English and Haudenosaunee established a complicated alliance, known as the Covenant Chain.

The English liked to proclaim that the Haudenosaunee were politically "dependent" on them, specifically through the Haudenosaunee's relationship with the colony of New York, and therefore Haudenosaunee conquests became English lands. To the west, these alleged conquests extended to the Mississippi River. South to north, Haudenosaunee claimed lands ranging from the Ohio Country to what is now southern Ontario. These conquests dominated Mitchell's map and appeared in influential books. New York politician Cadwallader Colden articulated this imagined mix of conquest and dependency in *The History of the Five Nations of Canada, Which are Dependent on the Province of New York in America*, published in two parts (1727 and 1747). The expanded edition amended the title to include "*and are the Barrier between the English and French in that Part of the World*," which reflected the essential geographic and political position of the mid-eighteenth-century Haudenosaunee.[6]

Yet this empire within an empire was not a purely English fantasy. The Haudenosaunee did much to shape English views of this empire's geography and function. For example, at a 1701 conference at Albany, Haudenosaunee representatives helped to draw a map outlining allegedly conquered lands near the Great Lakes that they placed under English protection. Supporting these claims during the 1740s and 1750s, Haudenosaunee representatives dubiously claimed that the Mississauga, inhabitants of those and additional lands to the north, had joined the league. Mitchell later added this land to his imagined empire that pushed well into New France (see fig. 1, which depicts present-day Ontario, north of Lakes Erie, Ontario, and Huron). By the mid-eighteenth century, Iroquoia's boundaries were a tangled mix of British and Haudenosaunee designs.[7]

Historians have long debated the extent of actual Haudenosaunee power over their neighbors, but they generally conclude that both the British and Haudenosaunee overstated this reach. Moreover, to be sure, the Haudenosaunee had no centralized state, let alone a king in the European fashion. However, like the powerful Comanche in the Southwest and the nineteenth-century Lakota on the Great Plains, the Haudenosaunee leveraged their geography, access to European technology, and political skill to establish one of several long-lasting "shapes of power" in North America, as one historian has recently put it. Haudenosaunee influence radiated far beyond Iroquoia and helped to shape the imperial contest for North America from the seventeenth century through the American Revolution. Most infamously, a group of well-connected Virginia land speculators, the Ohio Company, relied upon alleged Haudenosaunee control of the contested Ohio River Country to begin building forts on land the French (and other Indian nations) claimed, which, in turn, sparked the Seven Years' War. Consequently, there are no easily defined geographic boundaries for Iroquoia or its meaningful places. Nevertheless, the imprint of the Haudenosaunee became clearer as one traveled closer to their traditional homelands near the Mohawk River valley and the Finger Lakes.[8]

Again and again Mitchell's map suggests that if we want to understand eastern North America in the eighteenth century, we need to follow the road to these homelands and specifically Onondaga, the village at the heart of the Haudenosaunee's political world. But how do you get to this "capital" and what was there? Surprisingly, for a cartographer who built a British empire on Haudenosaunee claims, Mitchell had relatively little information to convey about Iroquoia itself. Few Haudenosaunee villages or trails appeared on his map. He was not alone in lacking detail on Iroquoia's built environment. Despite having been guided into Iroquoia, Mitchell's contemporary, Lewis Evans, also suffered from a lack of knowledge. In his *A General Map of the Middle British Colonies in North America* (1755), Evans included a few notable villages, such as Onondaga, which he had visited. Seneca country, however, remained relatively blank, with only a few notable settlements (see fig. 2). It was only with the appearance of Guy Johnson's map in 1771 that outsiders caught a glimpse of the extent of Iroquoia's villages and trail networks (see fig. 3). These maps consistently revealed Haudenosaunee power over geographic knowledge, as few Euro-Americans gained access to Iroquoia and its secrets.

This relatively blank space—on European maps but not in reality—reflected the paradox of Iroquoia at the height of the imperial contest for North America: it was simultaneously the heart of that struggle

Fig. 3. Guy Johnson, *The Country of the Six Nations* (1771).
New York Public Library.

and relatively unknown to outsiders. For more than a century, from New France south through the English colonies, Europeans had come to know and fear the Haudenosaunee. Yet few of them knew much of the Haudenosaunee's homeland itself: the history of its villages, the names of its places, and the stories attached to this landscape. Whatever was there, as the significance of an "Iroquois empire" hinted, it must be important and full of history. Of course, the Haudenosaunee knew that their homelands contained much meaning, ranging from places connected to their origin mythologies to recent village sites, but only a few Euro-American travelers and missionaries caught imperfect glimpses of this landscape as it existed prior to the Revolution. This mix of storied history and outsider ignorance would prove to be fertile ground for a contested process of imagining and reimagining Iroquoia's past, present, and future.[9]

Beyond structures and fields, Haudenosaunee settlements contained important cultural meanings and history. Historians, anthropologists, geographers, and other scholars emphasize that humans create an imagined landscape to correspond with the physical one. As individuals and as societies, people connect memories and even their identities to specific places, landmarks, buildings, and monuments. Naming, shaping, remembering—all societies were engaged in these activities, but this process is especially important for nonliterate cultures who can point to physical reminders of their remembered past. Uncovering this history requires access to networks of storytelling. Even obvious marks upon the land, such as a monument, pose challenges to visitors who must depend on the willingness of Native guides to share stories about the meaning of such an object. More challenging still, the less physical traces of the past easily escape notice. Scholars have emphasized the richness of place-names, which are essential aspects of people's attachment to the land but require cultural-specific knowledge to decipher. For example, remarkable recent scholarship on the Pacific Northwest has documented Cayuse, Umatilla, and Walla Walla place-names that speak to centuries of human occupation and understanding of the landscape, ranging from natural resource use to locations associated with mythical stories. The study of place-names points to the challenges in attaching history to landscape. For an outsider, a visit to such a location may be unremarkable. A natural feature—a hill, a tree, a bend in the river—may be indistinguishable from its surroundings. Yet if an important event occurred at that spot, those who know the story have no difficulty pointing to the obviously distinct landmark.[10]

Here is where the usefulness of British maps ends. They established the significance of the Native American landscape to the broader Atlantic world but could only hint at the layers of stories written onto the built and natural environment of eastern North America. These layers of history were anchored by specific places, with often overlapping and debated meanings among Native Americans and European newcomers. For instance, on his map, Lewis Evans suggested some of these layers as well as the limits of cartographic interpretation. Near the Ohio River he wrote, "Elephants Bones found here." More than a simple curiosity, this place was what Europeans and Native Americans eventually called "The Big Bone Lick," not far from present-day Cincinnati. Naturalists would eventually examine mastodon remains found there to prove that these remains belonged to an extinct species (that is, not elephants). Europeans knew of the location as a landmark during travel and as a source of natural history. For some of the Haudenosaunee, however, the place had a profoundly different meaning, at least by the years surrounding the Seven Years' War. Their oral traditions pointed to an apocalyptic mythical being, confined within a specific nearby hill, who could eventually be unleashed upon inhabitants of North America who had grown too close to Europeans and their ways. Or perhaps this hill marked doom for the unsuspecting Europeans, depending on the storyteller. In effect, this place represented the uneasiness of Native peoples at a temporal and geographic crossroads of empire in North America. With its terse explanation, Evans's map could hardly convey the true meaning of this and other Native American places.

Beyond specific places, the built and natural landscape as a whole played a profoundly important role in imagining and reimagining the Native American settlement and European conquest of North America. The eventual Euro-American conquest of North America, which took more than three centuries to complete, has greatly shaped who gets remembered as a *settler*, a label typically reserved for Europeans moving westward. Yet eighteenth-century evidence indicates that both Natives and newcomers spent much time thinking about the distinction between farming (settlements) and wild areas (the "woods") of the Northeast. The Haudenosaunee traced the arrival of agriculture back to their mythological origin stories, some centered on specific places within Iroquoia. They also distinguished between the forest, the domain of powerful, supernatural, other-than-human beings, and the clearing, where humans settled. On the other hand, historians have emphasized that the English viewed North America as an empty continent, as an unused wilderness in need of farming settlers. To be sure, this powerful cultural strain had a long history in the English colonies. Yet the English also knew better, as Mitchell demonstrated in his awkward attempt to incorporate hundreds of Native American villages into an imagined British empire. Across North America, Indian paths connected hundreds of villages with each other, significant waterways, and the encroaching settlement of colonists. Mitchell's map pointed to an obvious truth, hidden by Euro-American rhetoric about wilderness: Europeans sought knowledge of specific Native American settlements and how to get there. Europeans were not wandering through woods bumping into nomadic Native peoples—they were traveling on Native American paths and looking for Indian settlements.[11]

As Native American political power declined, Euro-Americans became less inclined to acknowledge Indians as settlers or farmers of any kind, and so among Euro-Americans—but not within Native American communities—a view of Indians as living in a state of nature eclipsed a more complicated view of the early American landscape and its Indian settlements. On maps, this shift meant the erasure of Native American towns. On the ground, this erasure entailed physical destruction. For the Haudenosaunee, like many of the other indigenous peoples in eastern North America, the American Revolution marked the turning point in their ability to define the nature of settlement. To at least attempt to maintain peaceful relations between Indians and colonists, the British government had endeavored to limit the expansion of colonial settlement onto Indian lands in the interior. Beginning with the Proclamation of 1763, and subsequently clarified through negotiations with Indian nations, the Crown barred colonists from settling roughly west of the Appalachian Mountains. Negotiated between the Six Nations and the British government, the Treaty of Fort Stanwix (1768) allowed colonial settlement east of a north-south line located slightly west of Fort Stanwix (near present-day Rome, New York). This policy lasted until the American Revolution, when the British government lost control of thirteen of its North American colonies. Throughout Iroquoia and the New York frontier, warfare targeted the built environment and reached its destructive peak with the 1779 invasion of Iroquoia by Continental army forces under the command of Maj. Gen. John Sullivan and Brig. Gen. James Clinton. The Sullivan-Clinton campaign systematically burned Haudenosaunee villages and crops. Following that destruction and series of treaties from the 1780s through the 1790s, Euro-Americans reinvented the Haudenosaunee's landscape to imagine how Indians had always lived in a wilderness and could not coexist alongside American farmers. In this imagined scenario, Indians would go extinct like the animal predators that American farmers hunted in the woods they so eagerly cleared.[12]

Significantly, the Revolution's erasure of the indigenous built landscape was not complete. Throughout Iroquoia, signs abounded of previous and enduring occupation, from the ruins of villages and fields to mysterious monuments. These traces composed a landscape of violence and suffering, where battles and raids of the war generated a trail of memories. Like other pivotal moments in world history, the Revolution left a complicated, sometimes contradictory, and always debated legacy. For many New Yorkers and residents of New England, the war opened opportunity to pursue happiness in the lands of Iroquoia, now part of New York State. Their independence came at the expense of the Haudenosaunee—even the Oneida and Tuscarora, allies of the Americans during the war—who eventually lost significant portions of their homelands and much of the political power they had once enjoyed as Britain's "Indian empire." Across these homelands, the Haudenosaunee had long erected their own records of war, ranging from painted figures to monuments of stones and wood, which spoke to Haudenosaunee heroes and significant events. These monuments, and specifically a famous "Painted Post" in western New York, served as the focus for the Euro-American invention of the essential popular memory of westward expansion: "heroic" frontiersmen employing their sharpshooting ability to take revenge against "savage" Indians for alleged atrocities committed during war. Before this enduring frontier myth appeared in history books and popular media, from novels to Hollywood movies, New Yorkers had established the myth's foundation by appropriating the Haudenosaunee landscape as sites of heroic conquest. In reality, frontiersmen play a minimal role in the conquest of Iroquoia, and evidence exists of an alternative history of the Revolution, a story of Haudenosaunee endurance and coexistence with white neighbors that challenged assumptions of inevitably "vanishing" Indians. All these stories traced their origin to one mysterious post.[13]

After much of Iroquoia lay in ruins and Euro-Americans claimed vanishing Indians had done little to shape the landscape of North America, seemingly grand, ancient sites puzzled educated Euro-Americans. From the 1790s onward, travelers across central and western New York encountered places where the earth had been moved. In the minds of Euro-Americans, these works appeared to be related to "mounds" found all along the frontier of the early republic, especially along the Ohio River and Mississippi River watersheds. Historians have studied how late eighteenth- and early nineteenth-century Euro-Americans searched for a "lost race" of "Mound Builders," responsible for monumental works such as the earthwork pyramids of Cahokia, near present-day St. Louis, Missouri. Yet within this infamous moment of dubious archaeology, Iroquoia's essential story remains largely overlooked. New York State's most powerful politician, DeWitt Clinton, popularized his own account of Mound Builders that recast the Iroquois empire as invading Huns, who destroyed a previously established advanced civilization. In this narrative, Indian power reflected destruction and Europeans came as restorers.[14]

As with the contested meanings of the Revolution's landscape, the Haudenosaunee had something to say about their ancient landscape and what it meant for understanding Iroquoia's past, present, and future. A surprising rebuttal to Clinton's interpretation came from the Tuscarora Reservation, where a pioneering Native American historian named David Cusick published his own account of ancient America. In *Sketches of Ancient History of the Six Nations*, Cusick claimed many of Iroquoia's ruins as part of a powerful, ancient Haudenosaunee confederacy—essentially a revived Iroquois empire on Tuscarora terms—at the moment when his Euro-American contemporaries were most dismissive of Indian abilities to change and asserted that Native peoples had little knowledge of America's ancient occupation. Cusick's history provides an essential Native American voice to scholarship on the "Mound Builder" myth, which typically privileges Euro-American writings.[15]

Although this is a story about landscape, only people can give meaning to that land. Most of these individuals, even the relatively famous intellectuals of their time, are largely unknown to the American public today, who have forgotten the debate about ancient America's "mounds." But the legacy of that cultural moment endures. Not coincidently, America's most successful new religion, the Church of Jesus Christ of Latter-day Saints (Mormons), emerged from the hills of Iroquoia—a specific hill, actually—during the peak years of speculation on the ancient American landscape. Less than one hundred miles to the east of where David Cusick published his history of ancient America, a young man named Joseph Smith claimed to have found an equally compelling history of ancient Christian America, written in an extinct language on golden plates. Avowing to have used divine magic to translate these plates, in 1830 Smith published the Book of Mormon, which his followers came to view as an essential addition to the Bible's accounts of Christianity. Although the Book of Mormon's chapters echo the style of biblical accounts, its history of North America follows the overall conclusions of contemporary Euro-American archaeological theories: the ancestors of Native Americans became destroyers of civilization, leaving a ruined landscape across the continent, which early believers could read as evidence of their religion's truth. Unsettled by the rapidly expanding capitalist landscape and a series of religious revivals, known as the Second Great Awakening, early Mormons sought religious truth and eventually refuge in their own New Jerusalem. Here they would await the Second Coming of Christ. From one apocalyptic place, the Big Bone Lick, to another eighty years later, Zion, visions of the Native American landscape reflected the dreams and fears of individuals caught up in eras of revolutionary change.[16]

Iroquoia is an especially significant place to rediscover essential but unfamiliar stories from a seemingly familiar land. For a time, beginning in the early nineteenth century, New York State contained the most recognizable landscapes in America, as Romantic-era painters sought sublime nature in the young republic's hills, mountains, and waterfalls west of the Hudson River valley. America's first great novelist, James Fenimore Cooper, captured the same spirit in books such as *The Last of the Mohicans*, which popularized the quintessential western hero, Nathaniel "Natty" Bumppo (Hawkeye), whose adventures contained vivid descriptions of nature, such as Kaaterskill Falls and Otsego Lake ("Glimmerglass" in Cooper's novels). Yet these familiar scenes, fixated on spectacular natural features, were but one reading of a place with an ancient history, where the Native American landscape was central rather than peripheral to the land's importance. *The Storied Landscape of Iroquoia* follows the transformation, appropriation, and continued struggle over North America's indigenous built and natural landscape from the height of Haudenosaunee geographic influence in the middle of the eighteenth century through the first decades of reservation life in the nineteenth century. By those years, maps of New York State had very little to say about the Haudenosaunee who had once dominated the geography of colonial America, and Indians appeared as small figures in Romantic paintings—a fleeting glimpse of a "vanishing" people in their wilderness home. Yet the indigenous built environment had not simply vanished, and neither had Iroquoia's original inhabitants. From monuments to the Revolution to the ancient landscape and the emergence of Mormonism, Iroquoia's storied landscape continued to shape American culture for Americans and Native Americans, who struggled over the meaning of conquest. This contested transformation was central to the making of a new nation, its distinct culture rooted in the exchanges and struggles of diverse peoples and the efforts of indigenous nations to maintain connections to their ancestral homelands.[17]

| Chapter One

Visions of the Great Island

In the beginning, waves of water rolled across a world of perpetual night. Above this world, in the Sky World, dwelt humanlike beings. One such being, known to the Haudenosaunee as Sky Woman, became pregnant by some mysterious means. She fell through a hole in the Sky World and plummeted toward the water below. From beneath the water's surface, the animals took note of the falling woman. Swimming to the bottom of the sea, Mink procured dirt and placed it on Turtle's back. Supported by Turtle, this expanding earth became an island, where Sky Woman landed safely. On the island, Sky Woman gave birth to a daughter, who, in turn, became pregnant with twins. These twins, Flint and Sky Holder, debated a means to exit their mother. Of a more sinister disposition, Flint exited through the mother's side, killing her. After some time, Sky Holder met his father (perhaps Turtle), who gave him the gift of corn and warned that Flint harbored evil intentions. The brothers fought, and Sky Holder prevailed. Into this world emerged humans, perhaps from the ground, who had Sky Holder as their benefactor.[1]

In September 1750, an Onondaga chief named Gaschwechtioni told this story to two Moravian missionaries, David Zeisberger and Henry Frey. For three days, the three men had been diligently working together, crafting a canoe in the forest near Onondaga. Taking a

break, Gaschwechtioni explained "much Indian history" to the curious missionaries. In his diary Zeisberger later wrote, "He said it must
have been more than 1,000 years since they were in this country. . . .
This account, he said, had been handed down to them by their ancestors, from very remote ages, before any whites had been in the country,
and they, in turn, told it to their children, so that it might not be forgotten." Gaschwechtioni emphasized the deep connections between
history, place, and identity.[2]

What are we to make of this encounter? Here was an Onondaga
man building a canoe with a missionary from Pennsylvania (Frey)
and another originally from Moravia (Zeisberger) in the middle of
what, upon first glance, seems like a remote wilderness at the margins of the British empire and the Atlantic world. Bringing their interpretation of a religion that originated in the ancient Middle East, the
missionaries listened to a man who explained a truly American set
of religious beliefs. From the perspective of a post-Enlightenment,
empirically minded worldview, we can often miss truths unlocked
by contemplating the myths and religious traditions that these men
shared. Although the world may not be resting on Turtle's back, for
more than ten thousand years Native North America truly was an
island that developed separately from Eurasia. Far from a wilderness,
the Great Island was an Old World of its own, where Native Americans had developed their own agriculture, societies, and cultures long
before the arrival of Europeans.[3]

Yet the presence of Zeisberger and Frey, well-meaning men who
nevertheless sought to change Indian culture, indicated that the Great
Island had become something of a "New World," characterized by the
mixing of people, diseases, technologies, and beliefs from America
and Europe. The missionaries were not the first Europeans to venture
into Iroquoia hoping to shape its future, nor would they be the last.
Since the seventeenth century, Europeans had visited the Haudenosaunee's lands to invade, trade, and proselytize. Across Iroquoia, from
the charred remains of destroyed villages to the tools used to craft
new homes, material evidence revealed the costs and benefits of the
European presence in North America. But like Zeisberger, who would

eventually abandon his efforts in Iroquoia and move westward, Europeans did not permanently settle in the lands of the Haudenosaunee prior to the American Revolution—even as Iroquoia itself remained forever connected to the encroaching world of Europeans.[4]

To follow the missionaries and their Indian guides is to travel through a landscape still defined, in large part, on Indian terms. We can best understand eighteenth-century Iroquoia as a land with layers of history: ancient sites associated with myths, the remnants of early villages and the formative years of the Haudenosaunee's Great League, and a relatively new colonial-era built environment. None of the layers marked a replacement of one culture by another. Iroquoia's layered history reflected the evolving and enduring homeland of the People of the Longhouse, who built their New World on the cultural foundations of America's Old World. Men like Gaschwechtioni knew stories of this ancient land, but they were not relics of that past. His homeland's evolving built landscape reflected the efforts of a people who embraced their history while planning a future connected to Europeans but not defined by them. All was not well, however, on the Great Island. Underneath this dynamic landscape, the ancient landscape spoke to stories and assumptions about the limits of cross-cultural exchange. The central question of this period was whether all peoples could continue to build upon that layered history or if a great cataclysm would destroy that world and replace it with a truly New World.[5]

Although relatively unknown to Europeans, the Haudenosaunee homelands had long been an interconnected world, both within and to peoples outside of Iroquoia. The Haudenosaunee maintained trails through the forest and between the numerous waterways that linked Iroquoia to European and Native American settlements throughout eastern North America. Although Haudenosaunee trails existed for centuries, it was only in 1771, with the creation of Guy Johnson's *Map of the Country of the Six Nations*, that they appeared in any detail on Euro-American maps. Even then, Johnson's trail lines were suspiciously straight for a landscape full of hills and waterways, which suggests the existence of this trail network but also a continued reliance on

Haudenosaunee guides to actually traverse it, as the Moravian missionaries had done in the 1750s. When Haudenosaunee chiefs needed to
send news quickly along these routes, they relied on specially trained
runners, who acquired great reputations, such as the Seneca chief
Cornplanter's runner, Sharp Shins, who reportedly ran ninety miles
during daylight.[6]

Looking backward, following centuries of intense ecological change
and population growth, it can be difficult to comprehend how significant the built landscape of Iroquoia was for eighteenth-century Americans. To be sure, extensive forests did cover much of America east of
the Mississippi, a region scholars often call the Eastern Woodlands.
Yet nobody, Indian or European, simply found him- or herself adrift
on an "ocean of woods," as eighteenth-century cartographer Lewis
Evans once described the East. The purpose of any such journey was
to reach an Indian settlement, where diplomacy, trade, or religious
exchange could occur. As such, the built landscape was as important
as the natural one for any traveler. The Haudenosaunee maintained
a dynamic system of towns, which periodically relocated when soil
became depleted, buildings fell apart, firewood became scarce, or
insects infested crops. Even then, these former sites remained visible to travelers and were remembered by the Haudenosaunee. First
occupied around 1710 and relocated in the early 1740s, the village of
Onnahee, near Canandaigua Lake, exemplifies a typical eighteenth-
century Haudenosaunee settlement, its significance to colonial powers, and a lasting memory of that settlement. During the 1720s, the
village first appeared in the records of British colonial officials, who
worried that French threats and gifts would lure the Haudenosaunee
away from their British alliance. Reports indicated "that the principle Sachims of one of the Sinneke Castles, called Onnahee have
given a large belt of Wampume to the Governor of Canada to pitch
one a place for them near him." The British would suffer if the village relocated closer to the French in Canada, the imperial rivals of
British North America. This village was important to Europeans and
Native Americans alike, but its people were not fixed in place. By the
mid-1740s, travelers encountered signs of abandoned habitations. In

1750, near Canandaigua Lake, Cayuga chief Hahotschaunquas and Moravian missionaries John Frederick Cammerhoff and David Zeisberger "reached an Old Indian settlement, where a city by the name of Onnachee is said to have stood, but which is now uninhabited." Traveling with several Seneca chiefs in 1788, the Presbyterian missionary Samuel Kirkland noted: "came to open land where was formerly a seneka settlement called anaye." While villages moved, lineages and clans continued at the new village. These movements created a network of places and memories across Iroquoia.[7]

Settlement patterns and locations shifted over time in response to strategic and ecological needs, but during the eighteenth century the Haudenosaunee restricted their villages and fields to the fertile alluvial soil of river valleys, reserving much larger tracts of hilly hinterland for hunting. The forest was the domain of men, who hunted deer, bears, beaver, squirrels, rabbits, and turkeys. The Haudenosaunee required tens of thousands of square miles of forests to sustain deer as a food source. Consequently, visitors to Iroquoia saw lofty old-growth forests, especially stands of hardwoods such as elm, maple, beech, and oak trees, but also some conifers such as white pine and hemlock— seemingly a land begging for productive use. Yet appearances could be deceiving. This extensive forest remained because it served the needs of its human inhabitants, who cleared as much land as their crops required but also used fire to burn the dense undergrowth of forests, which, in turn, provided good habitat for the large mammals that Indians hunted. Lofty trees represented a human-shaped landscape rather than an untouched wilderness.[8]

By the 1770s, the approximately 9,000 Haudenosaunee lived in villages stretching from the Mohawk River valley, on the east, to the Genesee Valley, on the west. Along the Mohawk River, the Mohawk had two principal villages, Tiononderoge (Fort Hunter) and Canajoharie. West of the Mohawk, the Oneida had two villages, with the main settlement at Kanonwalohale, located on Oneida Creek, eight miles south of Oneida Lake. An older settlement, Oneida Castle, lay eight miles southeast of Kanonwalohale. In the heart of Iroquoia stood the village of the Onondaga, on the southeast shores of Onondaga

Lake. Southwest of Onondaga, on the northeast shore of Cayuga Lake, was the principal Cayuga settlement. The largest Haudenosaunee village, Chenussio or Genesee Castle, belonged to the Seneca. Located on the west bank of the Genesee River, Genesee Castle contained approximately 128 homes (housing one to two families). Located on the northwest shore of Seneca Lake, the second-largest Seneca village, Kanadesaga (Canadasegy on Guy Johnson's map), contained approximately 50 homes. Across Iroquoia stood these substantial villages and many smaller settlements, especially in the Seneca territory.[9]

For centuries, visitors to these villages would see variations on the Haudenosaunee's famous housing, known as longhouses. The development of longhouses was a cultural watershed for the ancestral Haudenosaunee—the People of the Longhouse—and it became an enduring symbol linking the people to their homes and homelands. The earliest longhouses probably date from the thirteenth century. Archaeologists have uncovered traces of these early homes, but the most thorough firsthand descriptions are from much later dates. The famous naturalist John Bartram, visiting Onondaga in 1743, described what he saw (and suggested the perceived importance of his visit): "the cabin is about 80 feet long, and 17 broad, the common passage 6 feet wide; and the apartments on each side 5 feet, raised by a foot above the passage by a long sapling hewed squared, and fitted with joists that go from it to the back of the house; on these joists they lay large pieces of bark, and on extraordinary occasions spread matts made of rushes, this favor we had." In a residential longhouse, families were related through the mother's line and belonged to a larger clan (typically Wolf, Bear, or Turtle). A husband often moved into his wife's home, a practice scholars call matrilocality. Although the length of longhouses varied over the centuries, the basic design remained consistent into the eighteenth century.[10]

Housing represented one aspect of a broader colonial world defined by both fluidity and tradition, where Native peoples retained their identities even as they were forever connected in an Atlantic network of trade and communication. Located on the Susquehanna River, the multiethnic town of Onoquaga featured the most dynamic built landscape in Iroquoia. Revolutionary War soldier Erkuries Beatty wrote, "This town was one of the Neatest of the Indian towns on the Susquehana, it was built on each side of the River with good Log houses with Stone Chimneys and glass windows it likewise had a Church & burying ground and a great number of apple trees." In other Haudenosaunee towns, scholars have noted descriptions of "log houses" as evidence that the Haudenosaunee no longer resided in traditional longhouses and instead adapted housing similar to their European neighbors. When soldiers described Haudenosaunee towns, they sometimes distinguished between family homes and a "Council House," that is, a traditional longhouse used for ceremonies and special occasions. For example, at Kanadesaga, Maj. John Burrows noted "forty dwellings and a Council House." However, recent archaeological work in the Seneca homelands has demonstrated that even as villagers shifted to smaller homes, many of these dwellings were constructed using internal support posts, which larger longhouses had also featured. That is, they were not cabins in the Euro-American sense, and brief Euro-American descriptions need to be read carefully against archaeological evidence. This evolving built environment pointed to a powerfully symbolic historic past, represented by the longhouse, and an ability to accommodate European tools and materials as Indians had done for well over a century.[11]

The Haudenosaunee conceptualized their homeland as a symbolic longhouse, which had always been a land of selective exchange. The Mohawk watched the eastern door, and the Seneca watched the west. The Haudenosaunee spoke of the need to keep the paths clear as a metaphor for open communication and harmony among the Haudenosaunee and their neighbors. Everywhere that the Haudenosaunee ruled, a great tree of peace stretched its branches of protection. At peace within the longhouse, the Haudenosaunee channeled their aggression outward. No Algonquian-speaking peoples joined the league, and seventeenth-century Iroquoian-speaking nations such as the Huron, Petun, Erie, Wenro, Neutral, and Susquehannock remained outside the longhouse. During destructive seventeenth-century wars, the Haudenosaunee acted most aggressively against these Iroquoian speakers who had refused the message of peace promoted by the Five Nations but were the most culturally similar (and therefore adoptable) neighbors.[12]

While all of this land existed within a symbolic longhouse, it had taken centuries after the development of their signature housing before the People of the Longhouse lived in peace. This history was grounded in a particular place at the center of the symbolic longhouse: the village of Onondaga. This village hosted the Council Fire of the League, at the center of the Haudenosaunee's identity as a peaceful league of related villages. Although the village location shifted over the years, the Haudenosaunee associated the region around Onondaga Lake with the coming of peace to the Five Nations centuries earlier. Evidence indicates that the Haudenosaunee of the colonial period possessed extensive knowledge of the League's formation, which they connected to well-known places in Iroquoia. In the early nineteenth century, an intriguing cultural figure, Major John Norton (Teyoninhokarawen), a Mohawk leader of Scottish Cherokee heritage, recorded an Onondaga account. Before the formation of the League, many ancestors of the Onondaga lived at "a very extensive village at up Salmon Creek, a River about eighteen miles to the Eastward of Oswego." Following a disagreement, the villagers decided to part ways and resettle elsewhere. As the villagers parted, an elderly woman paused and informed them that she would become a burden during the long travels ahead and would be "distressed myself in being taken from my native place, and in beholding you separate." She told the younger people, "I command you therefore to lay me between the parting canoes, that when you separate, I may be let fall into the pure and transparent waters of the Lake." The people obliged, and as the old woman sank to the bottom, she became a sturgeon.[13]

The drowning elder marked the end of unity among the ancient people of the Onondaga. One group "pursued the route toward Cataraqui, and before they got out of hearing of each other, they had begun to speak a different language." (Cataraqui lies on the St. Lawrence River, near present-day Kingston, Ontario.) According to Norton's source, "From these, they say, have sprung the Nations of the Algonquin or Chippawa language, which the Five Nations call Dewakanka."

Geographically Algonquian-speaking peoples surrounded Iroquoia, a fact that required some explanation. Norton's story offered an Iroquoia-centered view: all peoples of the northeast had their origins in Iroquoia, sharing a common ancestor. Iroquoia remained at the center of their worldview and of the Great Island that they all shared, a land of diverse but related histories.[14]

According to Norton's legends, the ancestral Onondaga debated a course of action, and new leaders emerged to head two factions. The Onondaga remembered this quarrel with a place-name that recalled the story. "The other party took a western course, till arriving at a Creek (still called Ondatshaigh from the circumstance of disputing there) about nine miles west of Oswego; some were inclined to ascend it, and others to continue westerly along the shore of the Lake. This difference of inclination caused a dispute, and they separated, each following the bent of their inclinations: those who went up the Creek were headed by a Chief called Hayouwaghtengh." The chief later became known in history as Hiawatha, and his story constitutes the foundation myth for the Great League of the Five Nations.[15]

Unable to conquer one another, the villages of Iroquoia remained in a state of constant conflict. This shadow of violence emanated from the "lofty hill of Onondague [Onondaga], covered with its forest of oak, rising about the rest, and the smoke of Thatotarho's fire (the Chief of the village) ascending to the Clouds." Here dwelt a chief, angry and physically deformed by rage. For hair, Thatotarho had dreadful snakes. His name, also spelled Tadodaho and Atotarho, meant "the Entangled," and he reflected the rampant warfare detected by archaeologists during the period before 1600 CE, when the Haudenosaunee League apparently formed. During this violent time, Hayouwaghtengh experienced a series of tragedies that plunged him deep into the forest to escape from the anger of Thatotarho. A sorcerer killed one daughter, and Thatotarho killed the other.[16]

These wanderings left a trail of memories associated with particular places throughout Iroquoia, which Norton diligently noted. Hayouwaghtengh visited "one of the branches of the Susquehannok called Atchineankigh, and soon discovered the abodes of men." Here

Hayouwaghtengh resided for some time in a village but left when he did not receive a voice in their council. Traveling farther, Hayouwaghtengh "came to the confluence of another branch," which Norton called "Oghquaqa"—probably Onoquaga, the eighteenth-century settlement on the Susquehanna. Here, in a pool, Hayouwaghtengh discovered wampum beads. At the confluence of Schoharie Creek and the Mohawk River, Hayouwaghtengh discovered a Mohawk village inhabited by a chief named Tekannawitagh (Dekanawidah), or the Peacemaker, a great, mysterious figure who began a quest to heal the strife of Iroquoia. On his journey to meet the Peacemaker, Hayouwaghtengh visited locations well known to the eighteenth-century Onondaga. By including these places, Norton's storyteller connected the distant past to the present.[17]

In Norton's account, the Peacemaker taught the Haudenosaunee the condolence ceremonies used to ease the mind and so render warfare unnecessary. Accompanied by several chiefs of a reunited Haudenosaunee people, the Peacemaker confronted Thatotarho and offered "wampum until they had removed all his deformities: they then covered his body with a garment and put moccasins on his feet." To further appease Thatotarho, the Peacemaker appointed him "Keeper of the Council Fire of the Confederacy." At Onondaga, fifty chiefs from the Five Nations' villages annually met to renew the ceremonies of gift exchange and words of condolence, to maintain peace among the Five Nations. As the Tuscarora historian David Cusick later explained, "the Onondaga was considered the heart of the country." No longer the site of an angry, deformed chief, the village instead hosted the Council Fire of the League, where the Haudenosaunee maintained their peace.[18]

As the story of the Peacemaker and Hiawatha suggests, throughout Iroquoia particular places are connected to hundreds of years of history. Our knowledge of what the eighteenth-century Haudenosaunee knew about these places is limited but telling. Glimpses of this knowledge hint at a very large body of remembered history. Travelers encountered abandoned fortifications from the times of trouble surrounding the formation of the League. Earlier in their history, the Haudenosaunee had built villages with palisades and piled earth around the base. This digging left a trench in front of the palisade. Some earthworks may have also surrounded sacred burial sites rather than large villages. Travelers through Iroquoia encountered dozens of places where Indians had moved the earth for defensive and ceremonial purposes. The Seneca maintained that some of these ancient fortifications remained from battles against western nations. Seneca chiefs knew the history of fortifications found near Tonawanda ("Swift Running Water") Creek, northwest of their primary villages in the Genesee Valley. Accompanied by a Seneca chief, Kirkland rode out into the open fields and examined two fortifications called Tegatainedaghgwe, or "the double fortified town." Kirkland learned of an important battle said to have occurred 270 years earlier. He wrote, "Near the northern fortification, which is situated on high ground, are the remains of a funeral pile, where the slain were buried, in a great battle fought between the Senekas and the Western Indians, where the former won the day, as they affirm." Kirkland saw some human bones scattered on the surface. The missionary had visited the southern fort of Tegatainedaghgwe in the present town of Oakfield, New York. Our best archaeological data suggests a settlement date of around 1400 CE, give or take a century. The settlement lay to the west of the known village sequences of the later Seneca, so archaeologists believe that the ancestors of the Erie, an Iroquoian nation, probably occupied Oakfield.[19]

However, the ancestors of the *eighteenth-century* Seneca had, in fact, occupied Tegatainedaghgwe and neighboring settlements. From the 1630s to the 1650s, the Haudenosaunee engaged in brutal warfare against their poorly armed western neighbors, dispersing the Wenro (1638), Huron (1649), Petun (1650), Neutral (1651), and Erie (1657). The Haudenosaunee fought these wars to gain access to hunting land and to take captives as replacements for individuals killed by devastating epidemics and warfare. The Haudenosaunee took so many captives that in 1657 a missionary reported that Iroquoia contained "more foreigners than natives of the country." The Seneca took adoptees from the Erie, among others. Memories of this war persisted throughout the eighteenth century. Kirkland's old friend Mohawk chief Joseph Brant

understood that the region around Tegatainedaghgwe had belonged
to the Erie and others conquered by the Five Nations. Regarding this
land, in a 1794 letter Brant wrote, "the whole Five Nations have an equal
right one with the other, the country having been obtained by their
joint exertions in war with a powerful nation, formerly living southward of Buffalo Creek, called Eries, and another nation then living at
Tioga Point." Through conquest and adoption, the Seneca absorbed
the traditions of Tegatainedaghgwe as part of their own history and
incorporated the surrounding region into Iroquoia.[20]

The history of Tegatainedaghgwe points to the difficulties in tracing
oral traditions in the wake of devastating diseases and warfare, which
had profoundly reduced Native American populations and spurred the
creation of new nations and identities. The Haudenosaunee knew of
places where they had conquered and absorbed other nations into the
Five Nations, but some of these places and nations remain relatively
inexplicable. Traveling along the Susquehanna River, in what is now
northern Pennsylvania, Cammerhoff wrote, "we came to a place called
Gahontoto [tree or post standing up] by the Indians. It is said to be the
site of an ancient Indian city, where a peculiar nation lived. The inhabitants were neither Delawares nor Aquanoschioni [Haudenosaunee],
but had a language of their own, and were Tehotitachse." (The phrase
probably translates as "Stopped Them.") A few corn pits indicated that
a village had stood there. According to Hahotschaunquas, the Cayuga
"completely exterminated them." By "extermination," Hahotschaunquas
meant many had been killed and the survivors had been adopted into
the Cayuga. Cammeroff noted, "The Gajuka had many prisoners, who
remained among them, but there exists nothing more of their nation
and language." Farther north, the group encountered a related battle
site of special importance. The group reached the foot of a mountain,
where Hahotschaunquas said his wife had given birth to their child.
Climbing the mountain, "[Hahotschaunquas] pointed out a cross to
us, which marked the spot where the Gajuka's had fought with the
Tehotitachies." He concluded the only known story that survives about
a people known as the Tehotitachse.[21]

Scholars typically identify European colonialism as the catalyst for the type of truly destructive warfare described by Hahotschaunquas. Responding to losses from waves of epidemics and caught up in a transatlantic economy that demanded increasingly scarce furs, the Haudenosaunee fought violent wars during the mid-seventeenth century. Yet Hahotschaunquas believed this battle occurred before the Haudenosaunee had acquired firearms. By 1640 the Dutch had sold enough guns to arm most of the Haudenosaunee, who were geographically closer than their enemies to the Dutch colony of New Netherland. However, Hahotschaunquas's claim of extermination presents problems for the pre-1640 date, when the Indians of the Northeast possessed comparable weaponry. Hahotschaunquas's testimony cannot be read alongside the historical record to provide an accurate date for this battle.[22]

Because archaeologists have not yet uncovered any seventeenth-century towns in the upper Susquehanna Valley, the precise identity of the Tehotitachse also remains uncertain. During the early seventeenth century, a few Europeans made vague references to people possibly living near the Tehotitachse village. In 1615 the famous French explorer and administrator Samuel de Champlain apparently sent Etienne Brulé to find allies at a village called Carantouan, in the upper Susquehanna Valley. Investigators have never located this village with any degree of certainty. If the Tehotitachse existed, they probably spoke an Iroquoian language and were part of the Susquehannock, who originally lived on the northern branch of the Susquehanna and moved to the southern branch during the early sixteenth century. The Haudenosaunee and Susquehannock fought a war that ended in 1676 with the migration of the defeated Susquehannock southward to the Chesapeake. Some remaining Susquehannock joined with the Delaware, Cayuga, and Onondaga, while others, later known as Conestogas, remained in the Susquehanna Valley.[23]

Indian ancestries connected to vanished societies, including those that had risen and fallen before Europeans knew of America. Euro-Americans recorded frustratingly abridged accounts that hint at the possibilities of deep history known to eighteenth-century Indians. Leaders of the Illinois Confederacy, for example, recalled that great pre-Columbian pyramids of Cahokia had been built by their ancestors.

Bringing warfare and deadly pathogens, Europeans accelerated the processes of social collapse and reconstruction. The Haudenosaunee incorporated people from several nations, including the Susquehannock (who may have been the Tehotitachse). By the eighteenth century, most American Indian nations and identities were the recent creations of Indian survivors of peoples devastated by disease and warfare. In addition to its terrible human toll, colonialism also engendered the erasure of memories of Native places for both Americans today and, to an extent, Native peoples of the past.[24]

Yet stories about places helped the Haudenosaunee to understand and adapt to the fluid identity of their nations in the wake of these colonial wars and migrations. In 1722 the Five Nations became the Six Nations, when Tuscarora refugees joined the league. An Iroquoian-speaking people, the Tuscarora migrated from North Carolina during the 1710s. The Onondaga justified the arrival of the Tuscarora with an origin story similar to their league's formation, which had also referred to Oswego Creek. According to tradition, the Onondaga and Tuscarora once lived together at Oswego Falls. One day the Onondaga and Tuscarora attempted to cross the Oswego River by holding onto a vine tied across the river. The Onondaga made it across, but the rope broke before the Tuscarora finished crossing. Norton concluded, "This gave them such a chill that they immediately changed their speech, retaining but a slight resemblance to the language of the Five Nations. They then began their journey to the Southward." Cusick recorded a different account but also focused on Oswego Falls ("Kuskehsawkich"), where the ancient Haudenosaunee had emerged from a nearby mountain, having survived devastating warfare among Indian nations that followed attacks from horned serpents and other mythological foes. With the guidance of the Holder of the Heavens, six families migrated toward what became the traditional Haudenosaunee homelands in Iroquoia and then began speaking distinct languages. The sixth family, however, continued toward the Mississippi River. Although Cusick wrote this account during the early nineteenth century, it drew upon traditions that had existed since at least the early eighteenth century. In 1713, when dealing with New York officials, representatives from the Five Nations explained that they wanted their Tuscarora "kins-men" to "return home" to Iroquoia.[25]

Perhaps during a time of profound demographic change, the Haude-nosaunee engaged in what scholars have called "the invention of tra-dition," a myth-making process whereby nations achieve legitimacy and cohesion by emphasizing purportedly historic traditions, rituals, and bonds that are actually new. However, these traditions certainly spoke to deeper connections between the Tuscarora and Onondaga. The branches of the Iroquoian languages led back to a shared past, thousands of years old. The Tuscarora language more closely resem-bles that of their North Carolina and Virginia neighbors, the Nottoway (Cheroenhaka) and Meherrin peoples, than it does the languages of the Five Nations. Yet the Tuscarora speakers diverged from their northern "kinsmen" at a relatively recent date compared to the more distantly related Cherokee, who spoke a Southern Iroquoian language. Algon-quian peoples and hundreds of miles separated the Five Nations from the Iroquoian speakers to their south, but linguistic and archaeological studies suggest a hypothetical "Proto-Iroquoian" homeland that existed thousands of years prior to the eighteenth-century Tuscarora migration to New York. The breaking of the vine served as an apt metaphor for the long, related processes of linguistic development and migration.[26]

More easily followed than clues about the Tehotitachse or ancient Tuscarora homelands, signs of recent colonial-era conflicts dotted the homelands of the Haudenosaunee. European colonialism had entan-gled the Haudenosaunee within a transatlantic struggle among Native Americans, the English, French, and (until 1664) Dutch to control profits and land in eastern North America. Throughout the Eastern Woodlands, colonialism had produced a dynamic and complex mix of alliances among European powers and Native peoples. During the late 1670s and into the 1680s, the Haudenosaunee wars for captives and hunting lands continued against a host of Great Lakes peoples: Illinois, Ojibwe, Fox, and Odawa, among others. By the end of the 1680s, how-ever, the Haudenosaunee would be pushed back to their homelands. In 1687 the French and their Native allies invaded Iroquoia and burned down the Seneca villages of Cannagargo, Totiakton, Gannogarae,

and Ganounata. In 1693 the French and their allies burned all three
of the Mohawk villages. In 1697 the French struck at Onondaga. Finding the village already set ablaze by retreating residents, the French
burned the fields and a nearby Oneida town. To the west, over the
next three years, the Anishinaabe of the Great Lakes continued their
attacks, which likely did more than the French to weaken the Haudenosaunee. These destructive wars ended in 1701 with the Grand Settlement, in which the Haudenosaunee relinquished their claims to
western hunting land beyond Detroit and pledged to remain neutral
in future wars between the French and British.[27]

Throughout Iroquoia, many significant places spoke to conquests
or resistance to conquest. The Haudenosaunee long remembered the
French invasions, which left an imprint upon the land visible well
into the next century. In 1752 near Onondaga, Moravian missionaries
encountered ruins that they learned had remained from these troubled years. They later wrote, "We came to a place where many posts
were standing, from which we concluded that a town must have stood
there formerly." The missionaries joined with two Seneca hunters, also
traveling to Onondaga. One of these men "told Bro. David, that when
he was a child of eight years of age, Onondaga stood on this spot, but
was burnt by the French." This invasion spurred village relocation and
rebuilding, which left a trail of memories across Iroquoia. One well-
known eighteenth-century settlement, Kanadesaga, or "New Town,"
located on the northwest shore of Seneca Lake, traced its origins to the
1687 invasion. Following the Haudenosaunee pattern of periodically
relocating their villages, this settlement was actually a series of three
villages located relatively close to one another. The best known of the
"New Towns" appeared in 1754. Regarding this settlement's history,
Norton wrote, "Four Hundred Men escorted the women and Children to the Borders of a Lake now called Geneva [i.e., Seneca], and
which they named Kanadesgue or New Town, from there rebuilding
their village at that place."[28]

While the Haudenosaunee remembered their costly conflicts with
Great Lakes Indians and the French, well into the eighteenth century
they considered themselves the most significant Indian power in the

Eastern Woodlands and found ways to express their military might. Following the Grand Settlement, the Haudenosaunee channeled their aggression into less destructive raids against relatively distant southern Indians, including the Catawba. Near a creek called Gientachne, Cayuga warriors constructed a monument to their feats against the Catawba, which expressed the great pride the Haudenosaunee had in their skill as warriors. Hahotschaunquas explained to his Moravian companions, "When the great warriors go to war against the Gatabes [Catawba], they make a painting of themselves." Standing alongside Hahotschaunquas, Cammerhoff described the details of these paintings: "The one time he [Hahotschaunquas] had brought back 8 prisoners and 2 scalps, and on the other occasion 3 prisoners." Throughout the Eastern Woodlands, Indians constructed similar monuments. According to missionary John Heckewelder, these paintings displayed detailed information about battles: tribal affiliations, numbers involved, the duration of the campaign, direction traveled, and enemies encountered and captured. He concluded, "All Indian nations can do this, although they have not all the same marks; yet I have seen the Delawares read with ease the drawings of the Chippeways, Mingoes, Shawnoes, and Wyandots, on similar subjects."[29]

Even without a monument or a ruined village, a battle site remained memorable. Working their way toward Canandaigua Lake, not far from the abandoned community of Onnahee, Hahotschaunquas, Cammerhoff, and Zeisberger followed a creek named Otochtschiaco [red bearberry] to a place also named Otochtschiaco, which had been the site of a battle. Cammerhoff noted, "Forty or Fifty years ago, as the Gajuka [Cayuga, i.e., Hahotschaunquas] told us, the 5 Nations fought a battle there with the Zisagechrohne [Mississauga], and defeated and took them prisoners." Had the meeting of the Moravians and Hahotschaunquas never occurred, the written record would have been silent on this battle that the Haudenosaunee found important. As the men traveled, Hahotschaunquas had much to say, and he offered rare glimpses into how the Cayuga remembered Iroquoia's past, hinting at a more extensive but unrecorded body of knowledge.[30]

Although all Eastern Woodlands Indians may have built monuments to battle, the Haudenosaunee were especially proud of their historic military conquests. By citing the ancient fortifications and conquered landscape, the Haudenosaunee claimed sovereignty over a significant portion of America's Eastern Woodlands. In his 1794 letter Brant noted, "By our successes all the country between that [Tioga Point] and the Mississippi became the joint property of the Five Nations,—all other nations now inhabiting this great tract of country were allowed to settle by the Five Nations." Brant reiterated the long-standing concept of the Haudenosaunee as an Indian empire, a belief that the British had also emphasized throughout the eighteenth century. While the British represented this Indian empire on maps, such as John Mitchell's famous creation, the Haudenosaunee had oral traditions and monuments that confirmed their right of conquest.[31]

Battles, conquest, monuments—these events and places were reasonably translatable. To be sure, guides such as Hahotschaunquas spoke of events and peoples that could puzzle his traveling companions, but culturally much of what he said fit into European understandings of North American history and the nature of the world. Guides had little trouble speaking in historic time—"forty or fifty years ago," and so forth. Beyond the historic landscape, however, Native peoples saw a mythological landscape that was largely hidden to all but the most observant of visitors. The Haudenosaunee's supernatural landscape pointed to the enduring legacy of North America as an Old World of its own, where stories connected the present to a past that long predated the arrival of Europeans and their sense of calendar time. As their origin story suggested, from the beginning the Haudenosaunee had shared their land with other-than-human beings. In this regard, they were like many peoples throughout the Atlantic World who knew of an unseen realm that overlapped with the natural environment. Each culture, however, had particular stories and beliefs that distinguished it from others that respected the supernatural. For the Haudenosaunee, plants, game animals, the weather—all of these had other-than-human being representations who required ceremonies and tobacco offerings to secure their help. The forest was alive with spirits and meaning for those who knew its secrets.

Occasionally, a few Euro-Americans glimpsed the power of this hidden world. In the spring of 1765, Samuel Kirkland traveled with his adopted Oneida brother, Tekândie, across Oneida Lake. The pair became trapped in a thunderstorm, with fierce winds that rocked their canoe. Kirkland noticed his brother "untying a squirrel skin which contained his sacred or magic powder, which would produce a pre-ternatural Influence when offered in an hour of danger." Attempting to calm the storm, Tekândie loudly called out, "Do your best O wind I say, now then pull hard O wind I say—you cannot conquer now." Tekândie advised Kirkland that a prayer to Jesus Christ might also help. The missionary diligently complied. Through their combined efforts, the waters calmed and the pair reached the shoreline.[32]

Throughout the Eastern Woodlands, American Indians shared suggestively similar mythological beliefs that differed in detail, hinting at a deep and intertwined history within the cultural diversity that characterized Native North America. Many peoples had stories of giants of various origins and dispositions, but these giants connected to culturally defined places and ancient landscapes. Among the Haudenosaunee, these beliefs focused on "Stonish Giants," or Stone Giants, who long ago invaded and tormented the Haudenosaunee. Tuscarora historian David Cusick placed this mythical struggle at Onondaga. Responding to the plight of the Haudenosaunee, Sky Holder changed himself into a giant and put the other giants to sleep in a hollow during the night. Cusick concluded, "At the dawn of day, the Holder of the Heavens ascended upon the heights and he overwhelm[ed] them by a mass of rocks, and only one escaped to announce the dreadful fate." As Cusick noted, "The hollow is said not far from Onondaga. Some say the Giants retreated by way of Mountain Ridge and crossed below the Niagara Falls." At the heart of Iroquoia, the long-occupied region around Onondaga served as an enduring setting for tales of events. Cusick's account also indicated the existence of differing accounts about the fate of these invaders, which suggested their continued presence somewhere to the north or west. That is, perhaps the Great Island's ancient world still existed and could return in some form.[33]

Neighbors of the Haudenosaunee, but speakers of an Algonquian

Fig. 4. David Cusick, "Stonish Giants." From *Sketches of Ancient History of the Six Nations*, 2nd ed. (Lockport NY: Cooley & Lothrop, 1828). Library of Congress, France in America: Selections from the Rare Book and Special Collections Division.

language, the Lenni Lenape (Delaware) held traditions that mixed stories of giants with a shared history of migration with the Haudenosaunee. An experienced missionary among the Lenni Lenape, John Heckewelder, recorded these traditions from "many hundred years ago." Regarding Delaware migration, he wrote, "After a very long journey, and many nights' encampments [i.e., many years] by the way, they at length arrived on the Namœsi Sipu [River of Fish, i.e., the Mississippi River], where they fell in with the Mengwe [Haudenosaunee], who had likewise emigrated from a distant country, and had struck upon the river somewhat higher up." This migration was not without its dangers. Following their migration across the Mississippi, the Lenni Lenape and the Haudenosaunee encountered the Alligewi—giant enemies—who controlled the lands south of the Great Lakes, between the Mississippi and Iroquoia. When the Lenni Lenape tried to cross, the Alligewi attacked. Heckewelder concluded: "An engagement took place in which hundreds fell, who were afterwards buried in holes or laid together in heaps and covered with earth." The remaining Alligewi fled down the Mississippi and disappeared. The Lenni Lenape attributed to the Alligewi the earthworks and mounds found south of the Great Lakes. Located in many places throughout the continent, American Indian earthworks had widely ranging chronological origins. Some of the works in Ohio predated the Delaware tradition by two thousand years while others were much newer. A roughly parallel chronological comparison would be Europeans gazing at the spectacular ruins of ancient Greece or Rome and contemplating the history of these distant peoples without being able to draw upon their equally famous writings. On the Huron River, in present-day Ohio, Heckewelder found an earthwork associated with the Alligewi, but he astutely maintained that these giants were, in fact, Indians of some unknown people from the distant past.[34]

Although oral traditions may not correlate with archaeologically verifiable migrations (a continuing subject of debate among scholars), these stories speak to a general history of exchange and movement that long predated European arrival and even the formation of distinct tribal identities. Heckewelder's account followed very broadly defined populations of the Lenni Lenape, Haudenosaunee, and Alligewi rather than specific nations of the Haudenosaunee or their villages. The missionary Samuel Kirkland agreed that the Haudenosaunee and other natives had migrated long ago. In 1788, after speaking with several Seneca chiefs, Kirkland wrote, "I find by farther inquiry, that a tradition prevails among the Indians in general, that all Indians came from the west." The spread and adoption of agriculture testifies to the long-term inhabitation of Iroquoia and the complex movement of plants and people across the continent from the desert Southwest to the forests of the Northeast. Native peoples carried corn, beans, and squash from distant Mesoamerica, but these crops arrived at very different times and took many centuries to become widely adopted within Iroquoia. The people of New York cooked some squash by 1000 BCE. While evidence of widespread adoption of corn does not predate 1000 CE, new findings indicate the limited presence of corn in Iroquoia by 200 BCE. The arrival of these domesticated plants did not spur an immediate transition to clusters of semi-sedentary villages associated with specific nations. Instead, relatively mobile populations probably incorporated growing some of these crops into seasonal patterns of hunting and gathering. Within this fluid world, people, goods, and cultures long intermixed. Finally, perhaps around 1300 CE, beans arrived in Iroquoia. At this point, the well-known pattern of villages supported by the "three sisters" of corn, beans, and squash could take shape.[35]

By cultivating corn, beans, and squash, the ancestral Haudenosaunee created a landscape of impressive fields near villages. Reciprocal obligations between men and women defined the use of land in Haudenosaunee society. Men built the houses and cleared the fields, but women maintained them. Hunting passenger pigeons in the spring and deer in the winter, men ranged far from the village. Some women accompanied them to camps, but the village and fields remained the domain of women, and these fields left a significant imprint upon the landscape. In 1788 Kirkland described traveling through four miles of abandoned fields near an ancient Seneca settlement. During the Revolution, American soldiers admired Haudenosaunee crops. Erkuries Beatty described one field: "150 Acres of the best corn that Ever I saw (some of the Stalks grew 16 feet high) besides great Quantities of Beans, Potatoes, Pumpkins, Cucumbers, Squashes & Watermellons."[36]

By the second half of the eighteenth century, Euro-Americans observed that Haudenosaunee settlements had adopted some European imports such as watermelon, cucumbers, and apple trees, which grew well alongside the traditional crops. The intensification of agriculture must truly have been a formative period for the ancestral Haudenosaunee. Like many other Native American peoples, the arrival of domesticated crops figured prominently in the Haudenosaunee's original myths, and corn was central to this story. In Oneida and Onondaga versions of the origin, collected during the late eighteenth century, the Holder of the Heavens received the knowledge of corn from his father before presenting it to the Haudenosaunee. The Onondaga also connected the arrival of corn to Iroquoia with a particular hill near their village. An incredulous visitor, naturalist John Bartram, published this tradition in 1751. According to the tale, a hunter encountered a mysterious woman who claimed to be "from heaven"—that is, the Sky World. The woman promised that if the man came back in one year, he would find food. Bartram wrote that the man returned a year later and "found corn, squashes, and tobacco, which were propagated from thence and spread throughout the country, and this silly story is religiously held for truth among them." Bartram was one of the eighteenth century's great botanists, and he viewed the natural world through the lens of Enlightenment deism, which left little room for supernatural interventions in the natural world. While Bartram's empiricism aided the traveler in his pioneering scientific work, it missed the metaphorical truth that connected a people's origins to agriculture and place.[37]

Beyond these clearings, travelers of all nations encountered an eerie and potentially dangerous realm of spirits, or other-than-human beings. At certain secluded spots within the forest, beneath waterfalls, within caves, or under the waters of some lakes (especially those featuring steep cliffs), portals linked Iroquoia to the domain of other-than-human beings. Traveling on a trail near Tonawanda Creek in 1788, Kirkland encountered one of these portals at a small lake known today as Divers Lake or Spirit Lake (the eighteenth-century name is unknown), a shallow kettle lake formed by the retreat of a glacier. A limestone cliff looms seventy feet above the water, part of a lengthy rock outcropping across Iroquoia known today as the Onondaga Escarpment. Under the water dwelt a powerful being of Seneca lore. Kirkland visited "A small Lake at the foot [of] the mountain where Indian says resides a [large] snake or draggon which often discorges balls of liquid fire." Kirkland had discovered the abode of fire-dragon, a significant other-than-human being in Seneca and Huron-Wyandot mythology. Powerful sorcerers, the fire-dragons looked like a composite panther, eagle, and serpent. Covered in flames, fire-dragons could shoot light and fireballs out of their mouths and eyes. Because of their fiery nature, they usually remained in lakes to avoid burning the world. However, they could move to other bodies of waters, traveling across the sky as a meteor.[38]

The fire-dragon lived in a truly ancient site, which suggests how the Haudenosaunee maintained connections to the places and ancestors of their distant past through myths. For thousands of years before the formation of the Haudenosaunee's Great League, Native peoples had traveled to Divers Lake to procure flint from the only quarry in western New York. This valuable stone had traditionally been used in the crafting of knives and arrowheads, and it brought people back to this particular location. From a scientific view, of course, the fire-dragon did not exist, but its myth spoke to the truly valuable nature of the place that the dragon guarded. The Haudenosaunee had a long history of associating these flint-rich places with powerful other-than-human beings. While traveling with a group of Mohawks near Lake George in 1667, Jesuit missionaries wrote: "Arriving within three-quarters of a league of the Falls by which Lake St. Sacrement [George] empties, we all halted at this spot, without knowing why, until we saw our Savages at the water-side gathering up flints, which were almost all cut into shape." Puzzled, the Jesuits asked why their companions insisted on stopping. The Haudenosaunee explained that "they never fail to halt at this place, to pay homage to a race of invisible men who dwell there at the bottom of the lake." The missionaries noted, "These beings occupy themselves in preparing flints, nearly all cut, for the passers-by, provided the latter pay their respects to them by giving them tobacco." The Jesuits described these "invisible" beings as "little men" who traveled by canoe. Their description referred to the Little People or Djo-geh-onh in later Seneca accounts. Supernaturally powerful, the Little People often helped humans, traveled by canoe, appeared or disappeared at will, and sometimes received tobacco offerings for their assistance. The incident demonstrated the enduring importance of reciprocal relationships with all other-than-human beings, who would have to be reckoned with during changes to the Great Island's landscape.[39]

While the Little People befriended the Haudenosaunee, many of the other creatures of their mythology were dangerous. In one well-known story, a giant mosquito attacked the fortified village at Onondaga long before European contact. In David Cusick's rendition of the tale, written during the early nineteenth century but drawing upon older traditions, the giant mosquito attacked the fort intermittently. Although the warriors failed to repel the invader, the Holder of the Heavens came to the rescue: seeing the great mosquito, "he chased

[it] on the borders of the great lakes toward the sunsetting, and round the ground country; at last he overtook the monster and kill[ed] it near the salt lake Onondaga and the blood became small musquetoes." As any visitor to Iroquoia could testify, these insects continued to torment humans, though more as an annoyance than as an existential threat. At the end of the nineteenth century, the archaeologist William Beauchamp visited a stone commemorating a spot where the Holder of the Heavens rested during his pursuit. Beauchamp also learned of a swamp called Kah-yah-tak-ne-t'-ke-tah'-keh, or "where the mosquito lies," a reference to the place where the Holder of the Heavens had vanquished the great mosquito.[40]

More ominously, the Haudenosaunee believed that giant, menacing animals had long ago ravaged the Great Island and perhaps would someday return. Their most spectacular stories centered on "Big Bone Lick," a salt lick on the Ohio River in present-day northern Kentucky (at the time claimed by the Haudenosaunee), where native people found remains of the mastodon, an extinct large mammal from the Ice Age. In 1766 a Haudenosaunee chief told a fascinating tale of this place that mixed old and new ideas ranging from ancient extinctions to polygenism (the belief in separate creations of populations). According to this chief, the Great Spirit first created white men, who were too "imperfect" and "ill-tempered" and therefore placed across the ocean. As the second creation, Africans were better but still not fit for the Great Island. Finally, using red clay, the Great Spirit created the red men, perfectly suited for the Great Spirit's way of life. Unfortunately, after the Great Spirit had placed Indians on the Great Island, the chief continued, the people grew "ill-tempered and wicked," leading to a dramatic reckoning: "In consequence of this, the Great Spirit created the great buffalo, the bones of which you now see before us; these made war upon the human species alone, and destroyed all but a few, who repented and promised the Great Spirit to live according to his laws, if he would restrain the devouring enemy; whereupon he sent lightning and thunder, and destroyed the whole race, in this spot, two excepted, a male and a female, which he shut up in yonder mountain, ready to loose again, should occasion require." Putting his own age at eighty-four years, the chief explained that he learned of the bones from his grandfather, thereby confirming the ancient nature of this site with its fossils "the like to which are found in no other part of the country." A late eighteenth-century account attributed to the Shawnee also vouched for the destruction of the mastodon "Ten thousand moons ago." Yet the description of black, white, and red peoples indicated that this possibly ancient story had taken on new meaning during the mid-eighteenth century, by which point these formerly separate peoples had come together, often violently, in North America.[41]

Although it is tempting to speculate about the ability of these oral traditions to recall traces of a truly ancient past, the Haudenosaunee chief's story more clearly evoked contemporary Native American apocalyptic visions experienced in response to struggles against an expansionist British empire. Most famously, by the time of the Big Bone Lick's story, Indians of the Eastern Woodlands knew of the Delaware holy man Neolin, who had sought the Master of Life in a vision of a revitalization of Native American power. Much like the tale of the Big Bone Lick, Neolin's vision described separate creations of European and Indian peoples, but he clarified the laws of the Great Spirit, or Master of Life, for the Great Island. Indians had to resist the consumption of alcohol and the sale of their lands. By Neolin's reasoning, much of the blame for Indians' decline lay with Indians themselves, who had it in their power to choose the proper path and save their futures by returning to traditional ways, as he understood them. The holy man's message spread quickly during the uncertain closing years of the Seven Years' War, when the increasingly powerful and successful British forces seemed disinclined to respect the independence of Native peoples. This climate also fostered a diversity of interpretations and even additional religious experiences.

In September 1762 representatives from the Onondaga reported a similar prophet to the British superintendent of Indian affairs, Sir William Johnson. This vision also emphasized separate creations but shifted the overall blame to Euro-Americans for the problems on the Great Island: "[The Great Spirit] now saw the white People squabbling, and fighting for these Lands which He gave the Indians; and that in every Assembly, and Company of Governors, and Great Men, He heard nothing scare spoke, or talk'd of, but claiming, and wanting, large Possessions in our Country. This He said, was so contrary to his Intention, and what He expected wou'd be the Consequences at the time when the white People first came, like Children, among Us, that He was quite displeas'd, and would, altho their Numbers were ever so great, punish them if They did not desist." At first it seemed destruction would come from a diverse group of Indians throughout the Great Lakes region, who in 1763 attacked every British fortification within range. In response to what became known as Pontiac's Rebellion, after one of Neolin's followers, the British government implemented more generous policies toward Eastern Woodland Indians and attempted to enforce the Proclamation of 1763, which limited colonists to lands east of the Appalachian Mountains. For the moment, the Great Island would remain a shared land, but the widespread visions of destruction, which mixed pre-scientific understandings of race and extinction, revealed profound unease about the growing numbers of Euro-Americans and their influence in Indian country. During the second half of the eighteenth century, Haudenosaunee leaders increasingly saw management of European expansion as the most viable form of preserving their homelands and culture, which had incorporated European materials, tools, and crops to fashion a dynamic and evolving built landscape. Yet, given the Onondaga prophet's take on the Great Spirit's anger, it remained unclear who would face destruction if the mastodons someday emerged from their mountain slumber.[42]

During the eighteenth century, Euro-American visitors knew of Iroquoia's importance, but the land remained mysterious and intimidating. One night during his journey through Iroquoia, Moravian missionary John Frederick Cammerhoff wrote in his diary, "We went on til toward evening, when we came into a wilderness, and entered a wood so dark that we could not see farther than where we stood." But their guide, Hahotschaunquas, saw a familiar landscape with a rich history. The next morning, over a trout breakfast, Hahotschaunquas told the missionaries that "long ago, Tutelars [Tutelos] had lived in the neighborhood." Without Hahotschaunquas, the missionaries could have only dreamed of the history of "a wood so dark."

The feeling people ascribe to locations changes greatly depending on what they imagine happened there. Throughout their journey the missionaries named each campsite to commemorate and remember their journey: David's Castle in Gajuka Town, Rose Meadow, and Senneka Mail Station, among many others. By naming places, the missionaries temporarily transformed the dark woods into something more welcoming. However, these place-names left a fleeting imprint upon the landscape, shared only by the travelers. The land remained the domain of the Haudenosaunee. A few nights since the trek through the dark forest, after constructing a shelter from the rain, the travelers reflected on the challenges of a still unfamiliar land. In his journal, Cammerhoff wrote, "David [Zeisberger] and I remembered how wonderfully we had been led over strange and difficult paths, and then retired to bed." Prior to the Revolution, the relatively few Euro-American visitors to Iroquoia depended on guides like Hahotschaunquas to navigate the terrain and understand the Haudenosaunee's landscape.[43]

The Haudenosaunee shaped everything from the plants to the place-names of Iroquoia. Lofty forests stretched across a land frequented by hunters and shared with other-than-human beings. Gifts from the Sky World, corns, beans, and squash grew in alluvial flats near villages. Shifting locations over the centuries, villages left a trail of history, remembered in oral traditions. Monuments reminded the Haudenosaunee of their achievements in war. This landscape connected the Haudenosaunee to their myths, history, and identities.

As they sat and talked of that land's history in June 1750, Cammerhoff, Zeisberger, and Hahotschaunquas could not have foreseen the changes to come to Iroquoia within Zeisberger's own lifetime. They seemed unaware that not far to the south, supernatural mastodons waited to be unleashed upon the Great Island. To be sure, troublesome signs abounded—notably, the growth of white settlements near the longhouse's eastern door—but the Haudenosaunee remained Britain's most privileged and respected Indian allies on the Great Island. Unimaginable at the time, the most powerful Atlantic empire would soon face a rebellion from thirteen of its North American colonies. Consequently, during the 1770s, Iroquoia faced the greatest challenge of its history. The Revolution would set into motion a series of disasters for the Haudenosaunee, unleashing white "settlers" upon the already settled land of the longhouse. Iroquoia's large stands of forest, its wild animals, its mysteries, and its ruins provided fertile ground for a new vision of the landscape, one that sought to erase the homeland of the People of the Longhouse.

| Chapter Two

Predators of the Vanishing Landscape

Had Iroquoia and, more broadly, North America truly been a "virgin land," the American Revolution might never have happened. It certainly would not have unfolded as it did, with a series of crises in the 1760s and 1770s that spiraled out of control as the British Crown lost thirteen of its mainland colonies. Famously, beginning in 1764, the British government initiated a series of unpopular taxes to pay for the Seven Years' (French and Indian) War, a struggle for North America, waged against the French and Indian allies. More important to the Six Nations, in an effort to avoid costly future conflicts with Indians, in the Proclamation of 1763 and the Treaty of Fort Stanwix (1768), the British government limited colonists' access to land west of the Appalachian Mountains and in central and western Iroquoia, respectively. Among the complaints he listed in the Declaration of Independence, Thomas Jefferson included the charge that King George "endeavored to prevent the population of these states; for that purpose obstructing the laws of naturalization of foreigners; refusing to pass others to encourage their migration hither, and raising the conditions of new appropriations of lands." By "new appropriations of lands," Jefferson meant lands protected for the benefit of Indians, including the Haudenosaunee.[1]

Coming from relatively infertile and crowded New England, potential settlers eyed Iroquoia as a place to improve their lives as family

farmers. During the Revolution, the Continental army's young soldiers caught their first glimpses of central and western New York,
which they described in glowing terms. To a significant degree, soldiers would have witnessed the potential of these lands because the
Haudenosaunee were already farming them. However, local historian Orsamus Turner recalled that many of these soldiers would later
return "through a long wilderness, to the land of promise—the Genesee country." This interpretation emphasized that the landscape had
great potential but required the proper men to transform it. Other
nineteenth-century Americans even waxed poetically of a new age
of discovery: "When none had dared with impious foot intrude /
On Nature's vast unbroken solitude / When its rude beauties were
unmark'd by man." Emphasizing the wild nature of the landscape,
settlers made their transformation all the more heroic by erasing the
place of the Haudenosaunee in the landscape's past.[2]

This opportunity came with the Revolution, which divided the Six
Nations and eventually eroded their control of Iroquoia. The most
pro-British faction fell under the sway of Mohawk Joseph Brant, who
commanded Mohawks and loyalists. Initially hoping to remain neutral, the Seneca, Onondaga, and Cayuga of western Iroquoia allied
themselves with the British in 1777. Under the influence of American missionary Samuel Kirkland, the Oneida and many of their Tuscarora allies sided with the Americans. In the Peace of Paris of 1783,
the British government abandoned their Indian allies, who had to
negotiate separate settlements with the new U.S. government. Without the support of the British empire, the vastly outnumbered and
divided Six Nations lost most of their homeland in a series of treaties
from 1785 to 1797.[3]

Beginning in the late 1780s, and sharply increasing during the early
nineteenth century, white settlers began occupying lands previously
controlled by the Haudenosaunee. These settlers transformed New
York into the dominant commercial center of the early nation. By 1810
New York was the most populous state in the union, and by 1820 three-
fourths of its 1.3 million inhabitants lived in Iroquoia. Rapid growth
of the New York frontier reflected broader demographic trends of the

early republic. America's population surged from approximately 2.8 million in 1780 to 9.6 million by 1820. Pushing past the Appalachian Mountains, Americans settled more land from 1790 to 1820 than in the previous 160 years of colonization.[4]

Along this frontier, the Revolution and its outcome became a struggle to define the nature of settlement and farming in eastern North America. For centuries the Haudenosaunee had supported villages by farming corn, beans, and squash, tended by women, and by hunting and fishing, mostly undertaken by men. Native Americans had defined the terms of permanent settlement. This massive influx of Euro-American farmers transformed the complex ecology of Iroquoia's remaining forest into a landscape of Euro-American farms. Settlers cleared the mixed-hardwood forests for fields of wheat and corn and pastures for livestock to graze. Farmers also scoured the remaining forest of animals deemed dangerous to livestock, specifically wolves and mountain lions. As settlers caused localized extinction, naturalists uncovered remains of the mastodon in New York, and they subsequently proved that the bones belonged to a species no longer found on Earth. This discovery introduced the concept of extinction to Americans, who had believed that the earth's animal species had remained constant since creation. Americans then applied their new language of extinction to the Haudenosaunee and American Indians in general. Surveying the rapidly changing landscape, which they saw as the domain of dangerous predators, white observers concluded that the Indians had hunted and lived like those vanishing wild predators, who could not coexist with "settlers" in a landscape of farms. By waging a war of eradication against wolves and mountain lions, white Americans discovered the idea of extinction and imagined that Indians would eventually vanish like the predators of the wilderness.

Befitting a struggle between settlers—Indian and Euro-American—much of the Revolution's border warfare focused on destruction of the built environment. Following intermittent back-and-forth raids in 1778, an earnest assault on Iroquoia began in 1779. In April Col. Goose Van Schaick struck at the heart of the symbolic longhouse, destroying Onondaga. During the summer, the Continental army began a three-route invasion of Iroquoia. Col. David Broadhead invaded from the south, attacking the Seneca villages in the Allegheny Valley. Gen. James Clinton led his troops through the Mohawk Valley to the Susquehanna Valley. In August 1779 Gen. John Sullivan's troops moved north along the Susquehanna and rendezvoused with Clinton's men at Tioga. Numbering more than 3,000 men, Sullivan and Clinton's army constituted the primary American force against fewer than 1,000 Haudenosaunee and loyalists.[5]

By burning the Six Nations' fields and towns, the Continental army began the erasure of the landscape's native identity. A young adult at the time of the war, the Seneca chief Governor Blacksnake (Chainbreaker) later recalled killing members of the Continental army, concluding, "I have thought that it was done in honor to protect our own country where all the Indian nations were built forever." Greatly outnumbered, Blacksnake and the rest of the Seneca failed to protect their most significant villages, which were abandoned. On September 7, 1779, soldiers burned down Kanadesaga, the "New Town" occupied by the descendants of the French invasion. Kanadesaga impressed Lt. William Barton, who expressed surprise that the expedition met no resistance. On September 15 Sullivan's army burned Genesee Castle, the largest village in Iroquoia. At the conclusion of his seemingly successful campaign to destroy Iroquoia, General Sullivan noted, "Every creek and river has been traced, and the whole country explored in search of Indian settlements, and I am well persuaded that, except one town situated near the Allegana [Allegheny], about 50 miles from Chinesee [Genesee] there is not a single town left in the country of the Five nations."[6]

Shortly after the Peace of Paris in 1783, the Haudenosaunee faced pressure from settlers, speculators, and an ambitious New York government looking to profit from land sales. The Oneida sold much of their land in two treaties with the State of New York, the Treaty of Fort Herkimer in 1785 and the Treaty of Fort Schuyler in 1788. In 1788 Massachusetts land speculators Oliver Phelps and Nathaniel Gorham acquired much of the Haudenosaunee land between the Genesee

River and Seneca Lake. In 1797 the Seneca sold all but 200,000 acres of their land in the Treaty of Big Tree to the Holland Land Company. These treaties confined the Haudenosaunee to discrete reservations in an emerging terrain of white settlements. Within New York, the Oneida retained lands south of Oneida Lake. West of Oneida stood the Onondaga Reservation. The Seneca had two large reservations on the shores of Lake Erie: Buffalo Creek and Cattaraugus. Northeast of Buffalo Creek was the Tonawanda Reservation. Smaller reservations (Canawagus, Big Tree, Squawky Hill, Gardeau, and Caneadea) stood along the Genesee River. Another important Seneca Reservation occupied the banks of the Allegheny River, near the Pennsylvania border. In between the Allegheny and Genesee Reservations was the small Oil Spring Reservation. The Tuscarora received a reservation near Niagara, south of Lake Ontario. Finally, to the north of the Adirondacks, the residents of the Akwesasne (St. Regis) Reservation found their lands split by the Treaty of Paris, dividing their settlement between Canada and the United States. Divided during the war, the Six Nations experienced additional division between national borders. By 1789, most notably, 1,200 Haudenosaunee had resettled at the Grand River valley in Upper Canada. After 1800 these land cessions and migrations left the approximately 3,500 remaining New York Haudenosaunee within small enclaves.[7]

With some variation in a segment known as the "New Military Tract," the Six Nations' land passed into the hands of land speculators, who then opened the land to settlers. In 1782 the New York legislature set aside 1.5 million acres of land for settlement by soldiers, who often resold their allotments to speculators. Officially open to settlement in 1791, the New Military Tract stretched from Seneca Lake in the west to Oneida Lake in the east. During the 1790s settlement also began between Seneca Lake and the Genesee River, in Phelps and Gorham's Purchase. West of the Genesee River, to the shores of Lake Erie, settlers arrived in the Holland Land Purchase after 1800.[8]

Instead of walking blindly into a forest, settlers sought signs left by the Haudenosaunee along the main east-west trail that the Six Nations had once maintained. Developed into a road known as the Genesee

Turnpike, the basic east-west route across New York State remained the route of the Haudenosaunee's trail. Developers sometimes used routes branching off from the main trail as blueprints for roads. With great numbers and an equally great need to transport goods between markets, New Yorkers eventually cleared hundreds of new roads, but many of these had origins in the Haudenosaunee system. The Holland Land Company built ten of its twenty main roads along existing Haudenosaunee trails. Developers occasionally straightened routes, but the trails followed good terrain and facilitated early settling. Through road building, Americans erased signs of the Haudenosaunee's trails, even as they made them physically permanent.[9]

Settlers preferred the fertile alluvial soil near river bottoms and lake outlets, where the Haudenosaunee had built their villages. Despite the burning of Iroquoia, these settlers found obvious indications of recent Indian occupation. In 1792 Alexander Coventry purchased a tract of land near Seneca Lake, where he noted the Haudenosaunee's landscape. Exploring near his purchase, Coventry wrote, "I suppose there are 50 or 60 acres of Indian clearing on this Lot." In his travels Coventry noticed additional "Indian clearings," where the Haudenosaunee had cleared the land for their fields and housing. Lucky early arrivals found apple orchards recovering from ax blows or bypassed by the Continental army. It was obvious that the Haudenosaunee had planted these fields. Early settlers, especially those near the reservations, frequently encountered Indians. An early settler near Palmyra, Stephen Durfee, later recalled, "The Indians were hunting and trapping, camping in our neighborhood, in all the earliest years. The flats of the Ganargwa [Ganargua] and all the adjoining up lands were favorite hunting grounds." Beyond the hunting grounds, settlers shared the trails with Indian travelers, fished the same lakes and rivers, and traded alcohol and furs with their Indian neighbors.[10]

Many well-known places in Iroquoia became American villages or farm fields. Kanadesaga became the American town of Geneva, located about one mile from the Seneca settlement. The Genesee Valley, home to Genesee Castle, became the most famous farmland in New York State. In 1789, in a remarkable coincidence, the site of Onnahee became the farm of a former captive, William Wyckoff, who had been taken there in September 1779. Although few could match Wyckoff's dramatic story, many American soldiers likely saw their return to Iroquoia as a reward and continuation of victory.[11]

Eager to profit from their newly acquired land, settlers cleared trees for farming—or, as the founder of Cooperstown, William Cooper, put it, "the great primary object, to cause the Wilderness to bloom and fructify." Clearing the forest took months of arduous chopping, carrying, and burning. After clearing underbrush and smaller trees, settlers felled the larger trees. Wood from these trees could be used for fencing, or the settler rolled the trees into a pile to dry for burning in the fall. Farmers sometimes used the ash for fertilizer or sold it to a merchant for potash manufacturing. A family of four probably cleared approximately five acres of land per year. By 1825 the New York State Census estimated that within the Holland Land Purchase, farmers had cleared forest from 396,826 acres, or roughly 11.61 percent of the total land area. This total included land used for pasture and land left fallow. This clearing began the process of creating a patchwork landscape, where previously extensive tracts of forest were broken into smaller segments, divided by farm fields. Joseph Ellicott, the company's land agent, required that any settler who bought land on credit needed to clear trees, fence lots, and plant crops by an agreed upon time. Ellicott recognized that farmland was worth more than forest, but he also wanted the landscape to look less like a wilderness. In the village of Buffalo, Ellicott had a stand of trees cleared to reveal the view of Lake Erie. He hoped to attract settlers by showing a rapidly improving landscape.[12]

Where Americans had settled, visitors remarked on a startling change. In 1791 a weary Dutch traveler named John Lincklaen slogged through thick forest near Onondaga. In the darkness Lincklaen and his companion attempted to stay awake by telling each other stories, "fearing the approach of bears and wolves." Only nine years later, British tourist John Maude cheerfully lauded the speed at which settlers had conquered that forest: "quit the Onondaga Reservation, and enter[ed] Marcellus Township, which, five years ago, was totally in wood—now many thousands acres of wheat."[13]

Nevertheless, these years passed slowly for early settlers, who described feeling surrounded by animal predators lurking in the forest just beyond their small clearings. Stories of animal encounters became part of local lore. Settling north of Batavia in 1803, Maj. John Morrison constructing a small cabin and cleared five acres. A year later, Morrison brought his wife and children to the frontier. One summer night, when Mr. Morrison had left for Batavia, Mrs. Morrison awoke to the "terrible howl" of wolves surrounding the cabin. Grabbing the ax, she "stood sentry, for hours and hours, until, day light approaching, the wolves retired to the depths of the forest." Writing of his first days in Otsego County, Levi Beardsley also remembered a precarious home. When his father left to help his uncle move, young Beardsley and his mother heard "frightful" noises in the woods. He explained, "I suppose it must have been blue jays, with the hootings of the owls; but we converted them into the possible, if not probable, noise of lurking Indians." Using household furniture, his mother barricaded the doorway. Early arrivals felt ill at ease in a landscape of unfamiliar sounds, places, and people.[14]

In reality, predators caused more harm to domesticated animals than to humans. Wolves, mountain lions, and bears traveled extensively with no understanding of property lines. James Sperry later recalled that settlers learned to build large enough pens for their sheep. He concluded, "If left out by accident or carelessness, they were almost sure to be attacked." To construct pens, pioneers stacked logs in the form of a small house for the sheep, tight and high enough to prevent wolves from entering. Although they had entered a conquered land, early settlers felt under siege from elusive and determined animal adversaries.[15]

State sponsorship turned this struggle against animal predators into a potentially profitable endeavor. In 1797 the New York State Legislature offered a bounty for wolves and mountain lions, paid by the individual county's treasurer. The "Act to encourage the destroying of wolves and panthers" paid ten dollars for each wolf or mountain lion killed. To receive this bounty, enterprising hunters brought the heads and entire skins of each animal to the county justice of the peace. The justice of the peace then administered an oath, whereby the hunter swore that his kills occurred within the county. This act also stipulated that Indians could collect bounties as well. Following the oath, the justice of the peace produced a certificate for payment.[16]

These efforts received support from folklore that spread throughout the United States, which celebrated the eradication of wolves. Most famously, in 1788 Col. David Humphreys popularized a hunt undertaken by the Revolutionary War general Israel Putnam during the general's early years in Connecticut. In Humphreys's account, the young Putnam faced off against a formidable "she-wolf," who had for years preyed upon the livestock of farmers. Eluding torch-carrying townsfolk, dogs, and a black servant, the wolf hid in the depths of a cavern. According to the folktale, only the heroics of Putnam defeated the animal. Descending into the cavern alone, Putnam faced off with the "she-wolf" and shot her in the head, to the joy of the townspeople. The *Otsego Herald*, an Upstate New York paper, described Putnam's story as "so well known that we shall not tire the reader by repeating it."[17]

Occasionally New York frontier communities produced their own local heroes, who matched Putnam's exploits. A resident of Butternuts, John King told of his daring encounter with a pack of vicious wolves. Awakened early in the morning by a howling of wolves, King found his neighbor's flock of sheep missing. In a scene reminiscent of a battlefield, King spotted "nine wolves in a body, advancing toward him." The *Otsego Herald* commemorated this battle with a bold headline, "Defeat of the *Wolves!*" A later local historian for nearby Cortland County evoked a similar martial spirit, observing that settlers wage a "crusade" or an "exterminating war" against "more than savage beasts of prey." As recounted by the historian, the war was just. The animal's savage nature left the settlers with little choice but to exterminate all of them.[18]

Sometimes viewed as formidable opponents, predators also received the less charitable label of "pests" that needed to be eliminated. Near Geneva in 1800, John Maude noted the uncleared land was "infested by bears and wolves." In Cooperstown, George Pomeroy promised a solution. Taking out a recurring weekly advertisement under the bold headline of "RATS," Pomeroy promised "an effectual compound for destroying RATS, FOXES, & WOLVES, without the means of *Arsenic* (vulgarly called *Ratsbane*) or corrosive sublimate." Pomeroy never revealed the secret ingredient, but later offered an "Indian Scent, for scenting Traps—Composition to destroy Foxes, Wolves, Bears, Martins, Minks, Rats, in fifteen minutes." Evoking Indians as masters of wilderness knowledge, Pomeroy marketed a solution to conquer the very nature associated with Indians.[19]

To win their "war" against wolves, settlers employed a mix of strategies against their crafty opponents. Most commonly, they dug pits. John H. Hooker, a pioneer resident of Cortland County, later recalled his pit: "about six feet wide by twelve deep." He built up a "curb" of two to three feet in height around the edges of the pit. Hooker and his neighbors covered the hole with a "pan" that would spin when an animal landed upon it, sending the wolf into the pit below. To entice the wolves, Hooker hung bait over the center of the unstable cover. One night he and two neighbors caught five wolves, which they paraded before the community and then killed. In a classic example of psychological projection, humans proved to be colder and more violent than their supposedly dangerous adversaries.[20]

Most famously, settlers engaged in circle hunts, social events where groups of men went into the woods to surround and kill wolves. In Tompkins County, settlers participated in the "Grand Annual Hunt" of wolves, headed by "The Chief" of the "Tompkins County Hunting Tribe," Benjamin Drake. A local merchant and pioneer resident, with a flair for the dramatic, Drake also headed a "Moral Society," which safeguarded Ithaca from vagrants. As head of the society, Drake anointed himself "Old Tecumseh," after the famous Shawnee leader who led a coalition against the Americans in the War of 1812. In December 1823 "Chief" Drake placed a very large announcement for a hunt in the *Ithaca Journal*: "The Ground designated for this year, is in the town of Newfield. Great Care has been taken, to survey and mark out a section of country, embracing a circumference of twenty-five miles, abounding with Deer; and much infested with Wolves, Bears, Panthers, Foxes, and other enemies of the human race." As settlers carefully delineated their lines of property and their farms from wilderness, they also cleared animals from land untouched by the plow or ax.[21]

By temporarily embracing the perceived violence of nature, with a dash of excitement, settlers as hunters became heroic conquerors of nature. "Chief" Drake argued that his "Grand Wolf Drive" was needed, as "the repose of the settler is disturbed by the midnight howl of the Wolf, and yell of the Panther." By organizing such a drive, settlers could "perform in a day, what in the ordinary course of events, would be the work of years." He also promised adventure and glory, as the men could help conquer the gloomy wilderness with its midnight monsters. He warned that no man would wish to remember that "the monsters of the wilderness have been routed from their lurking places; and I was not there." Conquest of the wilderness was a one-time event—once gone, the wild landscape would not return.[22]

Americans cleared the forest at an impressive rate, but they killed predators at an even faster pace. Drake's hunt was probably one of the last near the Finger Lakes region. By the 1820s, from Cooperstown west to the Finger Lakes and the Genesee Valley, wolves and mountain lions became scarce. In 1822 the *Otsego Herald* reported a rare mountain lion sighting near the Genesee Valley, reprinted from a Batavia newspaper. Someone found a large mountain lion dead on the shores of Lake Ontario, and another roamed nearby. These mountain lions were "the first of their species that have been discovered in that part of the country for 12 or 13 years; and were believed to have been totally exterminated." Along the thinly settled and marginal farming areas near the Pennsylvania border and in the Adirondack Mountains, wolves and mountain lions temporarily escaped notice.[23]

By 1840 mountain lions and wolves had made their last stand in the Adirondack Mountains of northern New York. This rugged landscape contained more than forty peaks of over 4,000 feet in height, great forests, and poor soil for farming. The region became known as Couchsachraga, which has been interpreted as "their hunting grounds." In 1784 Thomas Pownall, a former governor of the Massachusetts Bay Colony, translated this word as "Dismal Wilderness or Habitation of Winter." Pownall's phrase reflected the unsuitability of the land for farming and the tendency of native people to hunt there in winter. Far away from the farmlands of central and western New York, wolves and mountain lions survived the rest of the century (but not the twentieth).[24]

This war against wilderness confronted the powerful, sometimes unseen supernatural world at the heart of the Great Island. Despite settlers being unfamiliar with Haudenosaunee mythology, some beliefs influenced early stories about nature. The *Otsego Herald* reported an encounter between a fisherman and a sea serpent on Canadarago Lake. This fisherman described a snake the size of a man, with "a spear, or a horn that had grew out between his eyes, three square, and much resembling about four inches of the point of a bayonet, with a yellow ring around his neck, to appearances about an inch wide." In Haudenosaunee folklore, horned water serpents often appear as antagonists. No additional reports of the monster in Canadarago Lake appeared, but strange noises associated with lakes continued. For two years prior to the encounter, settlers had heard the animal's "voice," which sounded like an echo traveling through a massive hollow log, struck by an ax. This description of a booming echo seems remarkably similar to the "Lake Guns" or "Seneca Guns," a mysterious phenomenon later associated with Cayuga and Seneca Lakes. As Americans moved westward, they encountered nature that hid secrets within its vast expanses.[25]

No monster captured the imagination of Americans like the mastodon, which became the first (imagined) predator that vanished from the wilderness and the most significant Haudenosaunee mythological figure to enter Euro-American literature. As settlers caused localized extinction (often called "extirpation"), New Yorkers gradually realized that these ancient animals had gone extinct. Intellectuals could read of ideas of extinction in scholarly publications in Europe and in America, but everyday Americans also could read in the newspapers or hear from neighbors about spectacular finds of ancient fossils. Known for his art and founding one of America's first great museums, Charles Wilson Peale emerged as the most famous promoter of the mastodon. Having unearthed a largely intact skeleton in the Hudson River, Peale and his son Rembrandt assembled a mastodon exhibit and tirelessly promoted it. On Christmas Eve 1801, in Peale's Philadelphia museum the exhibit opened with a viewing by members of the American Philosophical Society, followed by the general public. In Peale's museum stood a great monster of an animal, fifteen feet long and eleven feet tall. Not the herbivore known today, the Peales' mastodon was a ferocious carnivore. The lawyer and sometime assemblyman Sylvanus Miller believed that the mastodon had once been found throughout North America: "that in numbers, they equalled the other beasts of the forest; such as the bear, the wolf, the panther, &c. &c. In the proportion which larger animals bear to the smaller, in the order of nature." In this sense, the mastodon became an apex predator, the largest and most powerful of the predators on the continent.[26]

In 1806 the French naturalist Georges Cuvier employed techniques of comparative anatomy to prove the American mastodon was a distinct and extinct species. Cuvier noted that the mastodon fossils differed from living elephants and fossils of the mammoth, found in Siberia. By the 1810s, New York intellectuals knew the work of Cuvier well. In his inaugural address to the Literary and Philosophy Society of New York, Mayor DeWitt Clinton noted, "The indefatigable Cuvier has classed the fossil remains of seventy-eight different quadrupeds, of which forty-nine are distinct species hitherto unknown to naturalists." Prior to this empirical proof, most intellectuals had been uncomfortable with the idea of extinction, believing instead that God had designed a permanent order in nature. Called the "Great Chain of Being," this belief placed man at the top of a hierarchy of animals, plants, and finally elements of descending sophistication. Dismissing the Great Chain of Being as a "superstition of philosophy," Clinton pointed to Cuvier's work as proof that many animals went extinct, but nature continued to function with a kind of "harmony."[27]

With the acquisition of Iroquoia, naturalists had an extraordinary opportunity to study the natural history and wildlife of western New York. Formed in January 1814, the Literary and Philosophical Society held its first meeting in Clinton's offices. A signer of the U.S. Constitution and a longtime member of the American Philosophical Society, Hugh Williamson, played an important role in forming New York's organization. The society included both gentlemen scholars, such as Clinton, and an emerging class of professional scientists, notably former Columbia University professor of natural history Samuel Latham Mitchill and physician-botanist David Hosack, who headed Columbia's Department of Midwifery and Surgery. Noted for his groundbreaking maps of New York, the surveyor-general of New York State Simeon De Witt was also a member (see fig. 10). Senator Rufus King and a former senator and chairman of the Erie Canal Commission, Gouverneur Morris, rounded out the cast of notables.[28]

When investigating the mastodon's disappearance, researchers' thoughts often turned to Indians and their traditions about the fossils, which linked the vanished animal to their ancient homelands. According to the *Gazetteer of the State of New York*, "Chemung is said to be big horn, or great horn, in the dialect of the Indian tribes that anciently possessed this country. And that a very large horn was found in the Tioga or Chemung river, is well ascertained." This "horn" may have been a mastodon tooth. In 1786 on the Tioga River, surveyors had found a grinder tooth from a mastodon, and the find made news in the *Columbian Magazine*.[29]

In popular culture, Indian traditions and scientific explanations mixed to produce the same conclusion: mastodons had vanished long ago. These traditions included variations on Haudenosaunee and Shawnee accounts of the Big Bone Lick. In 1802 the *Otsego Herald* reprinted a legend used by the Peales in marketing their mastodon display: "According to a tradition among the Indians, this animal, which so long excited the curiosity of naturalists, ceased to exist more than *ten thousand moons ago*." Previous investigators assumed (and Thomas Jefferson held out hope) that the animal still roamed in the vast unexplored west. Of course, not everyone trusted the veracity of Indian claims. An always-skeptical Clinton observed, "It is certain that the Indians had some notions respecting the mammoth, which they might have derived from tradition, or, after seeing the remains, they might have invented the fables which exist."[30]

Ongoing discoveries kept the public interested in the mastodon for decades. In 1817 the *Otsego Herald* ran a small article, "Another

Mammoth Discovered," which reported of a find by Mitchill: "The Bones of another of these huge animals, have lately been discovered in the village of Chester, five miles east of Goshen, Orange County. They were disinterred from the earth in the presence of Doctor Mitchill, and several other gentlemen, by whom they were brought to New York, and deposited among the collections of the Lyceum at the New York Institution. One of the tusks measured *nine feet*." By the middle of the nineteenth century, one account estimated that between fifteen and twenty fossil remains of mastodons had been unearthed and documented in New York State. Readers could only imagine how much more difficult frontier expansion would have been had they been fighting mastodons in addition to wolves and mountain lions.[31]

But what could have caused the dramatic extinction of such a seemingly powerful animal? Clinton republished compelling climatic and environmental theories in a letter he received from Miller, which summarized a hypothesis developed by Mitchill. He theorized that in the ancient past the earth's axis had somehow shifted by 90 degrees—that is, the equator once had run through the Mississippi Valley. By this reasoning, the climate of America's interior had once been tropical and, therefore, fostered habitat suitable for "animals peculiar to warm climates." Under this model, the presently frigid lands of Siberia and Alaska would have once been warm enough to allow the mastodon to cross from Asia to America. During the early nineteenth century, Mitchill and other scholars struggled with reconstructing a distant past that they had only very recently realized existed. While these thinkers debated the precise means by which extinction may have occurred, Mitchill's speculations pointed to how Americans of the early republic began understanding the powerful relationships between environment, survival, and extinction.[32]

Many late eighteenth- and early nineteenth-century writers believed that the climate and environment also shaped societies and human behavioral traits. Writers had noted the obvious connection between skin color and warm climates, but they debated the degree to which any other physical and mental characteristics resulted from geographic chance—that is, to what degree a society's potential was linked to its location. Americans responded especially sharply to the writings of the famous French naturalist Georges-Louis Leclerc, Comte de Buffon, who had written of America's climate as being so cold and damp that it produced small and weak animals. Even animal stock from Europe eventually degenerated after leaving their ideal home. In an often-quoted passage, Buffon applied his theory of degeneracy to America's native population: "In the savage, the organs of genera- tion are small and feeble. He has no hair, no beard, no ardour for the female. Though nimbler than the European, because more accustomed to running, his strength is not so great. His sensations are less acute; and yet he is more cowardly and timid." Rejecting any criticism of their continent's climate, Americans emphasized the relationship of humans to the natural environment and within social institutions as the key factors influencing what later social scientists would call cul- ture. (Important Americans, notably Jefferson, already wrote of Afri- cans in more biologically racist terms.) The more optimistic thinkers suggested that people—more properly, societies—had it within their power to modify their surroundings, which, in turn, ensured the long- term success of a particular population. Although he already claimed America had an ideal climate, Hugh Williamson even suggested that clearing the forest would benefit America by increasing the conti- nent's average temperatures. In any event, Americans saw their con- tinent's climate and environment as perfectly suited for a successful civilization, namely, theirs.[33]

American Indians represented a potential flaw in theories that extolled North America's climate and environment: if the continent possessed great potential, why had Indians (according to Europeans) seemingly squandered their opportunity to improve it? One answer came from Williamson in *Observations on the Climate in Different Parts of America* (1811), which identified North America's immense size and its bountiful nature as key barriers to the development of civilization in the past. His declensionist take on world history proposed that ances- tral Indians arrived from Asia with knowledge of farming: "But there was no extensive tract of fertile land in that part of America, wherefore small colonies issued from the parent stock, who supported themselves by hunting, and in a short time became savages, as in every other part of the world." Finding a continent teeming with wild game, hunters could live a supposedly enticingly idle life. In other words, the Great Island had always been a wilderness inhabited by a small number of hunters. By the early American republic, in environmental theories of human development, the wild frontier's influence posed a threat to the social advancement of Indians and white American hunters. But most Americans came in the waves of migration during the early nineteenth century rather than as long-distance hunters who roamed the farthest from civilization, and so America's original inhabitants faced the greater challenge of transitioning from centuries of supposedly dispersed wilderness living to life in fixed farming communities.[34]

Within this environmental framework, Clinton positioned New York's newly acquired lands as exceptionally promising, featuring unsurpassed natural bounty as well as soil productivity. As such, even its Native American inhabitants had advanced beyond the average Indian society. In an unusually generous assessment, which he later downplayed in the same "Address on the Iroquois" (1811), Clinton noted that the Haudenosaunee had "passed over the pastoral state and followed agriculture as well as fishing and hunting." Clinton believed Iroquoia had the best soil in America and the most significant waterways and lakes. He concluded, "The selection of this country for a habitation was the wisest expedient that could have been adopted by a military nation to satiate their thirst for glory, and to extend their conquests across the continent; and if they preferred the arts of peace, there was none better calculated for this important purpose." Williamson would have added that warfare (and hunting) led to a degeneration of knowledge. Later in his address, Clinton noted, "War was the favorite pursuit of this martial people, and military glory their ruling passion. Agriculture and the laborious drudgery of domestic life were left to women. The education of the savage was solely directed to hunting and war." In this gendered take on learning and agriculture, it would be up to white Americans to practice "the arts of peace" in such a favorable environment, which would involve the violent task of purging the forest of its animals. By any reckoning, the long-term prospects for predators in the lands of New York State looked grim. In the distant past, a climatic shift had prepared the environment for human dominance, but by the early nineteenth century, American settlers had begun their own dramatic transformations.[35]

American intellectuals fit the human-initiated transformation of the frontier within an Enlightenment framework of social development. Beginning in the eighteenth century, European and American intellectuals concluded that societies developed in distinct stages of increasing sophistication. The moral philosopher and political economist Adam Smith argued that societies pass through four ages: the hunter, the shepherd, agriculture, and finally the age of commerce. Many other writers, from Adam Ferguson in Scotland to John Quincy Adams in America, wrote variations of the four-stage theory. In each stage, humans used the land in a manner that rendered the previous stage obsolete. In his four-stage theory Adams observed, "But from the moment when man becomes a shepherd, the forest can no longer be his abode. His flocks and herds can subsist only by grazing. Open fields and verdant meadows are the scenes of his habitation." As Drake had suggested in his wolf hunt advertisement, development went in one direction only.[36]

This striking and seemingly irreversible change appeared in four etchings included in Orsamus Turner's *Pioneer History of the Holland Land Purchase of Western New York* (1849). In each image, as the pioneer's homestead improves, the forest vanishes into a landscape claimed by the farm (see figs. 5–8). These sketches reflected the life cycle of the pioneer as much as the life cycle of the landscape. In the first scene, the young pioneer braves winter to create the abundance of summer found in the second and third scenes. In the final scene, both the pioneer and the landscape have matured. Once more in winter, the pioneer, now a wealthy old man, lives in a landscape where its spectacular days of growth have long passed. But this cycle would continue elsewhere, as Turner's imaginative captions indicated: "ten to one that he has secured lands for his sons in some of the western states."[37]

Pious settlers found divine guidance in the rhythms of progress, setbacks, and triumph over the wilderness. In 1806 Simon Pierson

Fig. 5. [Benjamin C. Vanduzee], "First Sketch of the Pioneer." From Orsamus
Turner, *Pioneer History of the Holland Land Purchase of Western New York*.
Buffalo NY: Jewett Thomas, 1849 [opposite p. 563].

Fig. 6. [Benjamin C. Vanduzee], "Second Sketch of the Pioneer." From Turner,
Pioneer History of the Holland Land Purchase of Western New York
[opposite p. 564].

Fig. 7. [Benjamin C. Vanduzee], "Third Sketch of the Pioneer." From Turner, *Pioneer History of the Holland Land Purchase of Western New York* [before p. 565].

Fig. 8. [Benjamin C. Vanduzee], Fourth Sketch of the Pioneer. From Turner, *Pioneer History of the Holland Land Purchase of Western New York* [opposite p. 566].

and his brother led their families from Connecticut to western New York. Later in life, Pierson began reciting hymns to explain his years in the wilderness: "We then supposed we had arrived at the western verge of civilization, and that we were now coming to a region—"

"Where nothing dwelt but beasts of prey,
Or men as wild and fierce as they."

But what has proved to be a region where—

"He bids th' opprest and poor repair,
And builds them towns and cities there.

They sow their seeds, and trees they plant,
Whose yearly fruit supplies their want;
Their race grows up in fruitful stock,
Their wealth increases with their flock."[38]

Better known today for "Joy to the World," Isaac Watts had composed this "Hymn for New England" or "Colonies Planted; or Nations Blest and Punished" in 1714, but his words resonated with early nineteenth-century pioneers. The hymn included two especially relevant comments on the New England landscape: Indians as animal predators, and prosperity earned by the "race" of hardy farmers. But the hymn also contained a warning, unquoted by Pierson: "but if they sin, He lets the heathen nations in." Watt then described the devastation of New England at the hands of these "heathen nations," who led raids to take captives, leaving the fields untilled and abandoned. Some New Yorkers had experienced such devastation during the Revolution at the hands of the Haudenosaunee and British forces. During the mid-eighteenth century, the Haudenosaunee had pondered similar questions of divinely endorsed destruction in the form of the mastodons found at the Big Bone Lick. In the end, however, white Americans regained confidence in their standing with God. The Puritan hymn recalled that a just God rewarded His faithful by making "their cities thrive." As the nineteenth century progressed, New Yorkers could see evidence of such development throughout what had been Iroquoia.[39]

Americans question the ability of Indians to move beyond a "hunter" stage and into the subsequent stages imagined for whites on the frontier. When settlers quoted Watt comparing Indians to "beasts of prey," they reflected attitudes toward Indians that shaped policy. The comparison of Indians to animals suggested that Indians inhabited the natural world as animals do. George Washington, for example, hoped for peaceful purchases of Indian land rather than conquest of Indians. He explained that fighting Indians "is like driving the Wild Beasts of the Forest which will return as soon as the pursuit is at an end and fall perhaps on those that are left there; when the gradual extension of our Settlements will as certainly cause the Savage as the Wolf to retire; both being beasts of prey tho' they differ in shape." Washington wrote metaphorically of Indians as animals. Yet the metaphor spoke to a perceived truth in the early American republic—that an entire "race," however poorly defined by emerging science, had acquired traits shaped by and for survival in a wilderness where predators stalked prey. Indians would be trapped in a landscape of legal lines that confined them to discrete reservations, which were surrounded by townships divided into private landholdings. As the forest became farms, hunters could not trespass to find scarce game (see figs. 7 and 8).[40]

Visitors to Iroquoia often expressed the same thought: the expansion of agriculture would eventually drive the Haudenosaunee to extinction. In 1785, after visiting the Oneida, the French diplomat François Marbois wrote: "Indeed Europeans who are curious to know them [Indians] must not lose time, for the advance of the European population is extremely rapid in this continent, and since these nations live largely by hunting and fishing, they cannot remain in the neighborhood of civilized people." Demographic trends supported his conclusion. In New York, the white American population expanded the fastest at the nadir of the native population. In 1630, approximately twenty thousand people lived in the Five Nations. During the early seventeenth century, the future state of New York also housed the large Neutral Confederacy, the Erie Confederacy, and the Petun, Wenro, and Susquehannock. To the east of the longhouse, in the Hudson River valley lived the Mahican people, who would later reside near

the Oneida by the end of the 1780s. By the time white Americans settled Iroquoia, disease, warfare, and migration had reduced the Native
population of central and western New York by perhaps 95 percent.[41]

The Haudenosaunee had always derived a substantial portion of
their food from crops tended by women. That is, they were farmers
who also hunted. However, coming from a relatively patriarchal society,
Europeans expected men to lead their families as farmers. During the
first years of settler expansion, Haudenosaunee men hoped to maintain
their traditional gender roles. Visiting Oneida in 1795, Jeremy Belknap
and Jedidiah Morse found "agriculture in its infancy, labor being performed almost wholly by the women." The pair counted three families
of subsistence farmers. At Buffalo Creek, a visiting French nobleman,
the Duke de la Rochefoucauld, also observed women working in the
fields. Approving of the crops, the nobleman nevertheless noted that
because the women maintained the fields and homes, the men had
very little in personal wealth in the European sense. The duke saw
only tomahawks, pipes, and war scalps: "More property they do not
want." Catching the Haudenosaunee in their post-Revolution struggles, the duke arrived at an especially bad time to find material wealth.
However, his sentiments captured the Euro-American understanding
that without a male-centered farm economy of private property and
possessive individualism, societies would remain in a more primitive
state of development.[42]

On the Allegany Reservation, however, the Seneca chief Cornplanter
(Kaiutwahku) promoted plow-based agriculture, undertaken by men,
as part of a plan to adapt to the changing social landscape of the New
York frontier. In 1791 Cornplanter initiated a relationship with the Society of Friends (Quakers), who then educated his son. An enterprising individual, in 1795 Cornplanter established the first sawmill near
the reservation and sold lumber to the United States Army in Pittsburgh. In 1798, with Cornplanter's blessing, the first Quakers arrived
and began work on a model farm that taught the methods of plow-
based farming. Locating their farm on the Allegany Reservation, the
Quakers also promised cash bonuses for especially industrious farmers who grew specified quantities of crops.[43]

The federal government hoped that by becoming Euro-American style farmers, Indians would require less land and, therefore, sell more of it for settlement. While Washington had compared Indians to the vanishing wolves, his and subsequent administrations nevertheless supported efforts to "civilize" Indians. Washington's commissioner to the Six Nations, Timothy Pickering, explained: "They [Indians] will find their extensive hunting grounds unnecessary; and will then readily listen to a proposition to sell a part of them, for the purpose of procuring, for every family, domestic animals & instruments of husbandry." To an extent, it did not matter whether federal officials sincerely believed Indians could adopt a new style of farming. Either Indians would vanish like wolves, or they would be surrounded by and indistinguishable from a landscape of settlers, as defined by white Americans.[44]

The Quakers received assistance in their promotion of farming from Cornplanter's half-brother, the prophet Handsome Lake. In 1799 Handsome Lake experienced the first of a series of visions that led to the creation of the Code of Handsome Lake, the foundational beliefs of the Longhouse religion, which is still practiced among some of the Haudenosaunee. Handsome Lake proposed social and spiritual reforms that combined traditional ceremonies with aspects of Euro-American social life. In 1801 he explained that Indians should farm, but "they must not sell anything they raised off the ground, but give it away to one another and to the old people in particular in short that they must possess everything in common." Handsome Lake attempted to chart a middle course, one that reduced the role of men as hunters but maintained traditional bonds within the community.[45]

From 1800 to 1815, a growing number of Haudenosaunee men farmed with plows. Visiting Buffalo Creek in 1804, Gerald Hopkins saw "many of them at work; they were preparing the ground for the plough by rolling logs, taking up stumps, etc." He also noted the nearby Tuscarora "have greatly declined hunting and are becoming agriculturists." On the Grand River Reservation in Canada, John Norton also reported that the Mohawk were "improving rapidly" and producing between three and four hundred bushels of wheat for the year. These Mohawk sought to maintain elements of tradition while adjusting to the changing landscape. A hybrid figure himself, Norton approved of the farming: "The most industrious at the plough, generally shew themselves the most persevering at the chase, when in Winter they throw aside the hoe and take up the gun." Working year round, these farmer-hunters countered the familiar complaint that Indian men did nothing outside of hunting season.[46]

Despite the substantial fields Haudenosaunee women had always tended and the steps toward plow-based agriculture, New Yorkers still viewed the Haudenosaunee as hunters, doomed to extinction. In 1811 Clinton noted, "A nation that derives its subsistence, principally, from the forest, cannot live in the vicinity of one that relies upon the products of the field." Clinton ignored the Quaker and Haudenosaunee work at adopting plow-based agriculture. He knew of Cornplanter and Handsome Lake but focused on the "superstition" of their followers, who "cherished the imposter" of a prophet. Dismissive of supernatural aid, Clinton saw the Haudenosaunee and Indians in general as inflexible and incapable of adapting to a changing landscape. Clinton reasoned, "The Clearing of the country drives off the wild beasts; and when the game fails, the hunter must starve, change his occupation, or retire from the approach of cultivation. The savage has invariably preferred the last." Possessing a sharp and sometimes visionary intellect, Clinton nevertheless replicated stereotypes common among white observers of Indian life. Most Indians east of the Mississippi had been farmers, but Americans almost always saw them as hunters. By labeling Indians as inflexible agents of their own demise, Americans avoided recognizing their own role in ousting the Indians.[47]

As early as 1810, an astute William Cooper predicted the forest would vanish to such an extent that "they, which were the first obstacles to his improvement, become scarcer, become more valuable, and he is at length as anxious to preserve as he was first to destroy them." As a developer, Cooper thought mainly of natural resources. Yet by 1820 New Yorkers already looked back with some nostalgia at the only recent transformation of the frontier. As part of this nostalgia, the Indian belatedly became a tragic, vanishing figure to be pitied rather than feared. Some settlers believed Indians would leave voluntarily to avoid the cruelty of their white neighbors. The *Otsego Herald* published such an account, purportedly to have occurred in Maine. According to the tale, a Kennebec Indian man attempted to live in peace with white neighbors. The man allegedly said, "When white man's child die Indian man sorrow—he help bury him—when my child die no one speak to me—I make his grave alone—I can no live here." According to the tale, the man dug up his child, gave his farm to his neighbors, and walked to Canada to join other Indians, never to return.[48]

The conquest of the frontier became one of the most enduring symbols of the young American nation. But memories rarely exist separate from thoughts of the present or visions of the future. In the May 11, 1819, issue of the *Cherry Valley Gazette*, the editor published a travel narrative that described the Mohawk Valley in 1757. Introducing the narrative, the editor marveled: "What a vast difference between its general appearance then and now. How rapidly has the flood of our population rolled toward the western wilds! When will it stop?" The editor noted talk in Congress of crossing the Rocky Mountains, a vision of continental expansion eventually called manifest destiny.

While Americans could lament treatment of the Indians, they also insisted that such treatment had, in the long run, been necessary for the good of the nation. Taking a tone of sad resignation, the editor wondered: "What is ultimately to become of the red man of the forest? Is he to be hunted westward until he drowns himself in the waters of the Pacific? Or will we ever learn to be just and infuse into his mind the arts of civil life?" Only two columns to the right of the retrospective travel account, the editor included an account on news from South America, which provided a stark contrast with the agricultural productivity of New York markets. A correspondent from Buenos Aires wrote: "The state of this place is truly deplorable—its trade is very much reduced in consequence of the communication with the interior being cut off by wandering hordes of Indians, well-armed and mounted, who traverse the country, driving off the cattle, and committing excesses that shock humanity." Although some Americans expressed concerns about the fate of Indians, these words about South America would have also fit with their written accounts of the war against the Haudenosaunee.[49]

At the Fourth of July celebration held in Syracuse in 1820, to the usual celebration of nationalism, New Yorkers added conquest of the wilderness and the arrival of market-oriented agriculture. This event marked the completion of the middle section of the Erie Canal, which would eventually link New York City to the Great Lakes. When completed, food and manufactured goods would travel to and from any point on the Great Lakes to the great commercial port of New York City. The middle section of the canal connected the relatively new American towns of Utica and Montezuma. Coming from the west and east, seventy-three boats carried the festive crowd along the newly dug canal. Near the halfway point, in Syracuse, nearly two thousand people gathered to celebrate three years of work. Some boats featured decorations, but none had the celebrity of the *Oneida Chief*, a passenger boat carrying the governor of the state, DeWitt Clinton, along with the attorney general, speaker of the assembly, and other notables. After the boats arrived at Syracuse, the event featured an appropriately patriotic reading of the Declaration of Independence. Following the reading, Samuel Miles Hopkins, a lawyer and member of the state house of representatives, delivered a rousing keynote oration on progress and "the successive stages of improvement" experienced by the young nation. Music and food followed.[50]

The thousands in attendance included one to two hundred Haudenosaunee men and women. Some dressed in traditional clothing, perhaps for the occasion. They probably arrived from the nearby Oneida or Onondaga Reservations, both very close to Syracuse. For one participant, the celebration marked the demise of the sadly doomed Indians. Enjoying the booming guns, festive music, and decorations, he concluded: "All of these things were indeed calculated to astonish the poor Indians, and induce them to think that a kind of supernatural spirit was changing the face of that country which was lately a wilderness." He imagined these Indians as horribly out of place in any landscape except a primeval forest. In the past they had courageously pursued the "monsters of the wilderness." These monsters had disappeared as well, consigned to an age buried in the fields in the farms of western New York. No monster represented this changing age better than the mastodon. Once an agent of divine retribution in Haudenosaunee culture, meant to punish those who went against the Great Spirit, the ancient animal became a symbol of the first (imagined) apex predator to vanish from North America. Neither this supernaturally powerful animal nor the Indians who spoke of its wrath could survive the unstoppable changes underway in Iroquoia.[51]

Ironically, as he imagined frightened Indians of the woods, the well-meaning observer failed to understand the "changing face" of the country. Significantly, during the early American republic, Indians encountered much more complex problems than "starving" after farms had replaced their forests, as Clinton had generalized. By viewing Indians as similar to animal predators, observers overlooked the Haudenosaunee's understanding of the changing landscape and efforts to adapt to these changes. White Americans sensed that massive demographic and ecological expansion would be inexorable. Pushing toward the Mississippi, the young nation offered great opportunities for white farmers. Envisioning little potential for Indians in this landscape of farmers, white observers laid the intellectual groundwork for future calls that Indians leave Iroquoia and, more broadly, America east of the Mississippi.[52]

| Chapter Three

The Many Deaths of John Montour and the Mystery of the Painted Post

Following the Revolution, memories of violence and destruction haunted the frontier, where warfare between Indians and whites left a landscape of burned villages, destroyed fields, and sites of alleged atrocities. The postrevolutionary settlement of Iroquoia attracted men who could envision a future in this landscape of suffering. In fertile alluvial plains, speculators envisioned prospering towns and fields. Between the waterways, they eyed routes for the future Erie Canal. Travelers found a particularly alluring stretch of land at the confluence of the Tioga, Canisteo, and Cohocton Rivers, which form the Chemung River. In 1797, a budding poet submitted his work describing this region to the *Albany Centinel*. The first part of the poem contained a prophecy of the region's future:

> A Plain, a rising Plain, extended wide,
> With tree-topt mountains hem'd on either side;
> Amid this Plain a gentle rise we find,
> With nature, doubtless, for a town design'd.[1]

Imaginations projected backward in time as well as forward. At this confluence travelers encountered a mysterious wooden post of indeterminate age and of Indian design. First noted by white Americans circa 1780 and well known by the 1790s, the monument became known

as the "Painted Post" and lent its name to the region and a future village. At a geographic junction, the post also marked a temporal crossroads between the landscape's Indian past and its white settler future.
But what could this mysterious object mean? When pondering the
future, settlers saw the landscape's beauty. When conjuring images
of the landscape's past, settlers' imaginations turned darker. In the
second part of the poem, the author dreamed up the Post's history:

> The *Painted Post* stands there—but
> rais'd for what
> No one knows—the tribe, unlettered have forgot
> But, if indulg'd the liberty to guess,
> Tis a triumphal pillar rais'd to express
> Some savage warrior's deeds, or captive's pain

The poet concluded that the poor captive probably had been tortured
with fire before dying.[2]

As the frontier expanded throughout the nineteenth century, Americans appropriated Indian landmarks, real or imagined, as part of the
process of dispossessing Indians. Some landmarks, most notably "lov-
ers' leaps" later found throughout America, probably had no connection to authentic Indian landmarks. At these spots, Americans dreamed
stories of romantic Indian maidens leaping to their deaths to avoid
some unwanted fate. Exciting and memorable, these stories replaced
the more violent and less romantic history of Indian-white relations.
Many Americans probably saw appropriated "Indian" landmarks as
faint reminders of a distant, heroic past. But these vague memories
connected to a larger and more powerful cultural legacy of inventing
an American future where Indians had no place.[3]

Often described as an intellectual struggle of competing ideologies,
the Revolution also involved significant carnage and destruction, notably along the northern frontier and throughout Iroquoia. At the height
of the conflict in 1779, Iroquoia from the Mohawk River west to the
Genesee Valley was largely empty. Most of the British-allied nations
had retreated to Fort Niagara, leaving their villages for the Continental army to burn. In Tryon County, New York, the westernmost

county during the war, at least two-thirds of the inhabitants became refugees. The Painted Post figured in the memory of these violent years. Here, the locals recalled, the Seneca buried a famous Indian chief who had been killed in 1779 during a raid on Fort Freeland, a small settlement on the northern borderlands of Pennsylvania. This seemingly terse story connected to a much larger web of memories of Indian raids, alleged atrocities, and American victories. When recalling these violent memories, settlers often spoke of one shadowy family in particular, the Montours. They recalled that John Montour was the chief buried at the Painted Post. Moreover, stories of Montour and the Post connected to another famous "Indian" landmark in the Wyoming Valley of Pennsylvania, the Bloody Rock. Here, in one of the Revolution's most macabre scenes, settlers claimed that members of the Montour family had butchered captive Americans. Yet this massacre may never have happened, and John Montour was not buried at the Painted Post.[4]

Selectively recalling atrocities committed by Indians, white Americans crafted a history of the Revolution that emphasized the heroism of the patriot forces and the cruelty of the Indians. In 1794 a surveyor named John Adlum visited the Seneca village led by Cornplanter along the Allegheny River. Adlum had come in response to worries over potentially renewed hostilities between the Six Nations and the United States. Recalling the recent Revolution, Adlum asked that if war came, the Indians would not again massacre women and children. Cornplanter stood and responded. He insisted that the history of the war, and Indian-white relations in general, had been grossly distorted. He spoke of the deaths of men, women, and children at the hands of white settlers. He spoke of Indians' corpses being skinned. He concluded, "As I suppose your books do not tell you these things, I will answer for you. NO. You in your books charge us with a great many things we were never guilty of. But if we were to or could write books we could tell you of things that an Indian never practiced and would be ashamed to be charged with." These decidedly one-sided books, written by white Americans, created a mystery about what really happened at the Bloody Rock and the Painted Post.[5]

Scholars have written much about the significant distinction between cultures relying on oral traditions for their histories—for example, American Indians—and cultures that rely on printed primary sources. This hard division obscures the important interplay between written and oral history during a time when an Indian like Cornplanter spoke of lies he had read and truth that he had heard, all swirling about in lands occupied by Indians and their former wartime enemies, now neighbors. When writing the history of the early New York frontier, early historians relied as much on the oral traditions and memories of pioneer settlers and veterans as they did archival material. For much of the nineteenth century, if Americans wanted to know about the Revolution, they could ask someone who was there or find a descendant of a veteran who had heard the stories for years. As the pioneer generation and war veterans succumbed to old age, the second and third generations of settlers committed their parents' recollections to paper. Beginning in the late 1840s, many local histories of New York captured the local memories of the Revolution. These oral traditions survived beyond nineteenth-century histories, as recent scholarship has restated accounts of battles and alleged atrocities derived from these later memories. Verbal tale became written "fact." But before these books appeared in print, residents had already "written" their histories onto landmarks.[6]

As settlers cleared the forest and plowed fields, most Haudenosaunee landmarks probably disappeared without record because they had no discernible meaning for Euro-Americans. Occasionally local historians made passing references to landmarks of reputed Indian origin, especially regarding past adventures and buried chiefs. In Dansville, settlers recalled a stone pile that allegedly marked a chief's burial spot. According to locals, when the Indians traveled through the area, they would bring a stone from a nearby hill and toss it on the pile to commemorate the chief. The story seemed plausible, but nobody offered any proof of the story's authenticity. The pile disappeared, reportedly underneath the local Lutheran church.[7]

While taking an antiquarian interest in Indian landmarks, settlers altered the landscape and stories to the extent that the original meaning disappeared. This process of appropriation occurred on a prominent rock painting, along the Mohawk River, known as the Painted Rocks. The scholar Jeremy Belknap visited in 1796, and he saw a limestone rock formation about twenty feet in height, with a red picture of what locals claimed were Indians in canoes. A skeptical and astute observer, Belknap recognized problems inherent in interpreting any historical monument. He wrote, "Imagination may conceive the paint to resemble almost any thing; but judgment cannot decide without the help of testimony." Settlers apparently lacked Indian testimony, and they circulated their own stories instead. They claimed the rocks showed Indians leaving for a war expedition, never to return. At the eastern edge of Iroquoia, by the end of the eighteenth century, romantic stories of vanishing Indians had already taken hold.[8]

The rocks had enough meaning for locals that they maintained their appropriated landmark for decades. At some point between 1796 and 1810, someone probably repainted the rocks, but they followed the original pattern. When DeWitt Clinton visited in 1810, he saw a much clearer painting than Belknap had seen in 1796. In his journal Clinton wrote, "On an elevated rock was painted a canoe with seven warriors in it, to signify that they were proceeding on a war expedition. This was executed with red ochre, and has been there for upwards of half a century." By 1836 the painting had become barely discernible. Yet by 1840 the Painted Rocks reappeared, stronger in quality and quantity. Somewhere between twelve and fifteen Indians figured in the new painting, with two canoes, each carrying two men. Perhaps originally telling a story of warriors, then becoming an enduring symbol of the Indians' original claim to the land, the rocks became a tourist attraction for boat passengers.[9]

In lands to the west of the Painted Rocks stood a more famous landmark, the Painted Post, and its competing origin stories spoke to much more significant events than the unknown war party of the rocks. A man named Freegift Patchin recorded an explanation of this monument's origins. Patchin did not know if the Painted Post dated from the Seven Years' War, Lord Dunmore's War, or the American Revolution, but he understood that "an Indian chief had been victorious in battle, killed and took prisoners to the number of about sixty. This event he celebrated by causing a tree to be taken from the forest and hewed four square, painted red, and the number he killed, which was twenty-eight, represented across the post in black paint, without any heads, but those he took prisoners, which was thirty, were represented with heads on, in black paint, as the others." Given the allegedly major victory described, it seems unlikely that this post—at least the one Patchin claimed to see—spoke to the years surrounding the Revolution, as such a traumatic event would have been recalled by other Americans, especially the alleged captives. Patchin saw the post in the middle of this conflict, around 1780, when he himself was a captive of Joseph Brant. His account did not appear until decades later in a captivity narrative, by which time the post had become famous. Combining a vague understanding of the post's origin with a precise description and understanding of its painting, Patchin's account is wholly incompatible with later descriptions of the post and its supposed meaning. Therefore, it is possible that there were several Painted Posts.[10]

Vague stories of unidentified captives and Indian victories failed to capture the imagination of local residents, who described a much different post than the one Patchin claimed to see, and they insisted that their post had, in fact, been erected in 1779, prior to Patchin's arrival. In their version of its origin, a "numerous war party of Tories and Indians" arrived at the site of the Painted Post following "an incursion among the settlements on the west branch of the Susquehanna. They had suffered a severe loss in a conflict with the borderers, and brought with them many wounded." One of these wounded was John Montour. According to local historian Guy Humphrey McMaster, this story originated in a web of memories and information shared by four men:

> This account of the origin of the Painted Post was given to Benjamin Patterson, the Hunter, by a man named Taggart, who was carried to Fort Niagara, a prisoner of McDonald's party, and was a witness to the burial of Captain Montour, or at least was in the encampment at the mouth of the Tioga at the time of his death. Col. Harper, of Harpersfield, the well known officer of the frontier militia of New York in the

Revolution, informed Judge Knox of Knoxville in this county, that the
Painted Post was erected over the grave of a chief who was wounded
at the battle of the Hog-back, and brought in a canoe to the head of
the Chemung, where he died.[11]

In one way or another, these tangled threads eventually connected to
one place: Fort Freeland.

A minor footnote of the Revolutionary War, the raid of Fort Freeland nevertheless exemplified the deepest fears of the colonists, who
lived in constant fear of Indian attacks. Constructed by Jacob Freeland in 1778, Fort Freeland consisted of about half an acre of land,
surrounding by a fence approximately twelve feet in height. Within
the walls stood a two-story log house. Born in the fort, Mary Derickson later recalled that thirteen families shared the fort. These families
lived at the northern margin of the Pennsylvania frontier and gathered
for safety against an Indian attack. Nearby residents, such as Hawkins
Boone, employed a similar technique of garrisoning their homes. Their
strategy proved ineffective. On July 28, 1779, a British-Indian raiding
party led by Captain John McDonnell attacked and destroyed the fort
and its neighboring settlement of Boone's fort. This raid left a powerful impression upon future settlers, including Benjamin Patterson.[12]

Reportedly a distant relative of legendary frontiersman Daniel Boone,
Patterson possessed considerable talents as a woodsman, matched only
by his gift for storytelling. He played a key role in the settlement of
the Painted Post region. In 1792 he supervised the clearing of the first
road from the West Branch of the Susquehanna in Pennsylvania north
to Painted Post. According to local tradition, Patterson then guided
the famous French diplomat Talleyrand through the forests of New
York on a quest for a promising land speculation. In 1798 Patterson
built the first still in Painted Post and traded whiskey to the Seneca in
exchange for furs, which he then sent to Pennsylvania. Patterson also
maintained an inn at Painted Post and spent many hours entertain-
ing travelers with these stories of the early frontier. On account of his
knowledge of the terrain, brushes with fame, and narrative prowess,
Patterson became the pivotal figure in the legend of the Painted Post.[13]

Most significantly, Patterson stated that he fought at the battle of Fort Freeland, where John Montour had received his fatal wound. Patterson and his brother, Robert, fought alongside the ill-fated Hawkins Boone (also reportedly one of Daniel Boone's many cousins). In 1826 Patterson documented this service in an attempt to obtain a pension from the state of Pennsylvania. Responding to the patriotic mood of the early republic, beginning in 1812 Pennsylvania provided an annual pension of up to forty dollars for needy veterans. By 1817 legislation doubled this amount to eighty dollars, awarded to veterans who had served for at least a year and lacked "sufficient property" to live reasonably. Patterson stated that he had received three letters of discharge papers, but two of them were in Boone's fort when it burned down, and he later lost the third. The Commission on Claims rejected Patterson's pension application, noting "insomuch as his circumstances in life would not warrant your committee in granting him a pension, and finding no account to his credit in the Auditor General's office, they deem it inexpedient to grant the prayer of the petitioner." While denied a pension, Patterson had many supporters who vouched for his service and skill along the war's northern borderlands.[14]

Patterson's story of the Painted Post included names plausibly associated with the battle of Fort Freeland but difficult to verify. Researchers from McMaster onward have puzzled over the identity of "Taggart" without success. McMaster knew much of the public Benjamin Patterson, but he missed an obvious connections to "Taggart" in Patterson's personal life. Before arriving in Painted Post, Patterson had been married twice. His second wife was Mary Taggart, from a well-known family in Northumberland, Pennsylvania. During the Revolution, a Capt. Arthur Taggart served in the local militia. Detailed lists of captives taken at Fort Freeland do not exist, but among the fort's casualties was James Watts, whom later researchers identified as previously serving under Taggart. Fort Freeland's surviving men surrendered to McDonnell and then made the trek to Fort Niagara as prisoners. If a member of the Taggart family defended the fort, he would have gone to Niagara, as Patterson claimed.[15]

In his quest for wilderness, Patterson's life initially paralleled the story arc of New York's most famous fictional hunter, James Fenimore Cooper's Nathaniel "Natty" Bumppo, or "Hawkeye" in the *Last of the Mohicans*. Distrustful of civilization as constraining, Hawkeye continually moved west with the frontier in pursuit of freedom. Following the Revolution, Patterson's love of wilderness led him west to the Painted Post, where Taggert had allegedly witnessed Montour's burial. Unlike Hawkeye, Patterson found a permanent home and endeared himself to the prominent local residents, including Judge John Knox. Together, Knox and Patterson organized the local Masonic lodge in 1807 or 1808. As an early settler, Knox saw the original Painted Post and heard Patterson's accounts of its origins. When Patterson applied for his pension, Knox submitted a sworn affidavit in support. Noting that he had known Patterson since about 1796, Knox vouched for Patterson as "a good morall citizen honest in all his dealings and considered a man of unblemished truth and verasity in all his deportment." Compiling the tale of the Painted Post from stories originating with Patterson, Harper, and Knox, McMaster relied on information from a few men who inhabited the same social circle. They had all come to the frontier early and played important roles in transforming the landscape of Iroquoia and becoming respected pioneers in the process.[16]

This transformation depended on the defeat of the Haudenosaunee, who allegedly memorialized their loss at Captain Montour's grave. Montour was no ordinary captain. By identifying the Painted Post as a monument for him, settlers entangled their history with one of the most famous (or infamous) but frustratingly elusive families of the early Pennsylvania and New York frontiers. Contemporaries and later historians have continually conflated various family members. The Montours first appeared in public life with Madame Isabel Montour, born around 1685 in New France. Reportedly of French-Indian heritage, Isabel Montour crafted a complex persona, equally capable of engaging European and Indian audiences, which became the signature trait of the family. During the mid-eighteenth century, her son Andrew gained considerable notoriety as a "go-between," a man who employed his multifarious identity as a cross-cultural negotiator for colonists and Indians in colonial Pennsylvania. Colonists and historians have referred to "French" Margaret Montour as either Andrew's sister or cousin. She was likely the mother of "French" Catharine Montour. In local memories and histories, Catharine was often confused with her sister, Esther Montour. Born around 1750, John and Roland Montour were probably the sons of Catharine Montour or, possibly, Catharine's sister Molly, who briefly appears in local histories. Americans typically identified the brothers as Catharine's children. John and Roland's father was Edward Pollard, a prominent trader at the British Fort Niagara. It is unclear if or when Pollard had adopted Roland and John.[17]

During the Revolution, Americans knew of Catharine Montour's village, which they called "French Catharine's Town." (Fig. 3, the village at the southern end of Seneca Lake, is Catharine's Town, present-day Montour Falls.) In their diaries, soldiers indicated that they had heard much about the Montour family. William Barton heard that Catharine raised and sold horses. Regarding the village he wrote, "It derived its name from French Catharine, who in her infancy was taken from Canada by the savages, and became accustomed to their manners, marrying an Indian chief, who is said to be half French himself, from which marriage she claimed this part of the country." Barton likely crafted his composite from stories and rumors of multiple generations of Montour women.[18]

In many ways, the Montour family reflected the dynamic cross-cultural world of the early American borderlands, where men (and women) at the edges of empires were actually at the center of the struggle for the continent's future. Operating in the margins of imperial reach, these individuals were and are difficult to track. Complicating matters of identification, Andrew Montour had a son named John Montour, also a captain, who fought during the Revolution but for the Americans. This Montour won the attention of high-ranking Americans, including George Washington, who had known John's father. Best known as a captain serving under Col. Daniel Brodhead at Fort Pitt in 1779, this John Montour reportedly switched sides on more than one occasion. However, many of Montour's movements remain unclear, as mainly fleeting references survive. Simultaneously famous and unknown, the Montours could appear and disappear as any plot demanded, rendering them a perfect family for a monument of uncertain origins and meaning.[19]

While elusive, members of the Montour family were clearly present during the most significant action along the northern borderlands of the war. To a greater extent than their American counterparts, the British government depended heavily on the Haudenosaunee and loyalist recruits to fight campaigns in New York and Pennsylvania. In September 1777 Sir Guy Carleton, the governor of Quebec, authorized Col. John Butler to raise a corps of Rangers, a volunteer force of loyalists. Butler's Rangers often coordinated with Indian forces led by notable leaders from the Six Nations, such as Joseph Brant and Cornplanter, and also John and Roland Montour. The Rangers and their Indian allies acquired a notorious reputation because of their skill in raiding frontier settlements from 1778 to 1780.[20]

America's later celebration of its frontiersmen has obscured how poorly frontier militias did fighting against these and earlier Native American forces. From the Seven Years' War through the Revolution, Indian raids successfully emptied the northern borderlands, as terrified residents fled after their militias failed to protect them. Along the Pennsylvania and New York frontiers, the name Montour came to represent this terror, ready to emerge from the dark forest at any time. The family became most infamous for Esther's (or, alternatively, Catharine's) alleged participation in what became known as the Wyoming Massacre, one of the war's most notorious moments. Writing in the 1840s, the historian William Leete Stone observed, "Wyoming is mentioned in almost every book of American history written since the Revolution, as the scene of *the* massacre." During the 1820s and 1830s, the first textbooks of American history appeared in print. Works such as Emma Willard's *History of the United States* (1828) provided many Americans with an interpretation of their nation's relatively new history. As Alfred Young has argued in his work on the Boston Tea Party, these decades were an especially significant period for shaping popular memory of the Revolution.[21]

The basic facts of the battle are clear. In July 1778, Col. John Butler

led 110 of his Rangers and 464 Indians (mainly Seneca) to the Wyoming
Valley of eastern Pennsylvania, where they encountered stockades pro-
tecting the local residents and defended by the militia, commanded by
Col. Zebulon Butler and Col. Nathan Dennison. The first two forts,
Wintermoot's Fort and Jenkins's Fort, surrendered quickly. Potential
for bloodshed escalated when Forty Fort rejected surrender. Determined to fight rather than risk the destruction of their homes, the
patriots set into motion a chaotic chain of events that would shape
perceptions of Indians and the war for decades to come. Zebulon Butler and Dennison led four hundred militiamen to engage the Rangers
and Indians. Feigning a withdrawal, John Butler torched Wintermoot
and Jenkins's Fort and then set an ambush in woods along the patriot
militia's route. The Rangers waited on the left, and the Indians positioned themselves to the right. Tactically outclassed, the patriot militia marched into a bloodbath. Uncertain of their enemy's location, the
patriots fired their first volley at two hundred yards distance, and then
fired two more times without receiving a reply. At one hundred yards
out, the range of accurate fire, the Seneca opened fire. The Rangers
quickly followed with a volley of their own. In the chaos, some militiamen thought Zebulon Butler had ordered a retreat. In the ensu-
ing rout, the Rangers and Indians overtook many of the fleeing men
and killed them. On July 4 John Butler and Dennison (Zebulon Butler had fled) agreed on articles of capitulation, which stated that the
inhabitants would disarm for the remainder of the war, but their lives
and property would be spared.[22]

Immediately after the battle, and growing with each subsequent
year, fact and fiction joined in a dark and dramatic tale of torture and
slaughter that spread throughout America and across the Atlantic.
According to one contemporary newspaper account, after killing 70
men from Fort Wilkes-Barre, the loyalist-Indian force locked "up the
rest with the women and the children, in the houses," and "they set
fire to them, and they all perished together in the flames." The newspaper attributed this account to residents who, after the overwhelm-
ing defeat at Wyoming, fled the valley in what became known as the
"Great Runaway." Subsequent versions of the tale simply repeated the

newspaper's version. While claiming the information came from fleeing residents, early newspaper accounts already distorted the details
of the battle, claiming that Butler's men outnumbered the Americans
by 1,600 to 400. This gross exaggeration lent bravery to the inevitably
doomed smaller force, but probably seemed believable to panicked
people who had found themselves surrounded. Later histories, such
as Willard's *History of the United States*, included these numbers but
added more macabre figures. Willard claimed that prior to the surrender and subsequent burning to death of the men, women, and children, the "savages" had thrown "200 scalps, still reeking with blood"
at their future victims.[23]

While the Rangers and Indian force certainly killed a great many
people at Wyoming, including panicking militiamen, there is insuf-
ficient evidence of a general massacre of civilians. Immediately after
the battle, John Butler wrote to Mason Bolton, the British commander
of Fort Niagara, "I can with great satisfaction assure you that in the
destruction of this settlement not a single person has been hurt of
the inhabitants, but such as were in arms, to those indeed the Indians gave no quarter." In his report to the Board of War, Zebulon Butler mentioned nothing of civilians being burned to death inside their
homes. He estimated about 200 dead, close to John Butler's count of
227 scalps. Zebulon Butler noted, "I have heard from men that came
from the place since the people gave up, that the Indians have killed
no person since, but have burned most of the buildings, and are collecting all the horses they can, and are moving up the river." Butler
described a violation of the terms of capitulation, but not a general
massacre.[24]

Initial accounts blamed Butler and his Rangers for most of the alleged
crimes, but stories soon spread about atrocities committed by Indians.
As the best-known Indian leader of the Revolution, the Mohawk chief
Joseph Brant became a stand-in villain, responsible for such carnage.
Most famously, in 1809 British poet Thomas Campbell immortalized
the legend of "Monster Brant" in his epic romantic poem *Gertrude of
Wyoming.* Campbell described Brant as a "Mammoth" who laid waste
to the formerly beautiful valley. His comparison was timely. Newly

aware of the "Mammoth" (i.e., mastodon) as an extinct animal, Americans often imagined it as a ferocious monster of the woods. Away at Onoquaga during the battle, the proud Brant resented these accusations as an affront to his gentility and restraint. Americans readily accepted claims of atrocities, especially atrocities committed by notorious Indians. Word of mouth became fact, and uncovering the truth of Brant's whereabouts required prodigious research and continued debates well into the nineteenth century.[25]

While Brant's infamy spread through Campbell's invention, local residents identified the Montour family as at least equal monsters of Wyoming. Writing in the 1830s, Stone described these traditions, which he denounced as fictitious but widely believed: "It is related in the unwritten history of the battle that the celebrated Catharine Montour was present, with her two sons; and that she ranged the field of battle like a chafed tigress, stimulating the warriors of her adopted race to the onslaught, even in the hottest of the fight." Contemporaries (and later writers) often conflated Catharine and Esther, but by "two sons," Stone likely meant John and Roland Montour. In a letter written more than six decades after the fact, one early settler, Eleazer Carey, placed John and Roland at the battle:

> When a lad of fourteen years old, I resided in the Genesee country, and in 1803, became acquainted with the family of Kanchilak, eldest son of Blue Throat, or Talaguadeak. He had sons and daughters, not differing much from my age; and he said the boys must teach me to talk Indian, and I, them, to speak Yankee. We thus became intimate. Blue Throat could speak our language, understandingly. He assured me, as did Little Beard, who held the rank of captain in the battle, that Brant was not present. This statement was confirmed by Stuttering John, and Roland Montour, the latter a half-blood, who took my uncle, Samuel Carey, prisoner.[26]

Though soldiers could struggle recalling details decades later, John and Roland Montour almost certainly fought in the battle of Wyoming. In old age, Samuel Carey recalled that during the battle, he tried and failed to escape across the Susquehanna River. Captured by Indians

and taken to Fort Wintermoot, Carey saw it ablaze with a few bodies burning in the fire. As Miner narrated, "He then learned that the
Indian who had taken him was Capt. Roland Montour, who now gave
him food, unbound, and led him to a young savage who was mortally
wounded." As the fires burned, Montour spoke to the dying Indian,
an Onondaga man named Coconeunquo, and asked if Carey should
be adopted into Coconeunquo's family in his place. Coconeunquo
apparently agreed, and Carey subsequently underwent a ceremonial
adoption ceremony. Given John and Roland's association with Butler's Rangers, Carey likely saw Roland at the battle, even if his adoption story cannot be corroborated. The Gilbert family, later captives
of Roland, mentioned an unnamed captive at Fort Niagara, whom
they learned Roland had captured at Wyoming.[27]

Although Montour legends became widespread, they originated
with a few murky sources. Most—perhaps all—of the evidence for
Catharine or Esther's alleged atrocities originated with a single Revolutionary War soldier named Joseph Elliot, who claimed to have nar-
rowly escaped Esther's wrath at the battle of Wyoming. According to
Elliot, Esther arranged a group of sixteen to eighteen captives on a large
rock. (The number of captives varies in different versions.) Singing
a macabre countdown, Esther circled around the captives, occasionally stopping to smash the brains out of a victim with her tomahawk.
Elliot allegedly freed himself and escaped into the river. Some version of this story had spread among American soldiers by 1779, when
soldiers from the Sullivan-Clinton expedition passed through Wyoming. In his journal, the Reverend William Rogers noted, "It is said
Queen Esther, of the Six Nations, who was with the enemy scalped
and tomahawked with her own hands in cool blood eight or ten persons." Revealing the sketchy and prejudiced nature of his knowledge,
Rogers added, "The Indian women in general were guilty of the greatest barbarities." Roger's claim reflected the American conviction that
Indians were such savages that they inverted the proper gender order
and produced women who murdered. Rogers never named Elliot as
his source, but referred to an unnamed fortunate escapee: "Upon the
Indians beginning their work of cruelty, one of them [the captives]

providentially escaped, who reported the matter to Colonel Butler, who upon his return to Wyoming, went to the spot and found the bones of the fourteen lying as human bodies in an exact circle." As years passed, Elliot became the standard source for the tale of Queen Esther, and he apparently talked to quite a few people. In 1829 Israel Skinner published a poetic history of the Revolution (even its index was a poem), which contained a version of Elliot's tale, set in rhyming couplets:

> Those, who were taken by the Indians there,
> As Joseph Elliot doth to us declare,
> (Who did among the prisoners remain
> And was there appointed to be slain,)
> Were taken to a certain spot of ground,
> And stripped, and in a ring arranged around
> As victims of their rage, designed to be,
> A sacrifice of savage cruelty
> A squaw, the Indians did queen Esther call,
> Was set apart to tomahawk them all.
> (This right to her, perhaps they did extend
> To make atonement for some slaughtered friend.)

Residents called this "certain spot of ground" the "Bloody Rock" or "Queen Esther's Rock," and it became a great tourist attraction (see fig. 9). Visitors heard that "Esther's" rage actually stemmed from the death of one of her two sons—presumably John or Roland—who, in this nineteenth-century story, had been killed in the initial action at Jenkins's Fort. Some claimed that a close inspection of the rock revealed stains of the blood that had satiated her desire for vengeance.[28]

While historians and settlers such as Eleazer Carey exonerated Brant, clearing Esther and Catherine Montour of charges has been more challenging. Though well known, the Montour family lacked Brant's high-level public life and its resulting paper trail. Consequently, tracking their movements proves difficult. Conflating various family members, later settlers compounded the challenge of historical verification. Plus, as "half-breeds," the Montour brothers were exempted from the "Noble

QUEEN ESTHER'S ROCK.[2]

Fig. 9. Benson John Lossing, "Queen Esther's Rock." From *The Pictorial Field-Book of the Revolution*, vol. 1 (New York: Harper & Brothers, 1851), 357.

Indian" interpretation, which Brant's defenders employed. "Half-breeds" appeared in nineteenth-century literature, notably in James Fenimore Cooper's works, as possessing the worst traits of each race. In the end we have the story of Joseph Elliot. But like Brant's imagined participation in the battle of Wyoming, word of mouth became fact, leaving little room for doubt in the minds of locals. Decades later, according to local historians, Colonel Dennison claimed that Esther led the Indians at Wyoming. The historian William Lyman collected an equally plausible denial of the massacre from the Seneca chief Blacksnake, who was present at the battle of Wyoming. Lyman wrote that Blacksnake had "No knowledge of any prisoner being placed in a ring &

tomahawked by Kate Montour, or by anyone—does not believe it."
In another account, Blacksnake added that the Indians spared the settlement's children: "I know what came of them we left them un take
care off just as the general was orders to Do no more."[29]

Wyoming escalated the vicious cycle of back-and-forth raids between
the Haudenosaunee and the American settlers. In late September of
1778, from Fort Muncy Col. Thomas Hartley led two hundred Pennsylvania militiamen to exact revenge for Wyoming. Hartley led his
men north to burn the villages of Sheshecunnunk and Tioga. Hartley
described the expedition as an arduous journey into a savage wilderness inhabited by equally savage Indians. He noted, "We saw the Huts
where they had dressed and dried the scalps of the helpless women
& Children who had fell in their hands." Searching for the villains
of Wyoming, but failing to capture them, Hartley's men settled on
burning down Esther Montour's village. (Hartley called her Queen
Hester.) Overshadowed in memory by the Sullivan-Clinton invasion
of Iroquoia of the following year, Hartley's expedition still provided
opportunity for stories of heroism, especially among locals devastated
by the battle of Wyoming. Robert Covenhoven insisted that he was
the first to place a torch on Esther's home.[30]

Patterson and Covenhoven followed the same path of frontier adventure to local renown. Like Patterson, Covenhoven acquired a reputation as an expert scout and guide. The two men knew each other well.
When Benjamin Patterson later applied for his pension, one of the
supporting letters came from none other than Robert Covenhoven,
who stated that he knew Patterson from the expedition against Esther
Montour. Covenhoven confirmed that Patterson served under Captain
Campleton in Hartley's expedition. (Hawkins Boone also served on
the expedition.) Though obviously a friend of Patterson, Covenhoven
staked out his own claim to regional fame. Never stingy with praise
for frontier adventurers, J. F. Meginness, a local historian, later wrote:
"Few men in those stirring times passed through more hairbreadth
escapes, few encountered more personal perils in deadly encounters
with savages than Mr. Covenhoven." Settling in Lycoming County,
Pennsylvania, Covenhoven entertained the younger generations with

stories of his adventures. Like Patterson, his most enduring claim to fame involved a victory over the Montour family.[31]

One month after Esther's house burned, on November 11, 1778, John Butler's son, Capt. Walter Butler, and Seneca warriors descended into Cherry Valley, New York, and continued the cycle of revenge. Located south of the Mohawk River and about six miles east of Lake Otsego, Cherry Valley hosted soldiers and militia, and residents had built an inadequate garrison, which Col. Ichabod Alden commandeered and renamed Fort Alden. Over two days, the Rangers and warriors defeated the militia and burned the settlement. During the battle, the inexperienced Butler lost control of the Seneca, who massacred civilians. Sixteen soldiers and thirty-two civilians died at Cherry Valley. News spread throughout the colonies. Unlike the battle of Wyoming, colonial newspapers accurately reported the number of civilian deaths. In the aftermath, Butler attempted to explain the embarrassing massacre to his superior at Fort Niagara: "The death of the women and children upon this occasion may I believe be truly ascribed to the rebels having falsely accused the Indians of cruelty at Wyoming. This has much exasperated them and they were still more incensed at finding the colonel and those men who had there laid down their arms soon after marching into their country intending to destroy their villages, and they declared they would no more be falsely accused or fight the enemy twice, meaning that they would not in future give quarter."[32]

Unmentioned by name, the Montour family figured in Butler's account. By "the colonel and those men," Butler meant Col. Nathan Dennison and the militiamen spared at Wyoming. In the articles of capitulation, Dennison and his men had promised never to fight again. Instead, the Seneca believed that Dennison and some of the militia had accompanied Hartley on the expedition that had burned down Esther Montour's town.[33]

In local memory, the Montour family helped to ransack Cherry Valley. Stories about the Montours at Cherry Valley appeared in William W. Campbell's 1831 *Annals of Tryon County; or, The Border Warfare of New-York during the Revolution*. A judge in New York City, Campbell was the grandson of Col. Samuel Campbell of Cherry Valley. During the raid, the Rangers and Indians had taken around seventy captives, but allowed half of them to return home. Notably Walter Butler captured Samuel Campbell's wife, Jane, and their children, whom he later used as exchange for his own mother, held prisoner by the patriots. One of the Montour brothers allegedly took Jane Campbell's parents, Matthew and Eleanor Cannon, captive. Before attacking Cherry Valley, Butler had reportedly sent Roland to Shamokin, a multiethnic village on the Susquehanna in Pennsylvania, leaving John as the unnamed Montour brother. According to William Campbell, at the start of the journey an unnamed Indian killed the elderly Eleanor Cannon on account of her inability to travel. Turning to Jane Campbell, who carried an eighteen-month-old child in her arms, "the same Indian drove her along with his uplifted and bloody hatchet, threatening her with the same fate, if she should be unable to proceed on the journey, with the speed he required." Campbell bestowed John Montour with a degree of compassion, allegedly lacking in his mother and unnamed comrade. Rather than kill Matthew Cannon, John Montour brought him to Niagara as a prisoner for exchange. At the fort, Catharine allegedly rebuked her son, asking, "Why did you bring that old man a prisoner? Why did you not kill him when you first took him?" Campbell concluded with an ambiguous comment on Catharine's fame, writing, "This creature was treated with considerable attention by some of the officers." Lacking any other sources, historians repeated this account from Campbell's history.[34]

Thus those who knew the Montour name from Wyoming and Cherry Valley would find justice in the tale Patterson spun of the battle of Fort Freeland, fought one year after the battle of Wyoming. As Patterson later recalled, Hawkins Boone's men, including the Patterson brothers, surprised the unsuspecting British and Haudenosaunee forces, who remained near the captured fort. As the Indians cooked dinner, Boone and his thirty-two men positioned themselves in bushes overlooking the encampment. This spot must have been the perfect vantage point, for in McMaster's telling of Patterson's tale, the skilled woodsmen then fired "coolly and rapidly by sixes, with the unerring aim of frontiersmen" and "shot down one hundred and fifty (so the story runs) before the enemy broke and fled." Only then did Boone make the mistake of advancing, which exposed his smaller force. McMaster noted that Boone and half of his men died in the fight, but the Patterson brothers proved too fast and elusive for their Indian pursers.[35]

Drawing upon an interview with survivor Mary Derickson, J. F. Meginness portrayed this skilled ambush as retribution for the alleged arrogance and dishonorable conduct of the Haudenosaunee, especially the women. Locals recalled that McDonnell had trouble controlling the "thievish disposition of the savages," who ransacked Fort Freeland's bedrooms. To the British commander's chagrin, one Indian woman even stole a handkerchief from a girl, which McDonnell replaced with one of his own. Mocking the victims of Fort Freeland, the Indian women proceeded with the rest of the party down to a creek, where they began to prepare dinner while reveling in their success. Meginness wryly observed, "Their enjoyment, however, was of short duration." Revenge came from the cool accuracy of the frontiersmen. Meginness described the scene: "Each man was cautioned to take sure aim, and when all were ready, at a given signal they fired, and at least thirty of the savages fell dead without a moment's warning." In memory, local historians elevated Fort Freeland from a minor but destructive raid by the British and Haudenosaunee to a significant blow against them.[36]

Although Montour had been wounded in the battle, the following day he apparently had enough strength for a final, surreal encounter with an unknown captive, who had attempted to escape while housed in an "ash-house near Muncy" en route to Fort Niagara. Sitting alone on the second floor of the building, the captive saw John Montour appear in the doorway and take aim at him. But then Catharine followed John into the room and yelled at the terrified captive, "Ah! you debil, you tschot me." The trembling captive denied this charge, but Catharine continued, "You lie, you debil; I got my wrist cut by you." Displaying her tomahawk, she threatened to scalp the man but did not. Apparently meant to discourage a second escape attempt, the scene left the relatively fortunate man shaken long after the war had ended. Slipping into the passive voice, Meginness concluded with a comment that suggested the extent to which this alleged exchange had become a local legend that rendered the forest more eerie as the haunt of the Montours: "It is said that such was the fright he received at this time, that for years he could not divest himself of the idea that the rustling of the leaves as he passed through the woods, was the noise of the tread of the Indians in pursuit."[37]

When writing the history of Fort Freeland and the Painted Post, local historians relied on shaky memories and hearsay. Meginness praised Derickson's sharp memory and ability "to relate the thrilling scenes enacted at Fort Freeland, with remarkable accuracy." Venturing into melodrama, Meginness observed, "She was very small at the time of the taking of the fort in 1778 [sic], but being a sprightly child, everything was so strongly impressed upon her mind, that death alone can obliterate it." Derickson's memory was indeed impressive, but the battle occurred in 1779, the year of Derickson's birth—"very small" was an understatement. Therefore her account and Meginness's retelling of its heroic scenes rely on what she heard had happened, not what she had witnessed. Meginness concluded his sketchy account with the same local lore Patterson apparently told of the Painted Post: "John Montour suffered much from the wound he received when attempting to scalp old Mr. Watt, and finally had to be carried on horseback. The second or third day he is said to have died. A post was erected near his grave, and painted red, and the place to this day is known by the name of the 'Painted Post.' Montour was a distinguished warrior, as his death was much regretted by the Indians." If the noises in the woods haunted the unnamed captive from Fort Freeland, it would have to be Montour's ghost.[38]

By the nineteenth century, Patterson (or the locals retelling his stories) greatly exaggerated the success of Hawkins Boone's men at Fort Freeland. Contemporary British and American accounts present the battle of Fort Freeland as a one-sided victory for the loyalists and their Indian allies. Boone's men did catch the Indians off guard, and they shot one man dead, but that was the extent of their short-lived victory. Following Boone's initial success, the Indians withdrew. An overly ambitious Boone committed the fatal mistake of pursuit. Abandoning their cover, Boone's small party of about thirty men became surrounded by the much larger British-Haudenosaunee force. All contemporary accounts agree that by the end of the fighting, Boone and at least ten of his men were dead. Militia colonel Samuel Hunter simply wrote, "Capt Boon and his party fired briskly on [the] Enemy, but was soon Surrounded by a large party of Indians." Contemporary accounts do not mention any slaughter of Indians prior to Boone's defeat. Prominent Northumberland patriot John Buyers wrote to Assistant Commissary William Maclay: "Capt. boon who went out for their Relief fell in with the enemy Capt. Kompeton who observed the first Indian on guard shot him dead on the Spot then a party Raled out of the mill and defated bo[o]n's Company." From one guard shot, locals later imagined dozens of deaths.[39]

Americans attempted to salvage some personal honor from the disaster at Fort Freeland. Patterson's friend Covenhoven later recalled shadowing McDonnell's forces prior to the attack. Covenhoven saw them near Lycoming Creek, a tributary of the west branch of the Susquehanna. In a close call befitting his adventurous reputation, Covenhoven hid behind a tree as two Indians walked by, humming a tune and unaware of the patriot spy. Covenhoven brought his intelligence to nearby Fort Muncy. The fort's commander, Colonel Hepburn, relayed the information to Fort Freeland. Allegedly, the occupants of Freeland and Boone's fort concluded that the reports of McDonnell's forces were exaggerated. In this account, Covenhoven would have singlehandedly saved Fort Freeland and Boone's men, had they only heeded his warning.[40]

Was John Montour the "first Indian" killed? No, but locals had not dreamed up his death from scratch. For all his exaggeration, Patterson told some truth, because on August 5, 1779, Capt. John McDonnell reported to John Butler: "John Montour received a wound in the small of the back scalping a man under the Pickets of the Fort: but is in a fair way to do well." McDonnell wrote his report nine days after Montour was wounded and six or seven days after settlers remembered him dying. Perhaps Patterson's exaggerations lent credence to the severity of Montour's wound, which was not so severe after all.

The Painted Post became a tribute to the American frontiersmen at Fort Freeland, who in Patterson's memory took revenge on a family that was the scourge of the frontier.[41]

Although the battle of Fort Freeland seems to explain the story of the Painted Post, it is in fact only one piece of the puzzle. By following John Knox and John Harper's claim that the Painted Post was a memorial to a "chief who was wounded at the battle of the Hog-back," McMaster actually deepened rather than solved the mystery of its origins. "Hog-back" described hills or ridges shaped like a hog's back. More than one battlefield in Iroquoia contained a "hog's back," but Harper meant the battle of Newtown, the only major engagement between the Sullivan-Clinton invasion of Iroquoia and the loyalist-Indian forces, fought on August 29, 1779, one month after John Montour's "death" at Fort Freeland.

Of the early investigators into Painted Post, Col. John Harper had the most extensive knowledge of Haudenosaunee culture. While very few white Americans ever learned much about Indian culture, Harper had attended Eleazar Wheelock's famous Indian School in Lebanon, Connecticut, during the early 1760s, where he met fellow student Joseph Brant. At some point Harper had been ceremonially adopted by an Oneida, acquiring the name Thaoughweanjawegen. (He later employed his intercultural skills to dubiously acquire 92,160 acres of prime real estate from the Oneida. This land included the former village of Onoquaga.) John Harper's brother, Capt. Alexander Harper, led the ill-fated expedition in 1780, when Joseph Brant took Freegift Patchin, Alexander Harper, and other captives past the Painted Post to Fort Niagara. During the Revolution, John Harper commanded militiamen and fought at the battle of Newtown, commanding volunteers as a captain under Gen. James Clinton.[42]

The Sullivan-Clinton expedition exemplified the type of traditional invasion that European warfare emphasized and the Indians usually avoided: large-scale battles designed to strike decisive victories with high casualties. On August 11, 1779, General Sullivan's men rendezvoused with Clinton's forces at Tioga in northern Pennsylvania. From Tioga, more than three thousand American troops followed the river to the north and west. Two nearby villages, Chemung and Newtown, stood between the invading army and the heartland of Iroquoia. On August 14 Sullivan's army attacked Chemung. Finding the village abandoned, they burned it. Brig. Gen. Edward Hand pursued the retreating Indians, and he marched into a trap. Roland Montour and twenty Delaware warriors laid an ambush on Hogback Hill near the village. Greatly outnumbered, Montour and his men managed to kill seven Americans and wound several more before retreating. No chief died at this battle of the Hog Back.[43]

With only six hundred men, Brant and John Butler proposed a retreat followed by small hit-and-run strikes. Their Delaware allies disagreed and decided that Butler's Rangers and the Indians should make a stand. Led by Old Smoke and Cornplanter, the Seneca sided with the Delaware. For their stand, the loyalist-Indian force chose another hill known as the Hog Back, a half-mile-long ridge near the village of Newtown. To the right of the hill, the trail passed through an opening, which narrowed near the Chemung River. Here Butler built a camouflaged breastwork to catch the patriots' left flank as they passed. Most of the Indian force, perhaps including the Montour brothers, occupied the hill. Joseph Brant and John McDonnell commanded about sixty men behind the breastworks. Between the hill and the breastworks, Butler stationed himself and the remaining Indians and soldiers. He hoped that the men behind the fortifications would distract Sullivan's left flank, while the main body of Indians would surprise them on the right. Butler devised a skillful ambush, but an advanced guard spotted it on the morning of August 29. As Gen. James Clinton later noted, "If we had proceeded as they expected, in all probability we should have been very severely handled." Instead of walking into an ambush, Sullivan worked on encircling Butler's men. After six hours of fighting, Butler and Brant's greatly outnumbered forces managed to escape.[44]

While notable for the forces assembled, the battle of Newtown produced relatively few casualties. In total, Butler counted ten dead and twelve wounded from his forces. General Clinton reached a similar count, but added: "The Enemy's loss must be considerable; nine of them were found dead on the field, and many of them must have been wounded, as they were tracked some three miles by the Blood, while others were seen sent off in canoes." Gazing at the trail of blood, American commanders awaited to hear of greater casualties than they had initially counted.[45]

Only seven days later, a rescued captive, Luke Swetland, provided the story the American generals desired. Swetland had been taken captive at Wyoming a year earlier. Sullivan's men found him at Kendaia, also called Apple Town, located four days from Catherine's Town, up the eastern side of Seneca Lake. Some of Sullivan's men may have questioned Swetland's loyalty. Although a captive, he had significant freedom of movement within Iroquoia and occasionally traveled twenty miles to a salt spring but never escaped. Overcoming any initial suspicions, Sullivan's men listened intently to Swetland's statement that the Indians were demoralized following their defeat at Newtown. Confirming Clinton's reports, Swetland claimed that he heard from the retreating Indians that many wounded had been taken away in canoes. In his official report, read by George Washington, General Sullivan noted: "It was his [Swetland's] opinion that the King of Kanadasega was killed as he saw him go down but not return and gave a description of his person and dress corresponding with those of one found on the field of action." Suspiciously, this "King" was never named, and Butler mentioned nothing of him.[46]

Swetland lived with the Haudenosaunee for a year, but he only possessed a minimal understanding of their leadership. In a captivity narrative published in 1780, Swetland wrote, "They seem to have some legislative order, I cannot fully tell in what method." He probably knew little of who wielded influence in Kanadasega. Never mentioned by Swetland, Sayenqueraghta (Old Smoke) was the most prominent chief from Kanadasega and the closest man to a "King." British general Frederick Haldimand called Old Smoke "by many degrees the most leading and the man of most consequence and influence in the Six Nations." Over six feet in height, a distinguished orator, and almost seventy years old in 1779, Old Smoke fought at Newtown but lived until 1786. The legend of the Painted Post originated in two fictitious deaths: John Montour's and Sayenqueraghta's.[47]

Although vague, Harper's understanding of the Painted Post's origins drew upon rumors of a wounded "king" or "chief" incompatible with Benjamin Patterson's story. However, by September 1779, word reached Fort Niagara that John Montour had been shot at the battle of Newtown. Edward Pollard's former clerk Francis Goring wrote to his erstwhile employer, now residing in England: "Your son, John Montour (not Roland) was shot in the back, and the ball lodges in him; however, he is likely to do well, for in a few days after, he, with twenty Indians stopped the pass of the advanced guard of the rebels, which was upwards of one thousand, and obliged them to retreat." Far from the battlefield, Goring's details revealed a shaky chronology. It is unclear if Montour had been wounded *again* at Newtown or if Goring's source had missed Montour's wounding at Fort Freeland. Despite Goring's insistence that John stopped the advanced guard after Newtown, Butler had correctly written that Roland led twenty Delaware warriors in the ambush at Chemung, *prior* to the battle of Newtown. Contemporaries, and not just later historians, had trouble sorting details from the chaos of battle.[48]

From this confusion, the patriots spun their own accounts of battles, which shaped later histories that celebrated Patriot victory and Indian defeat. Patriot accounts exaggerated the extent of their victories, first at Fort Freeland and then at the battle of Newtown. From small details—a wounded John Montour and a trail of blood at Newtown— grew larger self-serving stories. The Americans quickly jumped to the conclusion that the battle of Newtown had been a crippling blow to the Seneca, while Fort Freeland's importance grew over decades. In reality, the Seneca were not defeated in 1779 and Montour had not died—as unlucky settlers would soon discover in 1780.

Despite the substantial setbacks of 1779, the British-allied Indians remained committed to resistance. Following the battle of Newtown and Sullivan's subsequent burning of Iroquoia, the Haudenosaunee held up at Fort Niagara during the especially cold winter of 1779–80. Beginning in February 1780, the war chiefs prepared to continue the raids into the American frontier. By the end of 1780, Niagara forces had burned six forts, seven hundred houses, and vast fields of grain across the northern frontier. They had driven off almost seven hundred head of cattle and captured or killed 330 Americans. As a deterrent to frontier raids, Sullivan's expedition had failed.[49]

Remembered by some as dead (and then avenged) at Wyoming, killed again at Fort Freeland, reportedly shot once more at the battle of Newtown, and without a home village (Sullivan's men had burned it down), John Montour continued to haunt the frontier. On April 25, 1780, the Gilbert family saw a raiding party of eleven Indians approaching their farm, located on Mahoning Creek in Penn Township of Northampton County, Pennsylvania. The captives later identified the leader of the Indian party as "Roland Monteur, 1st Captain." Joining him was the quite alive "John Monteur, second in Command, who was also stiled Captain: These two were Mohawks [sic] descended of a French Woman." Across the northern colonies, newspapers reported the dire news of the Gilbert family's abduction, but they did not mention the Montour brothers by name. Roland and John took fourteen captives, including Benjamin and Elizabeth Gilbert, their children, a day laborer, and several neighbors. This sensational story demonstrated that after Sullivan's apparently decisive victory, danger still appeared without warning. Neighbors heard no gunshots. They saw smoke, but suspected nothing at first because the Gilberts had been clearing land. Roland and John swept in and out before anyone else knew of the raid. The brothers appeared in a captivity narrative published in 1784, which later local historians overlooked when writing accounts of John Montour's earlier demise.[50]

Presenting the Gilbert family as victims of savage raiders from the wilderness, this narrative deepened the tarnish on the Montour reputation. Through the dark forests, along rivers, and over formidable hills, the weary captives trudged to Fort Niagara. Appearing only briefly in the narrative, at the beginning of the raid, John Montour remained an enigmatic figure. The narrative briefly mentioned his unnamed wife, who, during the journey to Niagara, appeared with Roland, carrying food for the captives. Upon arriving at Niagara, Roland presented Benjamin and Elizabeth's daughter Rebecca to his wife, who adopted her as their daughter. Roland's wife was the daughter of "Siangorochti,

King of the Senecas," better known as Old Smoke, the "king" who did not die at the battle of Newtown. Rebecca later said little of Roland, who was probably away for most of her captivity. While Roland and John's personal qualities received little attention in the narrative, the brothers had ample courage, which perhaps bordered on recklessness. Their continued efforts at raiding reportedly cost Roland his life in September 1780, when he was shot during yet another raid in Pennsylvania. Later, some local historians read of his death and claimed that Roland Montour had been buried at the Painted Post in New York. If so, this burial would have reinvented the post's meaning. (Patchin had already traveled past it.) Once at the center of so many important events along the northern borderlands, and perhaps haunted by true sorrow over a death, the Montour family withdrew to the shadows of history as the war drew to a close.[51]

Following the Revolution, like John Montour, the Painted Post seemed to disappear. From his sources, McMaster heard that "the story goes that it rotted down at the butt, and was preserved in the bar-room of a tavern till about the year 1810, and then disappeared unaccountably. It is also said to have been swept away in a freshet." By the time McMaster spoke to local residents decades later, the original post had become something of a vague legend. However, his dating appears to be reasonably accurate. In the *Gazetteer of the State of New York*, published in 1813, Horatio Gates Spafford included the post in his description of the town, though perhaps he only assumed the original landmark still stood. By 1816, when British tourist Francis Hall arrived, it definitely did not. Hall complained, "I was disappointed at Painted Post, to find the post gone; broken down, or rotted, within these few years."[52]

Once a symbol of Haudenosaunee control of the region, the Painted Post actually fell victim to tourists and relic hunters, who pilfered pieces of the famous landmark. As they expanded onto Iroquoia, New Yorkers had begun collecting Indian artifacts. Intellectuals sought antiques, often called "curiosities," such as the copper medal DeWitt Clinton acquired in 1810 near Apple Town from a Mr. Davis. Found with some wampum in a burial ground, Clinton passed the medal on to the New-York Historical Society. But collecting was not the hobby of elites alone, as farmers continually plowed up artifacts.[53]

This collecting occurred at an especially significant time for the development of popular memory surrounding westward expansion. Nineteenth-century America witnessed the emergence of a vernacular history, a celebration of the achievements of the common white men who served as the foundation of an increasingly democratic republic. Public monuments and written histories had long extolled the virtues of powerful kings, aristocrats, and military leaders. During the early republic, Americans imagined their own heroes—frontiersmen—who blazed the trails that led to the Jeffersonian dream of westward expansion. No figure symbolized this democratic frontier more than Daniel Boone, a hunter who had famously led pioneers into Kentucky in September 1779, not long after his counterparts to the north had heroically battled the Haudenosaunee at Fort Freeland (or at least were remembered as heroes). Even as he lived, Boone lost control of the stories spun about his exploits, including killing Indians. As historians have noted, and as Boone tried to explain, he regretted violent actions against Indians and "never killed but three." Americans projected their own values on Boone's life, and if his exploits failed to match their expectations, they just invented new stories that did. As New York's local historians recorded heroic tales of the Painted Post, Timothy Flint's *Biographical Memoir of Daniel Boone, the First Settler of Kentucky* was America's best-known biography. Flint drew upon folklore that emphasized dramatic action scenes. The public loved it, but Boone's family thought it was more fiction than fact. Nevertheless, from 1833 to 1868, the book went through fourteen printings. Collecting relics went hand-in-hand with collecting stories. Well into the twentieth century, enthusiastic collectors looked for pieces of trees where Boone had allegedly carved his initials, weapons he had once used, and places he had stayed. Frontier oral traditions and the written word mixed and transformed into stories that Americans wanted to hear whether true or not.[54]

By the time of Andrew Jackson's presidency, as the country's urban population expanded and the first American frontier looked more middle class than wild, this popular history identified men like Daniel and Hawkins Boone, the Patterson brothers, and Covenhoven as the sources of the masculine independence needed in Jacksonian America, where the president himself had been an Indian fighter. During the colonial period, hunters had been eyed with suspicion as they ranged across supposedly savage wilderness while failing to farm it. This negative perception of wilderness lingered in late Enlightenment writings about social development, which warned of degeneracy in the forest. By the time of Flint's biography of Boone, the dangerous wilderness had also become a place for rugged frontiersmen to develop an appreciation of freedom, honing their skills against crafty Indian adversaries and fierce animals. Describing the legacy of Hawkins Boone's band of sharpshooters, Meginness wrote, "Many of their descendants still reside in Chilisquaque [Pennsylvania] and no doubt inherit the same patriotism and love of liberty that distinguished their heroic ancestors." This cultural shift influenced later historians, most notably Frederick Jackson Turner, whose influential 1893 paper "The Significance of the Frontier in American History" viewed American exceptionalism as rooted in its frontier experience.[55]

Lacking the stature of polished politicians like DeWitt Clinton or rugged heroes like Daniel Boone, local men nevertheless shaped and collected objects of this heroic frontier history. Overlooked by most investigators, Capt. Samuel Erwin possessed a piece of the Painted Post. Born in 1770, Samuel accompanied his father, Col. Arthur Erwin, to the Painted Post in 1792, apparently alongside the hero of Fort Freeland and foe of John Montour, Benjamin Patterson. During the Adams administration, Samuel Erwin obtained a commission as a first lieutenant. Married in Easton, Pennsylvania, in 1801, Erwin settled in Painted Post in 1803. He lived in a log house from 1803 to 1811, and then moved into a tavern until 1823. In 1853 Thomas Maxwell of Elmira, New York, recalled the most detailed firsthand account of the post's fate:

> I saw it in the garret of a log house which stood on the bank of the river, then occupied by Capt. Samuel Irwin about fifty years ago, a

post which was said to have been taken up as the original post, its place having been supplied by another. This, if I recollect alright, was in size about a foot square, its sides smooth, and had been painted a reddish brown. The names of visitors were cut upon it with a knife. There were several hundred of these names, and I had taken a list of them, but it cannot now be found.[56]

As Maxwell recalled, the original post may have been replaced prior to 1810. A later antiquarian stated that a replacement post had appeared in 1803, not coincidently the year Erwin settled into his log house. If Erwin replaced the original post, as Maxwell recalled, his version quickly deteriorated, or tourists stole pieces of an inauthentic monument, because Hall saw nothing left standing in 1816. A variation on this tradition blames Samuel's brother Francis ("Frank") for the eventual loss of the original post. In this tale, recorded in the late nineteenth century, the brother grew so annoyed at the demands of visitors "that in very pronounced language he ordered the stick thrown in the river and thus the relic passed away on the classic waters of the Conhocton." But the post clearly meant something to local residents. Missing a symbol of the region's history, local blacksmith John Wygant erected a new post in 1824, this time designed to last. Atop a red and white striped post, Wygant mounted a sheet metal weathervane of an Indian chief holding a raised arrow. According to legend, villagers paid Wygant one cow as compensation for his work.[57]

Ironically, as the townspeople erected a replacement to John Montour's alleged gravesite monument, the indomitable captain lived to the west at the Big Tree Village, a small reservation of two square miles near the Genesee River. Had they wanted to find him, New Yorkers would have had trouble locating Montour's home on a map. Possessing a tendency to deemphasize reservations, the cartographer Simeon De Witt excluded the Big Tree Reservation from his 1802 *Map of the State of New York*, but it was there. Montour joined many well-known Haudenosaunee, such as Cornplanter and Red Jacket, who chose to remain in the United States following the Revolution.[58]

Montour was quiet, but hardly anonymous. He had acquired a

"fierce" appearance from one final escape from certain death—or so the story went. To explain facial disfigurement, his white neighbors claimed that during the Revolution, the British had poisoned the Indians' flour supply at Fort Niagara. As one local historian recalled, "Many died. Montour lived, but the poison resulted in an ulceration of his upper lip, which was quite eaten away, leaving both teeth and jaw exposed." (It is also possible that the British distributed rotten flour, which had been ruined by water during transportation.) Montour spoke fluent English, and it is quite possible, perhaps probable, that he spread the story of British poisoning. Among the Seneca today, oral tradition recalls that the British had poisoned Niagara's flour stores. This tradition reflected bitterness toward the British, who had abandoned their Indians allies in the Peace of Paris at the close of the Revolution.[59]

Perhaps eighty years old, Montour finally met his end in 1830 during a brawl with Quawwa, a longtime foe also known as James Brewer. The nature of their rivalry remains elusive, but Montour had often gotten the better of his younger opponent. Standing six feet in height, tall for his time, even an elderly Montour cut an imposing figure, even without accounting for the fact that he seemed impossible to kill. However, one day Montour drank too much and Quawwa won, delivering a fatal kick to the downed captain. Montour died the same year as his old rival, Benjamin Patterson, who resided a few counties distant, unaware that his villain of Fort Freeland had escaped revenge for fifty years.[60]

It is only fitting that locals recalled some mystery about Montour's actual death. Apprehended after a brief flight, Quawwa faced manslaughter charges for killing a man allegedly dead since 1779. (He would be convicted, but released early because of failing health.) Horatio Jones, a well-known former captive turned interpreter, provided his services during the trial. A child at the time of Quawwa's trial, a future judge named B. F. Angel later recalled: "The first time I saw Horatio Jones was about 1831, at the trial of an Indian named Quaw-wa, who had killed a reputed witch." Had Montour really been a "reputed witch"? Traditionally believing in witchcraft, the Seneca had experienced a

surge in divisive witch hunting decades earlier, at the turn of the nineteenth century. Reviving older religious traditions with a mix of measured acculturation, the prophet Handsome Lake saw alcohol as a
means by which evil and witchcraft spread. Quawwa was ill, and sick
individuals had often blamed their ailment on witches. Perhaps Montour's drinking, "fierce" appearance, and apparent immortality ampli-
fied whatever feud he had. However, as Seneca gender roles began to
resemble those of white Americans, and tensions developed over these
changes, witchcraft allegations increasingly fell on women rather than
men. In 1821 western New York newspapers had reported a sensational
execution by the Seneca of an accused female witch named Kauqautau. In any case, Angel's memory marked one final slander against
the Montour reputation.[61]

It seems odd that a victorious nation would preserve and rebuild a monument constructed by their recent enemies in war, especially a monument reportedly to a notorious Seneca captain like John Montour.
However, by the first decades of the nineteenth-century, their monument represented the heroic conquest of the wilderness more than any
sort of tribute to Captain Montour. Early pioneers had already carved
their names—perhaps hundreds of them—into the original monument prior to its disappearance. The restored Indian imagery reflected
their memories more than the Seneca's. This reinvention spoke to a
larger process of remembering the frontier as the place where American character emerged. As early as the famous Boston Tea Party of
1773, when colonists dressed as Mohawk Indians to destroy the tea
of the East India Company, Americans had selectively appropriated
Indian imagery to denote freedom and independence. Remembered
as formidable opponents, as the nineteenth century unfolded, Indians became lasting symbols of the adventure inherent in westward
expansion and the forging of a new nation—but only as they came
to seem defeated. When Francis Hall expressed disappointment that
the Post had already vanished, he added: "It was, as may be supposed,
an Indian memorial, either of triumph, or death, or of both. A post is
not much, but, in this instance it was a record of the past, a memorial

of (may I be pardoned the expression) the heroic ages of America!" But was John Montour the hero or the villain?[62]

When crafting histories of Indians, nineteenth-century writers dealt in stereotypes, which reflected Americans' often dichotomous views of Indians. On the one hand, once dead or dying, Indians could be romantic, impulsive, noble, and doomed. In McMaster's rendition of the tale of the Painted Post, Captain Montour was a "fine young chief, a gallant warrior, and a favorite of his tribe." For years following Montour's burial, McMaster heard that chiefs traveled to the Painted Post and paid their respects to their brave, fallen friend. But living, fighting Indians could be savages poisoned with rage, resisting the inevitable white settlement. Pennsylvanians remembered these Indians at the Bloody Rock, commemorating the rage of Queen Esther, or perhaps Catharine and John and Roland, depending on who told the story. In the end, these stories were all celebrations of white settler victory. Indians appeared as foils for heroic frontiersmen to battle. In histories, Montour was more of a character in a novel—and not one he authored—than a real and complicated person.[63]

As time passed, and it seemed that Indians vanished with the forest, Americans softened their attitudes toward their formerly feared opponents, or at least the ones who lived within the borders of Euro-American settled states. In 1826 residents of Wyoming announced the construction of a memorial to the people killed in the battle (or massacre) of Wyoming. One newspaper noted that the memorial would honor the fathers, mothers, brothers, and sisters killed "by Indians, and a more merciless race of beings called tories." Perhaps intentionally, this writer inverted language from the Declaration of Independence, which had accused George III of inciting attacks by "merciless Indian savages." At the dedication of the memorial, the Reverend James May noted, "The Indian who in those days lingered in the mountains that surround us, has long ago retired." Many thought that the Indians had physically vanished from the region, but Americans observers also saw reservation Indians as fundamentally inferior to their ancestors. In his address "The Iroquois," delivered in 1811, DeWitt Clinton told the New-York Historical Society, "They are, in general, addicted to idleness and drunkenness; the remnant of their eloquence and military spirit, as well as national strength, is to be found only among the Senecas." When Clinton spoke, the Seneca lived in western New York, farthest from the advancing white settlement. An ardent supporter of state expansion, Clinton knew that eventually white settlement would surround Seneca lands as well. He continued, "Their [The Six Nations'] ancient men, who have witnessed the former glory and prosperity of their country, and who have heard from the mouths of their ancestors, the heroic achievements of their countrymen, weep like infants, when they speak of the fallen condition of the nation." Alive, but aging, these Indians clearly were not the feared warriors of the past.[64]

The descendants of pioneers crafted a narrative of settlement that celebrated the military defeat of Indians, the conquest of the wilderness by frontiersmen, and the inevitable disappearance of Indians. When bullets failed to kill Montour, white settlers erased him with words. Montour became one of the many "vanishing" or "last" Indians memorialized by American settlers, who sought signs that Indians had been vanquished. Monuments, especially alleged Indian graves, signaled the replacement of Indians by white settlers—in effect, the end of Indian history and the beginning of the American nation on the frontier. Yet we can see hints of an alternative history in the Montour legend. Perhaps the overall plot of this story described a people with their own war heroes, who fought to protect lands where their villages had stood for centuries and nearly succeeded, only to be abandoned—poisoned even—by their British allies. To be sure, as in any human story, this history was also violent, difficult, and far from perfect. But this history did not end at the Painted Post, Newtown, or with the Peace of Paris.[65]

Little survives of John Montour's postrevolution experience, but William Lyman recalled an intimidating, enigmatic, though sometimes funny and friendly man. A pioneer merchant in Moscow, New York, near the Big Tree Village, Lyman knew Montour "very well," and also knew his two "good looking daughters." He noted that despite Montour's fierce appearance, he "was a *good* Indian & a friend of mine."

Lyman wrote that he could "fill a sheet of anecdotes" related to Montour. Unfortunately, only a few survive. One summer, Lyman spotted Montour drinking from the Genesee River. Seeing Lyman, Montour said, "Lyman, the river is very low, very dry time." In return, Lyman joked, "Low, you have drunk all the water." Those who knew of Montour's lip recognized the humor in this story. In another encounter, Montour came into Lyman's store and noticed his pair of lost mittens hanging for sale. Before Lyman took the mittens off the wall, Montour wanted to prove his ownership. He explained, "I was at a certain place, a little drunk, staggered and fell, the hand covered by the mitten struck a burning log, which scorched it in such a part. Pull them down and see." Lyman took the mittens down, saw the burn, and handed them back to Montour at no charge. These quirky anecdotes humanize and lend some humor to a man who survives in history mainly as a distorted shadow of himself. The quotations provide rare words by John Montour, a legendary character usually left without a voice. In local histories and surviving documents, glimpses of Montour the brave, violent, and sometimes reckless raider survive. But he, like most Indians from the revolutionary period, actually spent the majority of his life trying to get by in a new world, dominated by white American settlers, who had already rebuilt a monument to a man (or a people) not yet dead.[66]

Chapter Four

The Decline and Fall of the Romans of the West

On September 1, 1791, as many Americans pondered a future move to Iroquoia, Elkanah Watson and Jeremiah Van Rensselaer left Albany, New York, by covered wagon and headed west. These men, however, were not everyday citizens. Watson had been a courier for George Washington during the Revolution and then became a successful merchant. He had traveled extensively throughout the colonies and to France but still had much interest in this local trip. Watson wanted to scout the western portions of the state for future development, especially for potential canal routes. He brought an important friend in Van Rensselaer, a member of one of Albany's most powerful families, a politician, and future president of the Bank of Albany. Near the start of the journey, the pair met with two prominent friends: Gen. Philip Van Cortlandt and Stephen Bayard. The four men helped lead the development of central and western New York. They had all speculated heavily in the New Military Tract's lands of central New York, which had just opened for settlement. The travelers also scouted land for the Western Inland Lock Navigation Company. Chartered the following year, this company became the first private corporation established to open waterways from Albany to Seneca Lake and then to Lake Ontario.[1]

Primarily a business trip, the journey was also an adventure into lands only recently opened to white Americans, who would have to wait another six years to read in Albany's newspapers of the fabled lands of the Painted Post. Foreshadowing the hardships to come, Watson and Van Rensselaer endured a constant rain before reaching Palatine, on the north bank of the Mohawk River. The explorers slept in tents for most of the expedition, and pouring rain soaked through the canvas. For their efforts, the travelers were able to meet interesting characters, from rough pioneers to prominent Indians. Near Onondaga, the "King" of the Onondaga, Kiadote and his wife, Kanastoretar, visited the travelers. The Onondaga brought "some excellent fresh salmon and eels," which they exchanged for some rum and biscuits. In his journal, Watson proudly noted that this visit marked the seventh time that he had met royalty.[2]

As newcomers seeking wealth by reading the landscape, the men were sharp observers. Along their route, the travelers took note of the types of trees, quality of soil, number of houses, the character of the pioneers, and even the cost of salt produced at Onondaga. They also possessed some imagination. Watson, in particular, saw potential cities everywhere if the canal that he envisioned should ever arrive. He foresaw these cities as connected to a much larger, prosperous network of commerce and agriculture, stretching west to the Mississippi and "overspread with millions of freeman; blessed with various climates, enjoying every variety of soil, and commanding the boldest inland navigation on the globe." This vision was nothing less than the total reinvention of the continent, with New York at the center of an American empire of liberty.[3]

But this new republican, continental empire was not the first that Americans had imagined as emanating from the lands of New York State. Since the eighteenth century, with the encouragement of Haudenosaunee leaders, Euro-Americans had viewed Iroquoia as the hub of an Indian empire that controlled much of America's Eastern Woodlands. They knew something of this empire's history stretching back into the early seventeenth century when the French had first encountered the Haudenosaunee. During the early republic, New York's governor, DeWitt Clinton, would bestow upon the Haudenosaunee an imperial title: "Romans of the western world." Yet travelers reported signs that an even more ancient empire had once existed, perhaps also centered in New York and connected to the same lands where future cities in Ohio would prosper, once the Erie Canal linked the Great Lakes states with New York City. On the eastern shore of Seneca Lake, Watson's party discovered seemingly ancient ruins, which the members interpreted as a fortification, measuring 220 yards long and 55 yards wide. The settlement was clearly long abandoned, for old trees grew upon its banks. Walking to the center of the ruins, they noticed a flat stone, situated on a small elevation. Someone had carved a design, perhaps some kind of hieroglyph, about a half inch deep into the stone. Watson and his companions puzzled over its meaning for some time before giving up. They then explored about a half mile to the south of the main ruins and found a crescent-shaped "out-work," which concluded their search.[4]

This exploration marked the beginning of public interest in Iroquoia's ancient landscape. In the October 1793 issue of the *New York Magazine*, Henry Livingston, a poet and Van Cortlandt's cousin, wrote an account of the discovery. While reasonably certain that "Indians" had built the ruins, Livingston nevertheless alluded to the emerging mystery about America's distant past. He noted, "It is remarkable, that in the enquiries the travellers made concerning these singular constructions, among the surrounding Onandagoes and other nations, they were so far from receiving any information, traditionary or otherwise, that the natives themselves had never noticed it." Subsequent Euro-American writers echoed Livingston's claims. Across Iroquoia, they found dozens of substantial ruins, but nobody knew who built them—or so the Americans claimed.[5]

Intellectuals searched for an ancient history comparable to Europe's, and they found it in Indian earthworks spread throughout the frontier. These discoveries raised the question of who the real "Romans of the West" had been. Early archaeologists largely dismissed the possibility of Indian origins for these ruins and instead searched for medieval European architects. After exhausting all European options, investigators searched for a supposed lost race, frequently remembered as the "Mound Builders." DeWitt Clinton became the most important proponent of this vanished race theory. The debate about the ancient landscape became a conversation about Iroquoia's future. By claiming that Indians lacked the ability to build these supposedly pre-Indian ruins, Americans denied a possible future of Native Americans on the new "civilized" landscape of America. However, the Indians remained, and they knew who really built the villages, fortifications, and burial mounds encountered by Euro-American settlers. Overlooked by historians, then and now, these Indian traditions eventually appeared in one of the earliest published Native American histories: David Cusick's *Sketches of the Ancient History of the Six Nations*. First published in 1826, Cusick's history paid particular attention to the landscape of Iroquoia, which recalled the past greatness of the Haudenosaunee as the true "Romans of this Western World." These two interpretations set the terms for debating the total reinvention of the Great Island, its origins, and its future.

Debates surrounding America's ancient landscape attracted attention from some of the most prominent individuals in American and Native American society. Born in 1769 to Gen. James Clinton and Mary DeWitt, DeWitt Clinton belonged to the most influential family in the history of the New York frontier. During the Revolution, James Clinton and Gen. John Sullivan had led the invasion of Iroquoia and the subsequent destruction of its built environment. In 1784, at age fifteen, DeWitt Clinton enrolled in Columbia College (formerly King's College), as part of its inaugural class. He graduated first in the class of 1786 and consequently received the honor of delivering the graduation oration in Latin. New York City was still the capital of the new nation, and the Continental Congress suspended operations and joined both houses of the state legislature in attendance at Columbia's graduation ceremonies. This honor foreshadowed the prestige Clinton would later achieve in politics and in letters.[6]

Clearly intelligent, Clinton made his entry into politics through familial patronage. From 1787 to 1795, he worked as a secretary for his uncle, George Clinton. As governor of New York from 1777 to 1795, George Clinton dominated state politics during a key period of Haudenosaunee land cessions. In 1785 he presided over the Treaty of Fort Herkimer, whereby the Oneida sold 460,000 acres of land for $11,500. Already facing a troubling economic future, the Oneida received only a fraction of their land's true value. Over the next two years, the state resold 343,594 acres for $125,955, a 1,467 percent increase in dollar per acre. In 1788 at Fort Schuyler, Clinton presided over an even more lucrative treaty with the Oneida. They received $14,500 from New York State in exchange for 5 million acres of land. New York only paid $5,500 of the total upfront. The Oneida received the remaining $9,000 in a yearly stipend of $600, which amounted to about a dollar a year per capita. While the Oneida could barely provide for their population of 600, Clinton managed to finance much of his state's government through his deal. From 1790 to 1795, New York earned approximately half of its public revenue—over $1 million—by reselling the Haudenosaunee's land, especially land obtained from the Oneida. From early on, DeWitt Clinton's family and career were deeply connected with the Haudenosaunee's land.[7]

Clinton's political apprenticeship prepared him for a successful career that focused on the related processes of remaking Iroquoia and developing New York into the most powerful state in America. After two failed attempts as a Republican candidate for the state assembly in 1795 and 1796, Clinton won election in 1797. Only a year later, he won election to the state senate. In 1803 the Council of Appointment made Clinton mayor of New York City, a booming port that had surpassed Philadelphia as America's most populous city. (New York City did not directly elect the mayor until 1834.) Clinton served as mayor until 1807. He returned as mayor from 1808 to 1810, and then again from 1811 to 1815. He had ambitions to become president of the United States and unsuccessfully campaigned as an antiwar candidate in 1812. His career would reach its apex as governor of New York from 1817 to 1822 and again from 1825 to 1828. During his second term as governor, Clinton witnessed the completion of the Erie Canal in October 1825, which fulfilled the dream of transforming Iroquoia into a market-oriented landscape at the heart of an increasingly integrated national economy.[8]

Throughout his career, Clinton fashioned himself a gentleman scholar, a political ideal of the eighteenth-century Enlightenment. Proud of their education, gentlemen scholars demonstrated their intellect in wide-ranging writings and supported public societies where such knowledge could be disseminated. They looked to Europe's numerous learned societies as models for America, which seemed lacking in comparison. Consequently, Clinton eventually assisted in founding the New-York Historical Society (1804), the American Academy of the Arts (1807), and the Literary and Philosophical Society (1811).[9]

As politicians, the men of these societies promoted the growth of New York State, but this frontier development threatened the very history and nature that they wished to study as scholars. As early as 1796, the *Albany Chronicle* published the concerns of a traveler who had explored some of Iroquoia's ruins: "Would it not be worth while to examine those before the plough renders their foundation invisible?" Responding to this vanishing landscape, in 1809 the New-York Historical Society sought "descriptions, drawings or other communications concerning *mines, mineral springs, ancient fortifications, caverns, mountains, rivers, lakes,* or other *natural curiosities*," and especially any information that "may throw light on their origin and history."[10]

Only a year later, as a commissioner for the Erie Canal, Clinton found opportunity to study Iroquoia's ancient landscape. The New York legislature appointed Clinton and five other notable men, including Surveyor General Simeon De Witt, to explore possible canal routes. Clinton left New York City on June 30 and did not return until August 23. His route took him across central New York State from Utica and Rome westward to the shores of Lake Erie and then Lake Ontario. On his return, he traveled through the Finger Lakes region, stopping in Ithaca, Auburn, and other newly settled towns in what had been the heart of Haudenosaunee homelands. During his explorations, he visited two Indian fortifications near Auburn (north of Owasco Lake), a fortification eight miles from Auburn in Camillus, and another site six miles from Auburn in Scipio. Clinton noted an additional fortification along the turnpike at Asahel Clark's home in Niagara County.[11]

Clinton's observations suggest that during this tour he remained uncertain as to who built the fortified settlements. He noted that "Indian earthenware" had been recovered from the site north of Auburn. However, the sites appeared ancient, perhaps older than the historic Indian nations. Speculating on the utility of the site's defenses, Clinton denoted their antiquity: "The mammoth would alone, if carnivorous, render necessarily such erections." Clinton recognized this animal as an ancient inhabitant of the forest but misunderstood it as a carnivorous contemporary of the settlements he visited. He remained skeptical that historic Indian nations knew anything of the mastodon, which suggested to him that the earthworks and ancient animal had predated the Haudenosaunee. Seeking answers to the ancient landscape's mysteries, Clinton immersed himself in the written literature on the subject. He presented his findings to the Historical Society on December 8, 1811.[12]

Clinton understood his research as connected to archaeological speculation underway along the American frontier, especially in Ohio and Kentucky. These early investigators possessed little scholarship or scientific methods to accurately investigate ancient America. Archaeologists have since developed sophisticated techniques for dating and categorizing cultures. With decades of painstaking work, by studying techniques used to craft weapons, artwork, and housing, archaeologists have uncovered cultural linkages and disjunctions among sites. They employ carbon dating to arrange the chronology of these cultures. Their research has revealed an extraordinarily wide chronological and cultural range for ancient America. For instance, earthworks at Poverty Point, Louisiana, date from 3500 BCE. While at Cahokia, near present-day St. Louis, indigenous people built America's largest earthwork pyramid around 1050 CE. This city's landscape reflected a stratified society and the rituals of its ruling elites. Most of Iroquoia's sites were newer than Cahokia, probably dating from two centuries before Columbus. However, some, such as a relatively rare burial mound in Lewiston, New York, were a thousand years older. In Iroquoia, Euro-Americans took interest in two types of sites where the earth had been moved: burial mounds and, more commonly, palisades surrounding previously occupied villages that dated from after the eleventh century.

Lacking twentieth- and twenty-first-century techniques, early writers often lumped together unrelated archaeological sites of varying chronologies and purposes, and separated by hundreds of miles, as the work of a single "Mound Building" people.[13]

To invent an ancient but lost civilization, Americans first needed to imagine that their landscape contained ruins of sufficient grandeur. Not everyone saw "mounds" as evidence of a great population that afforded skilled architects. In an often-quoted passage from *Notes on the State of Virginia*, Thomas Jefferson wrote: "I know of no such thing existing as an Indian monument: for I would not honour with that name arrow points, stone hatchets, stone pipes, and half-shapen images. Of labour on the large scale, I think there is no remain as respectable as would be a common ditch for the draining of lands: unless indeed it be the Barrows, of which many are to be found all over the country."[14]

Jefferson overlooked the extent and purpose of earthworks described in travelers' accounts. Indians built various kinds of earthen "monuments" including barrows (burial mounds), fortifications with trenches, and large ceremonial earthwork pyramids, such as those found from the Mississippi Valley to the southeastern United States. At many of the larger sites, Native Americans had constructed substantial villages composed of wooden buildings, which had later decayed. Settlers and explorers saw earthworks that varied in size, purpose, and condition.[15]

Jefferson's contemporary, Noah Webster, later of dictionary fame, recognized the differences among the various mounds that travelers had encountered, but he too saw the barrows as largely insignificant archaeological achievements. In three letters to Yale president Ezra Stiles, published in the *American Magazine* in 1788, Webster turned his attention to larger "fortifications" at Muskingum, Ohio (actually a ceremonial center built by what archaeologists call the Hopewell culture), which he viewed as the only significant ancient architecture within the United States. Webster argued, "Such remains are discovered in every part of America, but in none of them do we find such traces of immense labor and proficiency in the art of fortifications, as in the works at Muskingum." By treating Muskingum as unique, Webster limited the necessary "Mound Building" population. With a smaller population in mind, he avoided the obvious candidates, Indians, and looked for European builders.[16]

Webster proposed that between 1539 and 1542 the Spanish conquistador Hernando de Soto built fortifications in Ohio and along the Mississippi. Like most scholars of the ancient landscape, Webster championed a theory that favored implausible scenarios over a simpler explanation. In reality, de Soto was a destroyer and not a creator of civilization. In 1539 the conquistador led the first Europeans deep into what is today the American Southeast, where he pillaged Indian villages, took Indian slaves, and killed for sport. De Soto and his men passed through heavily populated, stratified societies of sedentary farmers, the very societies, or the descendants of societies, who had built the mounds of the Southeast. His route did not pass through Ohio, the focus of Webster's speculations. Moreover, the conquistador had not the resources, time, or reasons for leaving similar earthworks across America. Tellingly, in this interpretation, the only significant achievements in America's long history came from Europe. The rest of the continent existed in a static state of nature.[17]

Webster saw his reasoning as sound scholarly research, but his search for unlikely clues in European history suggested the blurred distinction between history and fiction in the search for America's Native architects. Hunting for fleeting references to increasingly improbable colonizers, other Euro-American writers credited the legendary Prince Madoc of Wales for building America's earthworks. In *Divers Voyages Touching the Discoverie of America* (1582), the English writer and promoter of New World colonization Richard Hakluyt wrote of Madoc's alleged voyage in 1170, when the prince had sailed to America with ten ships of colonists. During Queen Elizabeth's reign, at the height of the Spanish-English rivalry for Atlantic hegemony, Hakluyt's story of a pre-Columbian—that is, pre-Spanish—settlement of America served a kingdom staking its own claim in the Americas. After two hundred years passed, the tale found new life in a nation built upon the myth that Native Americans had lived in an unused wilderness. In 1790, a year before Livingston's article on the mysterious ruins of Iroquoia, the *New York Magazine* reproduced the Madoc folktale. Moreover, elsewhere travelers reported Indians speaking Welsh, sometimes looking "white," and occasionally possessing an unreadable book, understood to be a Bible written, of course, in Welsh. One story circulated that during the seventeenth century, the Doeg Indians of Virginia had spoken Welsh and saved several Englishmen from bloodthirsty Tuscarora warriors. These Welsh sightings moved west with American expansion, and by the later eighteenth century, the alleged Welsh Indians lived near or beyond the Mississippi—that is, into yet unexplored and, therefore, more mysterious lands. In some accounts, vicious Indians had driven the civilized "Indians" west, a plot similar to subsequent explanations of where the Mound Builders went. Of course, nobody ever found these Welsh Indians.[18]

As with the story of de Soto, the Welsh legends failed to explain how a small colony left so many large earthworks across such a vast space, which led Clinton to dismiss these theories as "fanciful." He added that the supposed fortifications had "been erected a long time before the discovery of America" and that "their form and manner are totally variant from European fortifications, either in [ancient] or modern times." Having ruled out European architects as too few, Clinton dismissed Indians as too lazy. Similarly, Jeremy Belknap wrote: "The form of material of these works, indicate the existence of a race of men superior to the present race, in improvement, in design, and in that patience which must have accompanied the labour of erecting them." In his published account, which Clinton read, Belknap left the identity of this race open to speculation. Unlike previous writers, such as Livingston, Clinton knew that the Indians claimed that their ancestors had constructed Iroquoia's ruins. He had read accounts taken by the missionary Samuel Kirkland, which had described past wars won by the Seneca. He had also learned from his 1810 tour that Louis Dennie, a French trader who had long resided among the Oneida, had heard "the Indians say that they erected many of the forts themselves." (For his part, Dennie believed that the fortifications required iron tools to construct.) Clinton dismissed all of these Indian accounts, noting, "Until the Senecas, who are renowned for their national vanity, had seen the attention of the Americans attracted to these erections, and had invented the fabulous account of which I have spoken, the Indians of the present day did not pretend to know anything about their origin." If Indians and Europeans had not built ancient America's landscape, then Clinton reasoned that the true builders had disappeared.[19]

Clinton's dismissal of Haudenosaunee knowledge lacked evidence and reflected his own biases rather than Seneca vanity. He often reached the same conclusions whenever Native peoples offered information of interest to scholars. Clinton's claims of the Seneca suddenly sharing knowledge of Iroquoia's fortifications echoed his beliefs that Indians may have dreamt up mastodon stories to satisfy Euro-American curiosity. He was oblivious to a logical explanation of why Americans had just learned of Seneca history: the relatively recent arrival of Euro-American settlers in Seneca homelands. That is, only following the Revolution could large numbers of white Americans have seen or asked about Iroquoian fortifications. And only during the first decades of nineteenth century did residents settle places such as Buffalo, which Clinton visited in 1810. Here, another such visitor, William King, recorded a conversation with Honayawas (also known as Farmer's Brother) that reveals what Clinton overlooked. Honayawas explained that nearby fortifications "were thrown up by the Indians from 2 to 7 hundred years ago that they was then at war amonge them selves, and that these redoubts were hove up to secure their corn, and that their houses were bilt in these redoubts." Although Clinton was suspicious of Seneca motives, Honayawas's general explanation has proven to be historically sound. From an archaeological perspective, Honayawas clearly established Iroquoia's sites as part of Iroquoian history that was distinct from the history contained within the Hopewell earthworks of Ohio or the Mississippian Mounds—regions lumped together by Euro-American investigators.[20]

In an age of extinction, and as investigators disparaged Native American accounts of their continent's history, a lost race seemed plausible (to Euro-Americans) due to uncertainty over the first peopling of the Americas. As one writer in the *New York Magazine* noted in 1793, "Many writers have laboured to find out by what means America was first peopled; but their different systems do not afford that conviction which removes all doubt." Clinton subscribed to an early version of what later became the "Bering Land Bridge" theory—that is, migration to America from northeast Asia. Increasingly scholars decided that American Indians probably originated somewhere in Asia. Clinton read the work of naturalist Thomas Pennant, who noted the close proximity of the two continents and suggested that they had once been connected at the Bering Strait, prior to a series of volcanic eruptions. Observing that humans could travel by canoes across water or walk across frozen seas, Pennant concluded that migration would have been possible both before and after the continents had split. He supported this migration with general anthropological observations that suggested an eastward migration across Asia and to the Americas. Pennant observed, "The custom of scalping was a barbarism in use with the *Scythians*, who carried about them at all times this savage mark of triumph: they cut a circle round the neck, and stripped off the skin, as they would that of an ox." Scythia encompassed a region north of the Black Sea, known to the ancient Greeks and, later, Europeans through the writings of Herodotus. Pennant concluded, "This usage, as the *Europeans* know by horrid experience, is continued to this day in *America*." Pennant also drew upon Cadwallader Colden's *History of the Five Nations*, which described an alleged incident of the Haudenosaunee eating some of their French enemies, a practice Pennant had read about among the "Scythians."[21]

Even with reports of such incidents, Clinton saw the Haudenosaunee as superior to other Indian nations, and consequently he argued that they must have descended from an equally noble Asian people. Clinton followed the observations of Pennant and concluded that the Haudenosaunee descended from the "Tschutski"—that is, the Chukchi people of far northeastern Russia. He praised the Chukchi: "They cherish a high sense of liberty, constantly refuse to pay tribute, and are supposed to have sprung from that fine race of Tartars, the Kabardinski, or inhabitants of Kabarda," which encompassed the northern Caucasus region. Clinton imparted this same sense of liberty on the original Haudenosaunee prior to their ruinous contact with colonists. Clinton noted, "The causes of their degradation and diminution are principally to be found in their baneful communication with the man of Europe, which has contaminated their morals, destroyed their population, robbed them of their country, and deprived them of their national spirit." Clinton rehashed a well-established view of the Haudenosaunee as "Noble Savages." Instinctual, honest, and violent, the Noble Savage thrived in the natural world, but not the civilized world of Europeans with its greed and vices. This self-serving construction allowed Euro-Americans to simultaneously praise past Indians while insisting that nothing could be done to help them in the present.[22]

In his description of the Haudenosaunee, Clinton revived all of the characteristics of the Roman Iroquois. For instance, these Roman Iroquois had famously great sages, a fact noticed by other writers. In *The History of the Province of New-York* (1792), William Smith declared: "The fierceness of their countenances, the flowing blanket, elevated tone, naked arms and erect stature, with a half circle of auditors seated on the ground, and in the open air, cannot but impress upon the mind, a lively idea of the ancient orators of Greece and Rome." However, the wisdom of Indians had limits, dictated by their experience in nature rather than civilization. Noting that the Haudenosaunee created no formal schools, as the Romans and Greeks had done, Clinton described Indian philosophers in the Noble Savage style: "Their rich and vivid imagery was drawn from the sublime scenery of nature, and their ideas were derived from the laborious operations of their own minds, and from the experience and wisdom of their ancient sages."[23]

Although they lived as Noble Savages, the Haudenosaunee had created an empire that absorbed other nations and radiated across the continent. Clinton cited histories that suggested the Haudenosaunee's military had ranged from Hudson Bay in the North to the "Isthmus of Darien" [Panama]. Truly the Haudenosaunee operated on an imperial scale beyond their relatively modest longhouses. Clinton even noted that the famous Puritan minister Cotton Mather had estimated the Haudenosaunee had killed upwards of two million Indians (a wildly exaggerated count that would have rendered insignificant the brutal wars fought between Puritans and Native peoples). By these conquests,

Clinton reasoned, the Haudenosaunee had exerted sovereignty over much of North America, with some exceptions, where people such as the Cherokee and Cree maintained power. Nevertheless, Clinton imagined that from Iroquoia the Haudenosaunee reigned as "the Romans of this Western world."[24]

But had the Haudenosaunee truly been the Romans of the West? Noting the continent's cultural diversity, late eighteenth- and early nineteenth-century scholars understood the peopling of America as occurring in waves, which allowed for the possibility of a civilized race that predated American Indians. Jonathan Carver had noted "the diversity of language which is apparently distinct between most of the Indians, tends to ascertain that this population was not effected from one particular country, but from several neighboring ones, and completed at different periods." Along these lines, Clinton imagined that the ancestral Haudenosaunee had arrived to find America already inhabited by an advanced civilization, contemporary with ancient Rome. Clinton examined the northern side of the Niagara Escarpment near Lewiston, New York, and found gravel along the ridge, similar to that found in lakes, and small mounds, which he attributed to fish spawning areas. He then noted that while many earthworks had been found south of the escarpment, none had been found to its north. Before the New-York Historical Society, he explained that "there can be no doubt that these works were erected, when this ridge was the southern boundary of Lake Ontario, and, consequently, that their origin must be sought in a very remote age." He estimated that the lake had receded from one to two thousand years prior. In fact, from later professional archaeological work, we know that those earthworks dated from after 1200 CE.[25]

Like many American and European intellectuals of his time, Clinton viewed the history of civilizations as cyclical, and he looked to the fates of classical empires for examples of these cycles. European philosophies of history came in two varieties: linear theories toward a perfected ending (or terrible destruction), and cyclical theories of rise and fall. The ancient Eurasian Old World offered the most obvious examples of rise and fall, and when imagining their landscape's past and

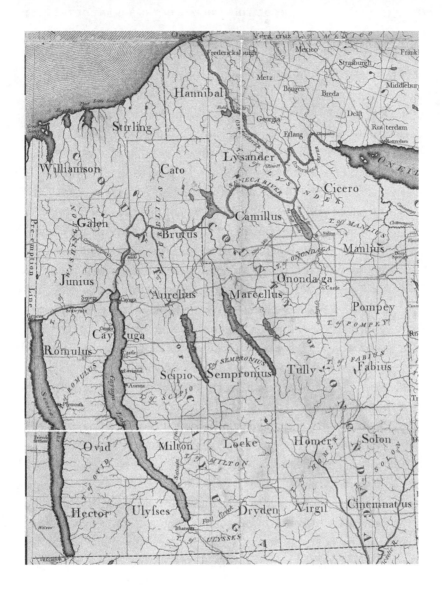

Fig. 10. Simeon De Witt, detail from *Map of the State of New York* (1802).
Library of Congress, Geography and Maps Division.

future, New Yorkers followed their young country's fascination with Roman history. Describing the discovery of ancient ruins in Iroquoia, Livingston had speculated: "Perhaps the day is not far distant, when some American Gabii or Herculaneum will astonish the world with a western history, great, important, and interesting as the oriental." Classical Roman and Greek place-names dotted Iroquoia, most notably in the "New Military Tract," which received its township names from Simeon De Witt's New York Land Office, as his map reveals.[26]

Clinton appeared to have cast the Haudenosaunee as the American equivalent of Rome, but viewed within his broader history, an entirely opposite conclusion emerged. Although some of the Haudenosaunee's conquests had been pre-contact, in Clinton's history they were relative newcomers to America. The real, earlier Romans of the West had lived in the high civilization, subsequently destroyed by the ancestral Haudenosaunee, who had actually played the role of the ravaging Huns. These Indian barbarians came in waves across the Bering Sea to attack ancient New York's civilization. Clinton imagined this civilization's collapse, "but like the Romans, in the decline of their empire, they were finally worn down and destroyed by successive inroads and renewed attacks." He returned to his cyclical understanding of history and noted that it seemed probable that given the lengthy history of America, some catastrophe had occurred—and would occur again. He concluded his address with a full leap into the romantic and, with a hint of guilt, imagined that a new invasion from Asia may someday take "revenge upon our posterity" for "the injuries we have inflicted on her sons." He ended with a new cycle of civilization pondering America's ancient landscape: "And when after the efflux of ages, the returning effulgence of intellectual light shall again gladden the nations, then the wide-spread ruins of our cloud-capp'd towers, of our solemn temples, and of our magnificent cities will, like the works of which we have treated, become the subject of curious research and elaborate investigation."[27]

Clinton's prediction was not so dire, as the collapse clearly lies far in the future. Americans must first build "magnificent cities" and conquer the continent. As with the trope of the romantic and vanishing

Noble Savage, Clinton's vision relied on a sense of inevitability that acknowledged past sins without actually critiquing America's emerging continental empire in any meaningful way. He also raised (but did not answer) the question of who would build the future civilization that looked back in wonder. But if his history were any guide, it would not be the Indians.

Clinton popularized the myth that a lost race built ancient Iroquoia's ruins while briefly noting and dismissing Indians traditions about the land, but other investigators had also caught glimpses of these native traditions elsewhere. Near Cahokia, Revolutionary War general George Rogers Clark had spoken to Illini Indians, who claimed mounds south of Cahokia were "the works of their forefathers" and had been "formerly as numerous as the trees in the woods." Favoring written sources, Euro-American writers largely ignored Indian traditions. Most scholarship that has discussed this "Mound Building" myth has followed this Euro-American trail. But this focus overlooks important Indian traditions that existed at the time and provided counternarratives of America's ancient past, grounded in the ruins found throughout Iroquoia. In one remarkable example, a Tuscarora historian named David Cusick collected and eventually published his own ancient history of America.[28]

Born during the early 1780s, Cusick embarked on a life that, while it could not match Clinton's in terms of fame and influence, was deeply intertwined with the same processes remaking Iroquoia. Like the Clinton family, the Cusicks had gained fame during the Revolution. David's father was Lt. Nicholas Cusick (Kaghnatsho), a Tuscarora chief, who served as a private in Col. Goose Van Schaick's New York Regiment. He later recalled serving as a lieutenant under "Colonel Louis of the St. Regis tribe of Indians" from June 1779 until the war's end. Nicholas Cusick also served as an interpreter and scout for the Marquis de Lafayette. By the early nineteenth century, Nicholas worked as an interpreter for the New-York Missionary Society, which stationed missionaries at the Buffalo Creek and Tuscarora Reservations. David Cusick's brother Dennis became a pioneering painter of Haudenosaunee folk art. Their brother James became a well-known

Baptist minister, whose son, Lt. Cornelius Cusick, later fought for the Union during the Civil War. By any measure, the Cusick family possessed impressive patriotic credentials.[29]

Although David Cusick could never have attended Columbia as Clinton had done, he received a prestigious education for an Indian of his day. In 1793 Samuel Kirkland sought potential Indian students for his newly established Hamilton Oneida Academy (now Hamilton College), located in Paris, New York. Kirkland hoped to train Indian and Euro-American teachers, who would then convert the Indians of the Northeast to Christianity. This approach fit Kirkland's Federalist political ideology, which favored class (or social standing) over race. Consequently, Kirkland focused on educating the sons of prominent Indian leaders. In turn, he believed, these Indians would spread enlightenment among the general population. Kirkland elaborated: "The education of the first class they wish to be such as shall fit them for politicians and schoolmasters, to introduce the manners and customs of the white people among them, which the famous Captain Brant has effected in a very considerable degree among the Mohawks." In 1799 Kirkland "adopted" David Cusick, who then lived with Kirkland and his wife while attending Hamilton Oneida Academy.[30]

Cusick wanted to learn about white American society, which proclaimed a desire to save Indians from "extinction" but failed to provide anything resembling equality of opportunity in education or economic advancement. Hinting at both the biblical obsession with wisdom that came from following God and the importance of a formal education, Cusick wrote to Kirkland, "I want to be a wise man. I don't think many Indians are wise." Kirkland replied that Cusick could be wise if he worked hard. While Cusick relied on Kirkland's sponsorship, the missionary's advice had limited applicability to other Indians. The Oneida Academy had fifty-two white students, but David was the only Indian. Having spent most of its funds on an impressive building, the academy had no money for scholarships. During the decade following Cusick's arrival, Kirkland would educate only two additional Indian students.[31]

Despite their connections and David's education, the Cusick family

struggled with economic hardships typical of Indians living in reservations surrounded by a remade landscape of private property. This
transformation enriched New York State and shrewd land speculators, but exposed Indians to potential fraud. While David focused on
his studies, a man named Peter Raymond swindled the Cusick family out of land, located in the New Military Tract's Junius Township,
that Nicholas had received in 1791 (see fig. 10). Reportedly insolvent
by 1797, Raymond's problems continued in 1804, when three men
sued him, claiming that they paid Raymond $750 for land that he did
not own. According to the plaintiffs, Raymond promised to let them
choose between "lot No. 65 or 76, in Junius, in Montgomery, (now
Cayuga county)." These had been Nicholas Cusick's lots. James Cusick
later wrote that his father "got cheated" out of his land. In 1808 Nicholas Cusick received another two hundred acres from "An Act regu-
lating the grants of Land appropriated for Military services, and for
the society of the United Brethren for propagating the gospel among
the Heathen." This federal land lay in distant Licking County, Ohio,
and Cusick probably had little interest in settling this lot, which he
also sold. To get by, the family farmed, and Nicholas Cusick received
a pension of $20 per month for his service during the war in addition
to payments from the Missionary Society.[32]

The Cusicks had acquired only modest wealth, but some observers saw significant improvement at the Tuscarora Reservation, which
they attributed to the "civilizing" efforts of the missionaries. Visiting the reservation in 1818, the Scottish traveler John M. Duncan estimated the reservation had about three hundred inhabitants and that
a "great many" attended services regularly. He singled out the Cusick
family as a success: "Kusick the interpreter, one of their chiefs, is a
decided Christian. Some of the other chiefs are still unbelievers, but
even they have been compelled to bear testimony to the beneficial
change which has been produced on the nation." By this reasoning,
the Tuscarora seemed best positioned to avoid extinction by embracing white American culture. Duncan found that Cusick possessed a
copy of the Gospel of John, translated into Mohawk by Joseph Brant,
and a copy of the Gospel of Luke, also in Mohawk, translated by John

Norton. A visitor in 1821 noted that David had collected "a variety of relics of their former implements and arms, such as stone axes, flint arrows, war-clubs, belts of wampum, and some curious ornaments." While the Cusick family cherished their Gospels, they also proudly preserved their Indian heritage.[33]

Drawing upon his cross-cultural training, and with encouragement from Kirkland, David Cusick developed an interest in producing Indian history for a broader American market. This effort brought Cusick into a long-standing debate about Indian origins and potential, which had also interested his mentor, Kirkland. In a 1787 letter, John Wheelock, the president of Dartmouth College, prodded Kirkland for information on America's ancient history: "I have ventured to indulge a conjecture, that the savages are the descendants of an ancient civilized people, who once covered a great part of North America, and that the present Indians are a degenerate race from former enlightened American ancestors, who in the course of many ages have devolved, like the eastern Tartars, from civilization to barbarism." Wheelock's speculation at least hinted that as creators of past glories, Indians could partake in future civilization as well. During a 1788 tour through western New York, Kirkland sought answers to Wheelock's questions from several Seneca chiefs. From his research Kirkland concluded that the Indians had built the abandoned villages and fortifications found throughout the New York frontier.[34]

This tour, however, only scratched the surface of a deep Indian history, still written on Iroquoia's landscape. Kirkland knew this history existed, but his own writings on the subject remained limited. Instead, he sought a comprehensive history from his old friend Joseph Brant, but the Mohawk chief never completed his projected work. In 1791 Brant wrote to Kirkland: "You express a desire to see my [Indian] history complete. I sincerely wish I could gratify my friends and the world with it, but the unhappy barrier which at present presents itself will either put a final stop to it, or furnish material for its enlargement, at any rate it will protract the work." Brant referred to the newly created border between the United States and Canada. A result of the Revolution, this border divided the Six Nations between two countries (and still does), with Brant residing on the Canadian side, where he maintained a separate Grand Council. Some of Brant's work may have found its way into the writings of his protégé, Maj. John Norton, who produced histories from the Haudenosaunee and other Eastern Woodlands Indians. However, Norton's history remained unpublished until the twentieth century, leaving Kirkland and his contemporaries with Eurocentric histories, such as Colden's *History of the Five Nations*.[35]

Into this intellectual void stepped the Cusick family, who would become the most prominent Indian voices in public debates about ancient America, which had been dominated by white intellectuals. Nicholas Cusick almost certainly began work on an Indian history. Hints of these studies survive in the 1802 annual report of the New-York Missionary Society. Extolling Nicholas Cusick as "indefatigable," the report noted, "He promises, should he again be employed [as a translator], to keep a more particular journal, to collect materials for making up an account of the present state of the Indians, as well as for a history of the ancient tribes inhabiting this continent." This promise foreshadowed the broad scope of David Cusick's *Sketches*.[36]

Missionaries found that translating history, or any other writing, was very difficult work, and so it would take decades for Cusick to develop the skills to write his ancient Indian history. In 1809 missionary Andrew Gray reported, "The tropes, figures, and most beautiful similitudes with which the sacred oracles abound, are in general lost to my Tuscarora hearers. Although I have made various attempts, I have never been able to point out, even to [Nicholas] Cusick, the usefulness of exegesis and improvement." To an extent, Gray's complaint reflected European missionaries' centuries-old concerns that Indians lacked a proper understanding of their new religion. But Indians were also newcomers to the world of books, and the prospect of intense reading and writing must have been intimidating. David Cusick would later recall that such fears of inadequacy delayed the start of his writing. In the preface to his history, he noted that he only wrote the history because nobody else would. Cusick believed that because of his "small" education, "it was impossible for me to compose the work without much difficulty." He continued, "After various reasons I abandoned the idea; I however, took a resolution to continue the work, which I have taken much pains procuring the material, and translating it into English language."[37]

David Cusick dedicated far more time to the acquisition of knowledge on ancient Iroquoia than his Euro-American counterparts. For years Cusick collected Indian oral traditions, performed at least some firsthand visits to ancient sites, and acquired familiarity with Euro-American scholarship. He certainly visited sites near the Tuscarora Reservation. He also mentioned an early visit to a fortification in Sidney, New York, where a giant of a man, "Soh-nou-re-wah, i.e., Big Neck," had once lived and tormented the nearby Oneida fortifications that stretched along the Susquehanna River. Cusick inspected this site in 1800, shortly after becoming Kirkland's student, but he likely had trouble visiting additional historical places as an adult. Surviving letters suggest that severe arthritis limited Cusick's mobility but fostered his interest in reading and writing. In an 1820 letter to missionaries, he wrote:

> I have long been in sickness, nearly two years; not able to do any kind of work. My chief time is occupied in reading. I am constantly desirous to hear the missionary labors from different parts of the world. How much the Lord has called in, to be his people amongst the different nations! My nation loves to hear the gospel; we have a Missionary sent to us, by the good people from N. York. I hope the rest of our red people will soon follow the example set them, to love the gospel, in every part of our western world. From your friend, David Cusick.[38]

By incorporating Indian traditions about places into a European-style narrative, Cusick crafted a unique book, which he completed on June 10, 1825. The following year, he copyrighted and published the book through a printer in nearby Lewiston. In the first section, Cusick related his version of the Haudenosaunee origin story, including the formation of the Great Island on the Turtle's back, the struggle between the twin brothers, Holder of the Heavens and Flint, and the creation of humans. The second part contains a history of ancient America prior to the formation of the Five Nations. The third, and by far the largest, section contains a history of the Five Nations, divided into ten reigns of Atotarho, the title of the keeper of the Council Fire of the League at Onondaga.

Cusick finished his history just as American and international tourists began traveling along the Erie Canal, through Iroquoia's ancient landscape, on their way to see the already world-famous Niagara Falls. Unable to perform physical labor, Cusick earned a small income by selling his book to these visitors. In 1827 British antiquarian collector William Bullock was standing on the banks of the Niagara River when an Indian man approached him and asked if he would be interested in buying a History of the Six Nations written by his brother. A fellow passenger took Bullock to David's house, which Bullock described: "His room was decorated with coloured drawings of his own execution, representing several subjects of the Indian history of his tribe; among the rest, was a drawing of the mammoth, which he informed me was so represented by his fathers, in whose traditions, it was stated more to resemble a hog, than any other beast." Cusick gave the drawing of the yet-famously extinct animal to Bullock. These pictorial works by David and his brother Dennis shared common techniques with American folk art of the time: two-dimensional profiles with even color distribution and distinct outlines. Dennis painted watercolors that depicted the missionary schools and Christian life, while David painted traditional subjects and included them in his *Sketches*. The diverse subjects reflected the Cusicks' syncretic cultural life.[39]

Trained by Euro-Americans who saw his culture as inferior, Cusick modestly discussed his abilities as a historian and his people's beliefs. His humble writing stood in stark contrast to Clinton's cynical take on Seneca national vanity and history. In his book's first paragraph, Cusick noted that he "found the [Haudenosaunee's] history involved with fables." By "fables," Cusick alluded to the supernatural elements of Haudenosaunee history. However, the book's second section promised "a real account of the settlement of North America and their dissensions." He hoped "to throw some light on the history of the original population of the country, which I believe never have been recorded." Within his modest writing, Cusick hid a claim of authority and knowledge of the truth. Even as Cusick emphasized his Christian identity in letters to the missionaries and wrote of "fables" in his introduction, he never disparaged Indian history in his *Sketches*.[40]

From the beginning pages, Cusick's work engaged contemporary Euro-American stories about the ancient landscape, including the lost race, which he connected to earlier Indian traditions. Cusick began with the familiar Haudenosaunee story of the twin brothers, Holder of the Heavens (Sky Holder), the good-minded benefactor of the Haudenosaunee, and Flint, the more sinister brother. When filling the World on the Turtle's Back, Flint tried to create humans but could only make "apes." As apes did not live in the Eastern Woodlands, this description was almost certainly Cusick's translation into a word that contemporary readers understood to mean human-like beings. Sky Holder fixed his brother's failed creation and gave them "living souls." Cusick noted in a footnote, "It appears by the fictitious accounts that the said beings became civilized people, and made their residence in the southern parts of the Island; but afterward they were destroyed by the barbarous nations, and their fortifications were ruined unto this day." Cusick's description evoked concepts of a lost "race" and connected this race to the same fate described in almost every account of America's Mound Builders. By Cusick's estimates, this fictitious lost civilization would have predated Columbus by more than 1,200 years.[41]

Following the creation myth, Cusick told a story of a great ancient Indian civilization, an account that contains enough detail—and mystery—that renders it tantalizing for scholars. Cusick related that in approximately 700 BCE the people of the north appointed a prince, who visited a "great Emperor who resided at the Golden City, a capital of the vast empire." This emperor extended fortifications toward the north, which threatened the peoples around the Great Lakes. Following this incursion, "long bloody wars ensued which perhaps lasted about one hundred years; the people of the north were too skilled in the use of bows and arrows and could endure hardship which proved fatal to a foreign people." Although successful in their defense, the northern peoples then turned on each other. These wars left the Great

Island empty for many years, until the Haudenosaunee emerged from a mountain, near Kuskehsawkich (Oswego) Falls.[42]

At this point in his narrative, Cusick emphasized a sacred connection between the Haudenosaunee and their homelands. After an initial six families emerged from the mountain near Oswego Falls, Sky Holder himself designated where each family would live. As Cusick described it, the ancestral Haudenosaunee traveled down the Hudson River and touched "the bank of a great water." Here they pledged friendship and alliance, but each family eventually settled elsewhere under the guidance of Sky Holder. The Mohawk settled in the Hudson River valley. The second family, who became the Oneida, continued to a creek named "Kaw-na-taw-te-ruh, i.e., Pineries" and settled. Cusick, or someone he knew, had investigated this location, as he noted: "The creek now branches off the Susquehanna River at the head generally called Col. Allen's lake, ten miles south of the Oneida Castle." As this note indicated, this ancient landscape remained visible and its memory endured. Continuing west, Cusick described the Onondaga, Cayuga, and Seneca homelands as well. Each of these places remained accessible. The Seneca settled "near a high mountain, or rather [knoll], situated south of the Canandaigua lake, which was named Jenneatowake." Only the ancestral Tuscarora continued west to the Mississippi before some of them crossed and became enemies, leaving the remainder to settle in North Carolina.[43]

Although the ancient "Golden City" had achieved much, in Cusick's history the Five Nations eventually established an equally impressive empire. To describe these achievements, Cusick emphasized the image of the Roman-like Iroquois empire. The Haudenosaunee projected their power by winning all of the wars that Cusick recalled. In Cusick's history, the Five Nations coordinated actions through a centralized government that resembled the classical governments in titles and leadership. Describing Onondaga, he tellingly wrote: "At Onondaga a tree of peace was planted [that] reached the clouds of Heaven; under the shade of this tree the Senators are invited to set and deli[b]erate, and smoke the pipe of peace as ratification of their proceedings; a great council fire was kindled under the majestic tree, having four branches, one pointed to the south, west, east, north; the neighboring nations were amazed at the powerful confederates."[44]

While Onondaga retained its customary position as the seat of Iroquoia, Cusick devoted a considerable amount of his work to the significance of western Iroquoia's fortifications. Kirkland had seen some of these sites in 1788 when he traveled near the primary Seneca village on Tonawanda Creek. Cusick confirmed Kirkland's general understanding that nearby fortifications derived from a war with western nations. Yet Cusick's *Sketches* contained more detail than Kirkland had recorded in his journal, indicating that Cusick had not simply repeated anecdotes from his mentor.[45]

By turning his attention to western New York, Cusick placed the Tuscarora Reservation at the center of Iroquoia's history. Specifically, he described wars fought just outside the reservation at a fort known as Kauhanauka, also called Kienuka. According to Cusick, the first of these wars, between the Mississauga (Messisaugers) and the Seneca, began "perhaps 400 years before the Columbus discovered America," during the reign of Atotarho VIII. When Kauhanauka's commander learned that the Mississauga planned an attack, he sent runners to neighboring forts and amassed a force of eight hundred warriors. Near the Niagara River, the Seneca laid an ambush and repelled the Mississauga. The Seneca then launched two attacks across the Niagara River, but the battles ended in a stalemate. On his 1810 tour, Clinton had traveled near the fortification, though he did not specifically name it. He certainly passed through the Tuscarora Reservation, where he "saw a chief with a cross on his back," the closest he probably came to the Cusick family.[46]

Kauhanauka's importance reached its apex during the reign of Atotarho IX, or approximately 1142 CE by Cusick's reckoning. According to Cusick, during this reign the Erie split from the Seneca and claimed the territory between the Genesee and Niagara Rivers. Just outside of Kauhanauka, Queen Yagowanea resided in a longhouse called the Peace House. She mediated between warring nations and acquired a reputation as the "mother of the Nations." However, she broke her neutrality and allowed a party of Mississauga to kill two Mohawk warriors from Canandaigua who had "killed a young prince." Before the leaders at Canandaigua discovered her betrayal, the queen traveled to build an alliance with the Erie commander at Fort Kauquatkay, located on the shoreline of Lake Erie. She also sent a runner to the "Naywaunaukauraunah, a savage tribe," who also resided near Lake Erie. As Cusick recalled, this amassed force planned to destroy the Five Nations' settlements east of the Genesee River. For unknown reasons, a woman from Kauhanauka betrayed the Peace Queen and stealth-ily traveled to warn the Haudenosaunee. Heeding her warning, Gov-ernor Sorihowane amassed fifteen hundred warriors and traveled to Fort Kawnesats, "situated on a small lake east of the Genesee River." Here they laid an ambush for the advancing Erie, who had been spot-ted by the chief's runners. A warrior disguised himself as a bear and waited on the path. Spotting the sitting bear, the Erie chased him into the Seneca ambush. After losing six hundred men, the Erie fled back across the Genesee River. The chief of Canandaigua declined to pursue, but shortly thereafter the "King of the Five Nations" ordered the Mohawk war chief Shorihowane to take a force of five thousand warriors and join the leader of Canandaigua in a siege of Kauquat-kay. A fierce siege ensued, which cost Shorihowane his life. After sev-eral days of fighting, the Peace Queen offered a truce, and the Erie retained control of the region.[47]

Memories of the Peace Queen reveal the possibilities and limits of oral traditions as evidence of the past. Cusick's traditions connected to a place with a storied and significant history. Archaeologists believe that the people of the Neutral Nation or their allies, the Wenro, inhabited Kienuka. Little historical evidence survives about the Neutral, whom the Five Nations had destroyed during the 1650s. Their European-given name derived from their impartiality in seventeenth-century wars between the Wyandot (Huron) and the Five Nations. Following a 1618 voyage, Samuel de Champlain explained, "Between the Iroquois and our tribe [the Huron] they are at peace and remain neutral. They are welcome with either tribe, but never venture to engage in any dis-pute or have any quarrel with them, although they often eat and drink together as if they were good friends." Descendants of the Neutral lived among the Five Nations. During the mid-nineteenth century, the

pioneer anthropologist Lewis Henry Morgan recorded an account of
the Peace Queen, probably obtained from Caroline Parker, the sister
of Morgan's well-known Seneca informant Eli S. Parker. In Morgan's
version, the Peace Queen was actually a hero, the mysterious woman
who warned the Seneca of the Erie's impending attack. Like the more
famous Hiawatha, the Peace Queen—or Queens—likely existed, but
time blurred her specific actions, and she too became an archetype.[48]

In Cusick's interpretation, the Five Nations fought just wars, which
made them the rightful rulers of Iroquoia. The Mississauga started the
first conflict fought at Kauhanauka. He recalled the mid-seventeenth-
century conflict with the Erie as a defensive war. Cusick recalled that
in approximately 1492, long after the original conflict with the Peace
Queen, "the Erians declared a war against the Five Nations; a long
bloody war ensued; at last the Erians were driven from the country, and supposed[ly] were incorporated with some of the southern
nations: after which the kingdom enjoyed without disturbance for
many years." Cusick struggled with chronology (although he chose
a symbolic year), placing the destruction of the Erie as the final pre-
Columbian conflict. In fact, European colonization propelled the conflict. Armed with guns supplied by Europeans, the Haudenosaunee
destroyed the Erie nation in 1657. Cusick mentioned nothing of the
Haudenosaunee's desire for hunting land for the beaver trade and captives to replace individuals killed by epidemics, the two factors historians have identified at the root of the conflict.[49]

Cusick's history glorified the Haudenosaunee's past in an ideal-
ized narrative of unity and strength meant to inspire the nineteenth-
century Six Nations struggling with division and marginalization. He
preserved traditions that connected the Tuscarora to a deep Native
history at Kauhanauka, a place where peace reigned. During the early
eighteenth century, the Tuscarora had fled to Iroquoia to escape warfare in North Carolina. The Tuscarora settled near the Oneida but
again suffered violence during the Revolution. After the war, their reservation near Kauhanauka became a new and permanent home for
the Tuscarora. Cusick made Kauhanauka familiar, important, and a
significant place to continue as a people.[50]

Cusick's book briefly caught the attention of Clinton, who was once again governor of New York State but who died suddenly in 1828 without publicly commenting on his historian counterpart from the Tuscarora Reservation. (A few newspapers did note Cusick's publication.) In 1827, while Cusick's brother promoted the hot-off-the-press history to tourists on their way to Niagara Falls, Clinton mailed a copy to his friend, the naturalist Constantine Samuel Rafinesque. Having visited the Tuscarora Reservation the previous year in search of Indian lore, the naturalist eagerly anticipated the final product of Cusick's research. Upon receiving the book, Rafinesque wrote to Clinton's son, George, and remarked, "Cusick['s] work is an interesting but very odd little work." In retrospect, this description appears misplaced, for Rafinesque's interest eventually incorporated Tuscarora history into a long and strange scholarly dialogue about the ancient world ranging from India to the Americas—some truly "very odd" work that included spectacular forgeries and wild speculations beyond anything that Clinton would have concocted.[51]

Even in an age of generalist scholars, few American intellectuals ranged as widely, both in location and in scholarship, as the eccentric and opinionated Rafinesque. He was born in a suburb of Istanbul in 1783 to a French merchant and a German mother whose family traced its roots to Saxony. After Rafinesque's father died of yellow fever in Philadelphia in 1793, his family could no longer afford to pay for tutors, and the future naturalist became largely self-educated. In 1802 in Livorno he met an American merchant named John D. Clifford. This meeting initiated an important friendship that brought Rafinesque back to Philadelphia, where he clerked for Clifford's family business. During his first stay in America, the budding naturalist took an interest in exploring the continent and cataloging its plants and animals. He even wrote Jefferson in 1804 to ask for funding to explore the American West. Before the year was over, however, Rafinesque returned to Europe, this time to Sicily. There he started a family and developed his skills and reputation as a naturalist. Apparently unsatisfied with family life in Sicily, he returned to America in 1815. After nearly perishing in a shipwreck off the Connecticut Coast,

Rafinesque made his way to New York City, an important stop during his many subsequent travels in America. While in Europe, he had corresponded with Samuel Latham Mitchill, and Rafinesque quickly became active in the city's intellectual circles, including the Lyceum of Natural History, New-York Historical Society, and the Literary and Philosophical Society.[52]

Rafinesque's New York friends provided him with an early opportunity to participate in their ongoing reinvention of America's ancient past into a tale of lost civilizations and Indian destroyers. In 1817 Rafinesque contributed a drawing of a mummified Indian, found in Kentucky's Mammoth Cave, for a short article by Mitchill, who mentioned Rafinesque as "that distinguished naturalist." The same year that Mitchill participated in a well-publicized excavation of New York's vanished mastodon, he published a theory that America's vanished race traced its ancestry to the Malay people. Mitchill arrived at this conclusion by comparing fibers from the mummy's wrappings with "fabrics of the Sandwich, the Caroline, and the Fegee islands." While employing an innovative approach to material remains, which echoed the emphasis on detailed comparisons that had uncovered the mastodon as a distinct species, Mitchill's erroneous conclusion nevertheless connected to the same big theory that hindered most Euro-American writings on the ancient landscape. Regarding the fate of this "exterminated" civilization he concluded, "They have probably been overcome by the more warlike and ferocious hordes that entered our hemisphere from the north-east of Asia. These Tartars of the higher latitudes have issued from the great hive of nations, and desolated, in the course of their migrations, the southern tribes of America, as they have done to those of Asia and Europe."[53]

Most Americans intellectuals knew Rafinesque as a natural scientist, but his proclivities made him an ideal candidate to build on these archaeological speculations. Rafinesque's prolific output resulted, in part, from an intellectual confidence that occasionally led him to take liberties with evidence. Notably, in 1817 Rafinesque published his first American book, *Florula Ludoviciana*, a work on botany in the lands of the American West. Printed by James Fenimore Cooper's publisher in

New York, Rafinesque's study immediately raised eyebrows because the botanist had never actually visited the environments of the plants that he described. Instead he relied on the published writing of a French traveler named Claude Cesar Robin. Rafinesque reworked Robin's descriptions of genera and even discovered new species. This willingness to make bold conclusions—even discoveries from text alone—foreshadowed features of Rafinesque's writing on the ancient Indian landscape. To some degree these speculative tendencies appeared in all writing on American antiquity, but Clinton had declined to take an intellectual leap to identify his lost race. In contrast, through a voracious and creative reading of his extensive library, Rafinesque eventually discovered an entire ancient world that never existed. Moreover, Rafinesque did not limit himself to authors of European descent. While Clinton and most Euro-Americans saw Indian traditions about the land as untrustworthy at best, Rafinesque championed a seemingly progressive understanding of oral traditions as histories that spoke to true events, which could be revealed by contemplating Indian traditions within supposedly accurate Euro-American narratives of ancient history.[54]

In 1819 Rafinesque found his opportunity to study America's ancient landscape when Clifford helped him to secure a position teaching botany and natural history at Transylvania University in Kentucky. Since their last meeting, Clifford had been busy. Deeply immersed in a study of nearby ruins, the merchant-cum-historian published a series of newspaper letters in 1819 and 1820 that identified alleged cultural and material connections between the ancient Hindu world and the substantial ruins of North America's lost civilization. He speculated that during the sixth century the spread of Buddhism had triggered social conflict and then migrations within and eventually out of Asia. Clifford pondered, "May not the immediate ancestors of our present race of North American Indians, the Lenni Lenape and Mengwe [Iroquois] nations, have been forced from North Tartary?" This Buddhist-instigated invasion of North America pushed the Hindu ancestors of the Aztec to the South, where they continued building relatively civilized cities.[55]

Clifford died shortly after completing his essays, leaving Rafinesque

to take up his work. Rafinesque's Kentucky home provided opportunities for the naturalist to see earthworks that Clifford had linked
to ancient Hindus. Over the next four years, Rafinesque claimed to
have discovered hundreds of uncataloged "monuments" and 123 additional ancient settlements in Kentucky. He sketched several of these
sites, such as the "Lower Alleghawee monuments on North Elkhorn
Creek," and sent his drawings to the American Antiquarian Society.
Following Clifford's lead, he remained interested in a Central Asian
haven for ancestral Native Americans surviving biblical floods, but
he shifted his interest in ancient civilizations to the Atlantic world.[56]

With his Atlantic focus, Rafinesque claimed to unite the archaeology of the Americas, Europe, and Asia into a coherent history. In 1824
Rafinesque published his conclusions in *Ancient History or Annals of
Kentucky*. He believed that an ancient northern African-Mediterranean
empire, the "Atlanteans," brought high civilization to eastern America.
Full of more imagination than evidence, Rafinesque described their
American empire with a capital "somewhere on the Ohio" that communicated with the Atlanteans in Europe and even with India. This
empire eventually divided, with the "Talegans" ruling over lands near
the Ohio River watershed. All of the Atlanteans would have to share
North America. The "Snake" people, who included the Mexican Indians, followed. Finally the Lenni Lenape (Delaware) and Haudenosaunee completed the migrations from Asia. Rafinesque imagined this
final migration as simultaneous with Rome's downfall. He explained
that "a swarm of barbarous nations emigrating from Tartary and Siberia spread desolation from Europe to America." This downfall echoed
Mitchill's work that Rafinesque had illustrated, as well as Clinton's
earlier writings.[57]

Although these theories originated in questions about North America's ancient landscape, they connected to wild speculations spreading
around the world alongside European imperial ambitions. Rafinesque
and Clifford's interpretations reflected the methodologies and shortcomings of their British orientalist counterparts, who employed tenuous
linguistic and historical comparisons to incorporate India's history with
biblical and classical European accounts. Clifford cited and admired

the work of orientalist Sir William Jones in the *Asiatic Researches*, a publication of the Asiatic Society of Bengal. (Transylvania University owned copies.) Yet by far the most interesting writing in this journal came from Francis Wilford, whose scholarship reveals the problems of authenticity and limits of believability in an age of historical conjecture and appropriation. His *magnum opus* was a nearly six hundred–page series of essays, "The Sacred Isles in the West," published between 1805 and 1810. Studying Sanskrit sources with the assistance of a pandit, Wilford claimed to have reconstructed an ancient Hindu understanding of world geography with a startling feature: sacred "White Isles" located in the west, where Vishnu had lived and the Vedas had originated prior to Krishna bringing them to India. Even more astonishingly, he uncovered tales that foretold of a savior to one day come from these isles—amazingly, the British Isles. In short, he discovered that Indian scriptures confirmed that everything significant about the subcontinent's past and future originated in Britain. Yet after years of work on supposedly ancient sources, but prior to publishing his essays on the "Sacred Isles," Wilford made a crushing discovery: "that whenever the word S'wetam or S'weta-dwipa the name of the principal of the Sacred Isles . . . was introduced, the writing was somewhat different, and that the paper was of a different colour, as if stained." In the end, Wilford blamed his hired pandit for possibly forging more than 12,000 lines of material that confirmed his employer's interests. Wilford claimed to have purged his essays of errors prior to publication, but the fact remained that his theories were based on spectacular forgeries.[58]

Although this was only one piece of Rafinesque's puzzle, Wilford's geography clearly influenced *Annals of Kentucky*, which labeled the Appalachian Mountains as the Locáloca Mountains, a range that Wilford had described as near the oceans at the edge of the ancient known world. (As he became more interested in Central and South America, Rafinesque later moved the Locáloca Mountains to the Andes.) In a telling example of orientalists' presumptions, Wilford had suggested a shared history of these mountains, named "by our own ancient mythologists *Atlas*," among other discoverable names in various cultures. Beyond these mountains, Rafinesque noted, was the "Great

White Land," where an Atlantic empire built great cities—that is, Rafinesque's own Sacred Isles of America, also once visited by the mythical Krishna (also known as Hercules, according to Rafinesque).[59]

During the second half of the 1820s, as Rafinesque worked on a more comprehensive ancient history, he wrote some shorter pieces that illustrated his orientalist methodologies at work. He became interested in Cherokee history as that Indian nation acquired a reputation as a so-called "civilized" tribe but nevertheless faced removal. In April 1828, writing to the *Cherokee Phoenix*, Rafinesque expressed admiration for the Cherokee people, urged them to apply for status as a federal territory, and encouraged them to follow David Cusick's example to preserve their ancient traditions in writing. Rafinesque boasted of his familiarity with more than twenty languages, and he indicated an interest in learning more about the Cherokee's language (Tsalagi Gawonihisdi): "I have a small vocabulary already and I think that I can trace some of its affinities to the Sanscrit, Etruscan and Atalantes. And in America with the Tala (or Tarasca) of West Mexico, Otolum, Muhiscas &c." We can only wonder what the Cherokee made of their newfound ancestors, the Atalantes. Three months later, in a series of letters published in the *Saturday Evening Post*, Rafinesque argued that the Cherokee—actually Iroquoian speakers distantly related to the Haudenosaunee—descended from his ancient Talega civilization, distinct from the "hunting Indians" such as the Haudenosaunee. Regarding Cusick's history, he noted, "We find in it that a people come by sea settled the Southern part of the United States more than 2800 years ago, and that they formed an empire extending to the Lakes, the capital of which was called the Golden City." To fit Cusick's Golden City into his textually constructed ancient world, Rafinesque had to creatively adapt the Tuscarora account. In *Sketches of Ancient History*, Cusick does mention in the most "ancient days" some people had "sailed from a port unknown" and shipwrecked on the southern part of the Great Island. They built settlements, but monsters had destroyed all of them. In a separate passage, unrelated to the vanished shipwrecked people, Cusick describes the Golden City to the south as existing "two thousand two hundred years before the Columbus," or approximately 708

BCE. Rafinesque believed that both of these stories, perhaps blurred by the limits of oral history, referenced his Atlantic empire, whose descendants still spoke related languages. To be sure, scholars today look for suggestive hints that match oral traditions with material findings and the printed record, but Rafinesque built an entire world history—in effect, a house of cards—using creative readings of text that supported incorrect linguistic classifications, which then confirmed inaccurate secondary literature.[60]

While writing his ancient history of Kentucky, Rafinesque had allegedly been working on translating his most controversial contribution to American Indian history, the *Walum Olum*, purportedly the history of the Haudenosaunee's neighbors, the Lenni Lenape, from an ancient migration through the period of European colonization. Rafinesque noted that the *Walum Olum* extended back through "96 successive kings or chiefs," which meant the history began approximately "1600 years before our era." Like a good creation myth from either Old World, the *Walum Olum* described the origins of the world and a flood. The ancestors of the Lenni Lenape and others survived this flood in the "Tula" land under the guidance of "Nanabush," the "grandfather of all, the grandfather of the beings, the grandfather of the men, and the grandfather of the turtles." After the flood, the peoples spread out across their ancient homeland, and the ancestors of the Lenni Lenape eventually traveled east to the edge of their continent. In a significant passage, the *Walum Olum* recalled their departure to the "Snake Island": "It was wonderful when they all went over the smooth deep water of the frozen sea, at the gap of the Snake sea in the great ocean." Rafinesque interpreted this passage as a description of a crossing of the Bering Sea. The *Walum Olum* then described travels across their new continent, including crossing the Mississippi River (*Nemasipi*) and great battles and victory over the Talegas, prior to the Lenni Lenape settling in their eventual homelands. The *Walum Olum* proper concluded with the Lenni Lenape pondering new arrivals from the east: "They were friendly, and came in big bird-ships, who are they?" A fragment of additional history provides the obvious answer. "Alas, alas! We know now who they are, these *Wapsinis*

(white people) who then came out of the sea, to rob us of our country." If genuine, the *Walum Olum* offered an unprecedentedly extensive history of a Native American nation and a startling counterpart
to Cusick's relatively recent work. Scholars had never (and still have
not) located any comparable artifact of such detail that unites archaeology, Native American traditions, and European history.[61]

The *Walum Olum* took Rafinesque down an eerily similar path to the
one that had led Wilford astray in search of his "White Isles." Yet the
Walum Olumo's origins remain more elusive. Rafinesque later recalled
that in 1820 the "late Dr. Ward of Indiana" had given him wooden tablets, which the doctor had received from some Lenni Lenape Indians
in exchange for medical care. From "John Burns," Rafinesque received
"songs" that explained the tablets' pictographs, and he acquired an epi-
logue from an unidentified individual. Nobody has ever located these
tablets or the identity of the individuals who provided them. Rafinesque's most recent biographer, Charles Boewe, believes that these
elusive men pulled an elaborate prank on the opinionated naturalist.
During the 1990s, linguistic research demonstrated that, among other
problems, the *Walum Olum* had been translated *from* English and into
the Lenape language. Acknowledging these problems, Boewe contends,
"Applying the principle of Occam's razor that the simplest explanation
tends to be the correct one, we should ask why Rafinesque needed to
waste ten years of his life trying to decipher the *Walum Olum* if he had
invented it himself." Boewe presumes Rafinesque actually received the
tablets in 1820 and spent a decade on translation rather than invention.
His argument raises the question of who exactly had the necessary linguistic skills or cultural connections to craft an artifact that not only
fooled Rafinesque but remained debated, if never universally accepted
as genuine, for the next 150 years. In other words, was creating a believ-
ably authentic Indian artifact the best way to "make a fool" of Rafinesque? In any event, in a strikingly similar scenario to the discovery
of Wilford's "Sacred Isles," Rafinesque received (or crafted) detailed
but forged ancient stories that confirmed his intellectual pursuits.[62]

Rafinesque published the *Walum Olum* in 1836 as part of the first
two volumes of *The American Nations*, which marked the culmination

of his efforts to combine archaeological investigations and linguistic studies with what he believed to be telling hints of shared ancient culture, scattered throughout thousands of pages of world literature. (Rafinesque promised but never completed additional volumes.) Much of his *American Nations* actually discussed ancient lands such as China, for these far-off realms all eventually connected to Rafinesque's ancient Americas. As he explained, "It is a positive fact that many ancient nations of the east, such as the Lybians, Moors, Etruscans, Phenicians, Hindus, &c. had heard of America, or knew nearly as much of it, as we did of Australia and Polynesia 100 years ago." Rafinesque believed that ancient islands had facilitated navigation across the Atlantic Ocean, but a cataclysmic series of volcanic explosions had sunk those islands and led the Atlantes to believe their colonies in America had been lost as well.[63]

In *American Nations*, Rafinesque greatly revised and expanded his previously published theories to include various migrations in a more extensive world history, but he remained committed to his ancient Atlantic culture, the Atlantes, who had colonized America (and southern Europe, northern Africa, and even Ireland beginning roughly four or five thousand years earlier. The progenitors of the Talegas (i.e., the Mound Builders) of North America and the ancient Mexican civilizations, the Atlantes left signs of their presence on both sides of the ocean named for them. Rafinesque asserted that the Atlantes brought almost everything of importance across this ocean to America: "Agriculture and Astronomy, the Maize brought from Asia and Africa, many kinds of pulse and guards, the peculiar months, weeks of 5 days, the civil castes, a glyphic writing, all the ancient monuments, the actual ruins of many cities and temples, the fine arts of Architecture, sculpture and painting." These achievements reached as far north as the Ohio Country. In contrast, most Native Americans north of Mexico traced their origin to a later migration from Asia, which brought destruction rather than civilization to North America. Rafinesque confirmed this destruction by noting Cusick's account of the Golden City and missionary John Heckewelder's earlier account of the Lenni Lenape meeting the Haudenosaunee at the Mississippi, their migration eastward, and their defeat of the formidable Alligewi people (Talega in Rafinesque's work).[64]

Within this framework, Rafinesque saw the *Walum Olum's* story of an icy migration as confirmation of the Lenape and Haudenosaunee's origins in Asia rather than as part of an Atlantic culture. Along with the *Walum Olum*, Rafinesque appropriated the Haudenosaunee and Lenni Lenape origin myth of the World on the Turtle's Back, noting that "although the tribes vary the tale, the holy song of the real Linapi [Lenape] alludes clearly to a great flood in Asia: where their nations at least were partly saved in *Tula* (the turtle land) in central Asia, by the help of a goddess, and Noah or *Nana-bush*." Relying on a large measure of conjectural etymology to craft world histories, writers like Rafinesque drew ingenious but incredibly flawed connections between unrelated times and places. As he explained in a note, "In Linapi the meaning [of Tula] is *Turtle* or *Tortoise*, names derived from *Thor* turtle in Hebrew. But all derive from strong and tall. *Tul-ap-in* is the real tortoise of Linapi meaning *strong-manly-thing*." He allegedly found additional references to this turtle refuge in Chinese and Hindu sources. As for Noah, Rafinesque referenced the Anishinaabe mythical figure of Nanabozho or Nanabush, whose name Rafinesque translated as "*Noah-Noah-hare*, or the *Great Noah* and *Hare*." Spinning these kinds of connections across thousands of miles and years, Rafinesque constructed an impossibly convoluted history of an interconnected ancient world that nevertheless arrived at the same conclusion as other writers: Indians had come to America as destroyers.[65]

Preoccupied with increasingly improbable archaeological theories, scholars failed to give Cusick's work the consideration that it merited during his lifetime. In addition to Rafinesque's appropriation, the book received a brief mention in Josiah Priest's popular *American Antiquities and Discoveries in the West* (1833), via an unauthorized reproduction of a book review Rafinesque had written. In Priest's sensationalist book, which reproduced nearly every theory of America's lost race, Cusick's work appeared as a curiosity alongside more earnestly argued passages describing allegedly Jewish customs found among the Indians. Even Cusick's obituary managed some parting shots on the alleged shortcomings of his work. Appearing in 1840, the obituary wrote of Cusick's book, "It is an illiterate and very crude affair, but embodies many curious though in general most absurd traditions of the people. Among other imaginary facts, he gives an account of a race of kings of the five nations, extending back centuries." The entire obituary was something of an insult, for, like John Montour before him, Cusick was not yet dead. The newspapers had conflated David and his father—the actual Tuscarora chief who had died in 1840. Frequently ill, David Cusick lived for only a few years longer, dying sometime before 1846.[66]

As American settlement progressed from the late 1780s onward, it became easier to forget the Native American imprint on the landscape. While Euro-American observers had always underestimated the role of farming for Native peoples, in 1779 the soldiers of the Sullivan-Clinton campaign had clearly admired the vast fields of crops surrounding the Haudenosaunee's villages. Following the American Revolution, the eventual rush of settlers and their livestock made it easier to imagine, as a writer for the *Albany Chronicle* recalled, that Europeans had found the Haudenosaunee living "in the forests" and that they had built nothing of note. Yet this same transformation provoked fears that settlers would also destroy New York's ancient history. This fear would later prove justified, as farming has destroyed or damaged much of the Native American built landscape from Iroquoia to the ruins of the great earthwork pyramids of Cahokia—destruction that has reinforced the enduring popular memory of America as an untouched wilderness.[67]

Before this destruction had advanced, intellectuals such as Clinton, whose father had initiated the destruction of Iroquoia, appropriated the ruins as the cities of a lost civilization. Recalling the subsequent transformation of Iroquoia by white settlers, mid-nineteenth-century local historians continued Clinton's imaginative but flawed history. One, Orsamus Turner, came close to articulating a vision of contact between Europe and America as two old worlds colliding rather than a new and old world—a view that professional historians have only recently adopted. Turner wrote, "We clear away the forest and speak familiarly of subduing a 'virgin soil';—and yet the plough up-turns the skulls of those whose history is lost!" Turner included Cusick's most important fortification, Kauhanauka, as part of this lost landscape. He praised its position, noting that "the mountain fastnesses of Switzerland are little better adapted to the purposes of a look-out and defence." Unfortunately, he attributed its lost history—and the history of Iroquoia's fortifications in general—to an equally lost advanced race. As they worried about losing their continent's ancient history, these historians perpetuated a myth which distorted that very history.[68]

As the "Romans of the Western World," the Haudenosaunee seemed like the obvious architects of its imagined ancient Roman landscape. Instead, during the early nineteenth century, at every opportunity Euro-American writers undermined the achievements of the ancestral Haudenosaunee. Although Clinton's writing referenced familiar images of an Iroquois empire, he actually cast them as the Huns who destroyed ancient America. After Clinton's theories rendered the Haudenosaunee as the "Romans" of only a second-tier world, Rafinesque's orientalist histories undermined the place of Great Island itself. Throughout the Eastern Woodlands, eighteenth-century Indian traditions had emphasized that the Great Island—the World on the Turtle's Back—was a land created for Indians. This world existed separately from Europeans, and their cultures were shaped for and by a different continent. In Rafinesque's account, the Turtle was not even North America but a Himalayan retreat, and Atlantes had been in America for thousands of years, even before the Haudenosaunee.

The decline and fall of the Roman Iroquois empire left Iroquoia's ruins as a blank canvas—not for Native Americans but for white Americans, who ignored Haudenosaunee traditions and projected their own self-serving interpretations onto the land. Cast as scholarly, even scientific, these Mound Builder explanations faded by the end of the nineteenth century as increased professionalization helped anthropologists to understand what the Haudenosaunee had already known. But for a time, writers wrote thousands of pages of elaborate theories on the ancient landscape from America to India, found tenuous connections with unrelated languages, grappled with allegedly ancient tablets, and tried to fit it all into something resembling a biblically compatible account of world history—an impossible undertaking. Consequently, even as Euro-American writers agreed that Indians had not built much, they failed to agree on who actually had. Barring a miraculous discovery hidden somewhere in America's vanishing ancient landscape, this debate seemed unresolvable.[69]

| Chapter Five

The Burned-Over District

From 1817 to 1825, when most New Yorkers thought of digging, they pictured the Erie Canal, which required the efforts of nine thousand men to complete. Its promoters desired a rational, predictable, and efficient landscape to hasten commercial agriculture to New York City. Nature failed to provide the necessary waterways, so New Yorkers built an "artificial river." Historians have argued that this canal marked the triumph of "art over nature," as nineteenth-century Americans' technology conquered the wilderness. This conquest required the expansion and improvement of the nation's roads, the building of canals, advances in steamship technology, and, eventually, the creation of railroads. Historians have labeled this unprecedented expansion of infrastructure and technology "the transportation revolution." In a single generation, Americans overcame centuries-old limitations on the speed at which people, goods, and ideas traveled. Lower transportation costs contributed to sharp declines in product prices by the middle of the century, allowing more Americans to purchase refined furnishings for their homes. Consequently, the canal marked a watershed in the development of American capitalism and the emergence of a middle class.[1]

Concurrent with capitalism's expansion, Americans participated in religious revivals and experimentation propelled by the stresses of

a rapidly changing society but rooted in varying intellectual traditions, collectively forming what scholars have described as America's
"Second Great Awakening." In central and western New York's rapidly growing towns, the upwardly mobile proved especially responsive
to revivals. In the canal towns, an emerging middle class promoted a
reform-oriented millennialist Christianity, which stressed perfection
of individuals, communities, and eventually the nation to prepare the
way for Christ's Second Coming. In 1830 this movement reached its
peak with the arrival of evangelical minister Charles Grandison Finney
in Rochester, where he drew crowds of people eager to hear his message of salvation through personal choice. As Finney later explained,
"Instead of telling sinners to use the means of grace and pray for a new
heart, we called on them to make themselves a new heart." Perhaps
not coincidentally, self-improvement and temperance also made for
better workers. Nineteenth-century Americans spoke of the intensity
of these revivals, especially those in central and western New York,
which they likened to spiritual fires. Following this custom, scholars
have labeled western New York the "Burned-Over District," a phrase
most famously applied by Finney in his autobiography. By first burning the Haudenosaunee's villages and fields, the Sullivan-Clinton expedition had set the stage for reinventing Iroquoia as a metaphorically
burned region, seemingly unconnected to the previous landscape. Yet
superficial glances proved misleading.[2]

In popular memory and intellectual models, landscape change
indicated supposedly linear progress away from the Haudenosaunee's
"wilderness" and its other-than-human spirits. But in reality, some
Euro-Americans looked for an equally magical world that overlapped
with the ancient places of the Haudenosaunee. On the fringes of the
Burned-Over District's emerging middle-class world, treasure seekers practiced their own art of digging to conquer the supernatural
rather than the natural world. Dependent on gifted individuals who
could manipulate the unseen world, treasure hunting was an American variant of older folk magic. Success depended on knowledge of
magical circles, magical numbers for the proper repetition of rituals,
and a seer stone or divining rod that worked with a specific individual.

Through these techniques, the hunter overcame guardian spirits, some very ancient, who protected the treasure by clouding the vision of the seer, moving the treasure, and frightening the living. Treasure hunting provided an opportunity for relatively poor men to seek the wealth and independence celebrated by the new middle class.[3]

In one extraordinary instance, a treasure seeker, Joseph Smith Jr., became the district's most influential prophet. In March 1830 he published the Book of Mormon, the foundational text of what became the Church of Jesus Christ of Latter-day Saints. Although usually not considered as such, the Book of Mormon represented the transformation of Iroquoia as much as the Erie Canal did. Originating in ancient plates that Smith claimed to have uncovered from the ground and translated, Mormonism became America's first new religious movement with roots in Native American archaeology. The Book of Mormon conveyed a religious history in a narrative that reflected (or employed) contemporary theories that ancient American civilization had been destroyed by the ancestors of the American Indians. As such, Smith's work offered an answer to the mystery of ancient America's ruins, which the Book of Mormon attributed to an early civilization called the Nephites, who had been conquered by ancestors of Native Americans, the Lamanites.[4]

Mormonism's origins were deeply intertwined with the early republic's social and economic developments, which eventually brought the Smith family to New York. Prior to Joseph Smith Jr.'s birth, his family, headed by Joseph Smith Sr. and Lucy Mack Smith, had owned a small store in Randolph, Vermont. In the developing capitalist nation, the rewards for success multiplied, but so too did the chances of failure. Joseph Sr. tried his luck in the lucrative ginseng trade with China. Rather than sell his ginseng to a local merchant, Smith shipped his product alongside the merchant's to China, cutting out the middleman and increasing his potential profit. The merchant's son apparently traveled on the ship, stole Smith's cargo, and claimed the whole operation had been a failure. He gave Smith a chest of tea as payment, which helped little with the family's debts. Lacking money, the Smiths sold their farm and moved between Turnbridge, Royalton, and Sharon, Vermont, where Joseph Jr. was born on December 23, 1805. In 1811 the Smiths briefly moved to Lebanon, New Hampshire, and then Norwich, Vermont, before moving to Palmyra, New York, in 1816. Here they opened a small shop that sold refreshments, and Joseph Sr. and his older sons worked as hired laborers. They earned enough money to purchase land less than two miles south of Palmyra in Manchester Township, where they moved by 1819.[5]

In Palmyra, the Smith family likely knew of the speculation regarding an ancient lost civilization, for their neighbors certainly did. Across the state, newspapers had reported on archaeological discoveries. The Smith family read the *Palmyra Register*, which covered such stories. Before writing local histories of western New York, Orsamus Turner worked as an apprentice printer in the offices of the *Palmyra Register*, where he recalled often seeing the younger Joseph Smith: "He used to come into the village of Palmyra with little jags of wood, from his backwoods home; sometimes patronizing a village grocery too freely; sometimes find an odd job to do about the store of Seymour Scovell; and once a week he would stroll into the office of the old *Palmyra Register* for his father's paper."[6]

On January 21, 1818, in a large front-page column, the *Palmyra Register* reported on the continued discoveries of "mounds" to the west in Harrison, Indiana. The amateur archaeologists concluded that enough bones existed for at least one hundred bodies to have been buried, which suggested a battle. On several occasions the investigators searched for iron tools but found none. New Yorkers found similar evidence of violence in their own ruins, and many great battles later appeared in the Book of Mormon. Regarding ancient battles, the column concluded: "We can safely infer from them nothing more, than that this immense tract of country, which has every mark of having been for centuries past a desolate wilderness, has been thickly inhabited at some former period by a warlike people, who had made much greater advances in civilized life, than any of the aboriginal inhabitants of North America, who have been known since its discovery by Europeans."

To explain this civilization's disappearance, newspaper accounts echoed a theory promulgated by DeWitt Clinton in his 1811 address before the Literary and Philosophical Society of New-York and reiterated in *A Memoir on the Antiquities of the Western Parts of the State of New York*, published in 1818: "From these and many other similar discoveries, the writer believes (and we think with good reason) that this country was once inhabited by a race of people, at least partially civilized, & that this race has been exterminated by the forefathers of the present and late tribes of Indians in this country."[7]

Newspaper articles reflected the eclectic early nineteenth-century views of ancient history that reached Americans through a mix of speculative books, religion, and folklore. Among other accounts, the *Palmyra Register* published an extended timeline of world history, which for the year 721 BCE read: "The Kingdom of Israel finished by Salmanaser, king of Assyria, who carried the ten tribes into captivity." In this pre-professional world of scholarship, religious views, mythology, and scholarship mixed. With story elements paralleling Smith's future discovery and C. S. Rafinesque's investigation into "Atlanteans," the August 20, 1820, issue announced a forthcoming book from Irish writer Roger O'Connor, *The Chronicles of Eri*, a history based on "authentic records" printed "in the Phoenician dialect of the Scythian Language," which the author had recovered from the ground. These records allegedly revealed an ancient migration to Ireland from the Middle East. If magic prepared Joseph Smith to believe in angels and hidden plates, widespread historical speculation cultivated a milieu where some expected to find plates written in an ancient language.[8]

Residents of the Burned-Over District also shared the common perception of Indians as either bloodthirsty savages or doomed, vanishing characters. In 1818 the *Palmyra Register* printed nearly seventy stories about Indians. Many described battles during the Seminole War in the southeastern United States. Local stories took a less threatening note, as these Indians had been defeated. In 1818 a published letter from Seneca chief Red Jacket to DeWitt Clinton emphasized the plight of the Haudenosaunee: "We feel the hand of our God has long been heavy on his red children. For our sins he has brought us low, and caused us to melt away before our white brothers, as snow before the fire." Red Jacket asked for action to prevent "wicked white men" from further harming the Indians, and he warned that perhaps God would take vengeance on the sinful Americans. Some news even hinted at hope for salvation among New York's Indians. With more than a touch of ignorance, likely referencing the Haudenosaunee's mid-winter ceremony of the "White Dog Sacrifice," one story proclaimed: "Renouncing the worship of dogs, we have heard some of those tribes confess the name of Jesus." Later the Book of Mormon spoke to simi-lar themes of humbled savages, wicked civilizations, and redemption.[9]

Meanwhile, Smith focused on the troubling religious disputes of his time and place, which the Haudenosaunee also observed and con-sidered. Young Joseph Smith viewed the diverse religious revivals with a mix of suspicion and anxiety. In an 1839 autobiographical sketch, Smith recalled: "In the midst of this war of words, and tumult of opin-ions, I often said to myself, what is to be done? Who of all these par-ties are right? Or are they all wrong together?" While the participatory impulses of the revivals attracted many new converts, they bitterly debated over which denomination truly understood the Holy Scrip-tures. Almost all believed that salvation required a certainty of belief and action rooted in the Bible, which was easier said than done. At the Buffalo Creek Reservation in 1805, Red Jacket cited this conflict to challenge the missionaries: "You say there is but one way to wor-ship and serve the Great Spirit. If there is but one religion; why do you white people differ so much about it? Why not all agree, as you can all read the book?" With salvation hanging in the balance, Smith decided to ask God for advice.[10]

An answer came in the spring of 1820, when Smith experienced his First Vision, a foundational event in Mormon history. Over time Smith provided evolving accounts of this vision, rendering the precise date and details uncertain. During this vision, God forgave Smith's sins. In 1838 Smith also recalled that he asked for guidance on which denominations spoke truly: "I was answered that I must join none of them, for they were all wrong, and the Personage who addressed me said that all their Creeds were an abomination in his sight, that those professors were all corrupt, that 'they draw near to me with their lips but their hearts are far from me.'" Smith's experience placed him outside Enlightenment rationalism, which saw the universe as operating by a fixed set of scientific laws, and mainstream Christianity, which assigned revelations and supernatural powers to biblical times. Smith recalled telling a Methodist minister of his vision. According to Smith, the incredulous minister told him that what he saw "was all of the Devil." The minister dismissed what Smith believed was true, and this rejection sent the future prophet on an individual quest to find religious truth.[11]

While Smith's questions focused on religion, the answers he sought led him back to Iroquoia's ancient mysteries. As Smith later recalled, late one night in September 1823 he prayed for forgiveness of sins and asked for a "divine manifestation" so that he could know his "state and standing before him." A light appeared and grew stronger until the entire room became exceedingly bright. A celestial being materialized and hovered next to Smith's bed. He wore white robes and his "whole person was glorious beyond description." This angel identified himself as Moroni and said that he brought a message from God. Moroni explained that "there was a book deposited written upon gold plates, giving an account of the former inhabitants of this continent and the source from which they sprang." Once Smith found these plates, the angel warned, he must hide them from prying eyes.[12]

This vision began a four-year quest for the plates, which Smith could accomplish only when he was spiritually ready. Moroni directed Smith to a hill about three miles south and east of the Smiths' farm. The main road between Palmyra and Canandaigua passed a few hundred feet to its west. Oliver Cowdery, an important early Mormon, noted that the hill's prominence "must attract the notice of the traveller as he passes by." No trees stood on the hill's steep northern end, but beech, maple, basswood, and some conifers grew on its other slopes. This picturesque road was framed to the west by a smaller hill. Smith had often traveled through here on his way to Canandaigua. Smith tried three times (an important number in treasure seeking) to obtain the plates and failed. He later recalled that the angel appeared again "and said unto me you have not kept the commandments of the Lord which I gave unto you therefore you cannot now obtain them for the time is not yet fulfilled." Smith had apparently seen riches in the golden plates and had been rebuked for his treasure seeking impulses.[13]

After Moroni's visit, Smith reportedly possessed detailed knowledge of the ancients. In her 1845 manuscript and the 1853 published history, Lucy Smith recalled that her household experienced great happiness as they awaited the "more perfect knowledge of the plan of salvation of the human family." In the meantime, Joseph entertained the family during the evening with "some of the most amusing recitals that could be imagined." Lucy Smith remembered: "He would describe the ancient inhabitants of this continent, their dress, mode of traveling, and the animals upon which they rode; their cities, their buildings, with every particular; their mode of warfare; and also their religious worship." Emphasizing the miraculous nature of this knowledge, Lucy added that her son told the stories with "as much ease, seemingly, as if he had spent his whole life with them."[14]

While he sought religious certainty, Smith also searched for the landscape's hidden riches, at least until he finally uncovered the plates in 1827. Often called "money digging," treasuring hunting was widespread across the northeastern United States, but its practitioners left little documentation. One Cooperstown newspaper, the *Watch-tower*, reprinted an article from Vermont whose author claimed, "We could name, if we pleased, at least five hundred respectable men, who do in the simplicity and sincerity of their hearts verily believe that immense treasures lie concealed upon our Green Mountains; many of whom have been, for a number of years, most industriously and perseveringly engaged in digging it up." One man's perseverance reportedly led to enough money to buy a house. Rumors of discoveries encouraged the unsuccessful to keep digging despite the odds.[15]

During his teenage years, Smith had acquired three seer stones to use in these hunts. Probably in 1819 or 1820, Smith obtained his first stone by using a stone borrowed from his neighbor, Sally Chase, who also hunted for treasure. Gazing into Chase's stone, probably in a hat, the ambitious treasure hunter located his future stone in the ground. Smith also found a green stone near the Susquehanna River.

His neighbors in Palmyra never noticed it, suggesting Smith rarely used it. Probably in 1822, digging a well for Willard Chase, Smith acquired his favorite stone, brown in color, which neighbors recalled him using in treasure hunts.[16]

With these magical instruments, treasure seekers saw past the settled landscape of farms and towns and imagined its more adventurous past. One study has uncovered more than forty instances of treasure hunting in the northeast between 1780 and 1830. Most hunters sought treasure buried by pirates, especially Captain Kidd, a Scottish privateer executed by the British for piracy in 1701. Drawing upon this widespread legend, Washington Irving featured Kidd's treasure in his short story published in 1824, "The Devil and Tom Walker," a tale about a money digger who sought the treasure buried in the woods since Kidd's day and protected by the Devil himself. Despite living inland, treasure hunters also sought Spanish loot. These improbable tales indicated the settlers' limited knowledge of their new homeland's history. Yet the well-read Noah Webster also imagined that Spanish adventurers had ventured far to the north of Mexico. Treasure hunters and amateur archaeologists understood the Native American landscape through a similarly shared ignorance, and they spun creative tales that revealed a limited understanding of Iroquoia's history.[17]

Locals claimed that prior to uncovering the plates, Smith had sought Captain Kidd's treasure and Spanish gold. In October 1825 Josiah Stowell of Harmony, Pennsylvania, hired Joseph Smith Sr. and Jr. to help find a lost Spanish mine. (Alternatively, in 1870 Fayette Lapham summarized an interview conducted with Smith Sr. around 1830 where he stated that this treasure "had been deposited there by the Indians or others.") In 1838 the younger Smith acknowledged this incident but downplayed the importance of treasure hunting in his life. Digging for one month, they found nothing, and Smith recalled that he "finally prevailed with the old gentleman to cease digging after it." Martin Harris later recalled that he heard Smith quit digging because "the enchantment was so strong he could not see." In March 1826 Stowell's concerned nephew filed a complaint with the South Bainbridge, New York, justice of the peace, which accused Smith of using his seer stone. New York law considered such treasure seeking a form of disorderly conduct. The outcome of these proceedings remains debated by historians, but Smith escaped any serious consequences.[18]

By the nineteenth century, the relatively educated middle-class and wealthy people viewed treasure hunters as lazy and unmotivated. Following the Book of Mormon's publication, Smith's newfound fame attracted enemies who collected testimonies of similar charges of laziness regarding Smith and his early converts. These same recollections suggested that allegedly lazy treasure hunters actually spent much time and energy on the perfection of their craft. In this interpretation, skeptics saw treasure hunting as a means by which gullible but otherwise hardworking men lost their way.[19]

After Moroni's visit, Smith saw the nearby hills with a mix of religious reverence and magical insight, a view reflective of his transition from treasure seeker to religious prophet. One skeptical neighbor, Roswell Nichols, recalled that during the late 1820s, Smith told him "the hills in our neighborhood were nearly all erected by human hands," presumably the Nephites. Nichols claimed that Smith "said that gold and silver was once as plenty as the stones in the field are now—that the ancients, half of them melted the ore and made the gold and silver, while the other half buried it deeper in the earth, which account for these hills." Nichols probably spoke to Smith in 1829, when the Book of Mormon translation neared completion. Smith's early convert, Martin Harris, supported this general claim of ancient treasure: "There was a company there in that neighborhood, who were digging for money supposed to have been hidden by the ancients." Thus the ancients—the perceived real inhabitants of America—competed with and eventually surpassed the seafaring pirates and distant Spanish as the sources of treasure. To an extent, this ancient wealth marked the transformation of Iroquoia, as locals developed (or discovered) their own traditions that replaced borrowed adventures from the coast.[20]

Another family acquaintance, Peter Ingersoll, recalled conversations with Joseph Smith Sr., which probably occurred shortly prior to the Book of Mormon's publication: "At another time, he told me that the ancient inhabitants of this country used camels instead of horses. For proof of this fact, he stated that in a certain hill on the farm of Mr. Cuyler, there was a cave containing an immense value of gold and silver, stands of arms, also a saddle for a camel, hanging on a peg at one side of the cave" It is unclear who Smith thought the ancients were when he spoke to Ingersoll, but camels do not appear in the Book of Mormon. In any case, Smith linked Eurasian-style treasures to the hills of New York but provided details incompatible with the golden plates, suggesting an evolving understanding of Iroquoia's ancient past.[21]

As they searched for wealth, treasure hunters employed their gift of seeing to solve the mysteries of the Native American landscape, and their visions evoked folklore and popular beliefs about "Mound Builders." During the 1820s, a seer in Rochester named Zimri Allen looked into his stone and saw that invading Indians had destroyed a race of giants, who had hidden their treasures within the earth. Allen reportedly uncovered some of their gold. Building upon popular views of contemporary Indians as invaders who lacked wealth and civilization, Allen's vision answered questions raised in archaeological speculation from the preceding decades. About forty miles to the west of Rochester, Clinton reported that bones of "unusual length and size" had been discovered in ruined fortifications. Local investigators speculated that conquering invaders had killed the fort's inhabitants and buried their remains. During the 1820s at Lockport, David Cusick published the Haudenosaunee's accounts of ancient struggles against Stonish Giants, but his history described the giants as ferocious invaders and mentioned no golden treasures. Even in their folklore about giants, New Yorkers and the Haudenosaunee debated the limits of Indian savagery and civilization.[22]

To uncover ancient secrets, seers needed to visualize an older landscape hidden by the forests and buried in dirt. Fortunately, their instruments could differentiate ancient from modern artifacts. In 1828 a onetime resident of Palmyra, the "Old Rodsman," or Stephen Davis, traveled to Grave Creek, near present-day Moundsville, West Virginia. Along with a companion, Davis sought a mine. Instead, they encountered a surveyor, who offered dinner in exchange for a demonstration of the Rodsman's ability to find some nearby "curious stone monuments." Davis found the stones on the surveyor's property. Reportedly, these monuments stood over six feet in height, appeared worn with age, and the two largest contained petroglyphs. The Rodsman asked his divining rod "whether the French, the Spaniards, the English, the Dutch, the Romans, and several other nations, had erected them; to all which the rod remained immovable. Finally, he asked if it was the Welsh, or the same people who had built the mounds." By moving, his rod confirmed his final inquiry. The rod also communicated that the monuments had been erected fifteen centuries before Columbus's arrival. These events occurred near what scholars now call the Grave Creek Mound, a great ancient American earthwork built around two thousand years ago by the Adena culture and the subject of much archaeological speculation during the nineteenth century.[23]

As repositories of unknown secrets and treasures, Native American fortifications and burial sites attracted treasure seekers. The protohistoric Haudenosaunee often built their large fortified villages on prominent hills. Visiting such a fortification south of Auburn, New York, in 1810, DeWitt Clinton noted, "We saw several holes which appear to have been dug within a few years, by superstitious persons, in search of money." At these fortifications, treasure hunters could easily find tangible artifacts that fueled imaginations and encouraged digging. Into the nineteenth century, visitors saw swords, axes, and gun barrels on the ground. Owing to its deep history, Iroquoia's ruins contained layers of history, sometimes at the same site, with European goods located beside ancient artifacts. In addition, these ruins contained enough mystery to allow for varying interpretations of their origins: European, Indian, or someone more ancient.[24]

Some treasure hunters even used Native American artifacts as seer stones. These stones possessed the same mystery that lured seekers to Indians ruins. Like Indian earthworks, the stones appeared both natural and artificial. Perhaps seers saw these stones as magically shaped, or they saw the stones' apparently ancient age and origin as a link to primordial magic, forgotten by modern civilization. Two significant early Mormon converts, David and John Whitmer, possessed seer stones that were probably Native American pendants. Smoothly polished, the Whitmer stones had drilled holes, as did other Woodland Indian pendants, which predated European contact.[25]

Other treasure hunters sought Indian secrets and wealth, but none of them matched what Smith allegedly uncovered. Some individuals had apparently sought wealth at the Hill Cumorah prior to Smith's discovery of the plates. Much later, at least two residents of Palmyra recalled that "money diggers" had left "a large hole" on the hill a year or two prior to Smith recovering the Book of Mormon plates. It is unclear if Smith had any involvement with what those neighbors had witnessed. During his treasure hunting years, Smith made annual pilgrimages to the Hill Cumorah. Finally, near midnight on September 22, 1827, Smith claimed to recover the plates that later constituted the Book of Mormon. Fearing angry townsmen and greedy treasure hunters who wanted a share of the wealth, Smith and his wife, Emma, left for Harmony, Pennsylvania. Arriving in December, they stayed in a house owned by her brother, where Smith translated the plates.[26]

The Nephites had composed their plates in "Reformed Egyptian," an extinct language that no American could read without supernatural guidance. Beginning in mid-April 1828, Smith translated the plates using the Urim and Thummin, a pair of stones fastened on an ancient breastplate recovered with the plates, while Martin Harris acted as scribe. By mid-June they had finished 116 pages, which constituted the book of Lehi. After Smith allowed Harris to bring the translation home, the manuscript disappeared, perhaps, as Lucy Smith suspected, destroyed by Harris's incredulous wife in an effort to discredit the project. If Smith attempted to retranslate the book of Lehi, and the manuscript resurfaced, any discrepancies would undermine his credibility. The Angel appeared and chastised Smith for letting Harris take the manuscript, and Harris lost his position. In April 1829 Smith met Oliver Cowdery, a fellow Vermont visionary who became Smith's primary scribe. Younger than Smith by one year, Cowdery had boarded with the Smiths in Manchester, where he learned of the plates. During his work with Smith, the plates remained covered on a table. While Cowdery wrote, Smith looked into a seer stone that he placed in a hat. In a burst of activity, the pair completed the translation by June. In March 1830 Smith published the book, and it was available for purchase in Palmyra.[27]

The Book of Mormon explains the migration, rise, and fall of an American Christian civilization, the Nephites, from 600 BCE to 421 CE. In the beginning, an Israelite named Lehi received a vision from God, warning him of the destruction of Jerusalem and the subsequent Babylonian captivity of many survivors. Lehi preached to the Jews, warning of their sins and their coming destruction, but they ignored his warnings. In a dream, God told Lehi to take his family and depart for the wilderness. He did so, accompanied by his wife, Sariah, and four sons, Laman, Lehi, Sam, and Nephi. The eldest brothers, Lehi and Laman, lacked faith in their father's visions and desired to stay in Jerusalem with their wealth. Nephi prayed for guidance, and God confirmed that Nephi should follow his father but added that Laman and Lehi would someday turn against Nephi and God. Joined by another family headed by Ishmael, Lehi's family traveled another eight years in the wilderness, finally arriving at a land somewhere near the Red Sea that they named Bountiful. Here Nephi received instructions from God to build a ship that would take them to the promised land. Divinely guided, the ship was "not after the manner of men," that is, its design exceeded the limits of contemporary builders. Laman thought Nephi was a fool for building a ship. During the voyage, he and Lehi bound Nephi and treated him poorly. Only after a near disaster in a storm, which they understood as the wrath of God, did the brothers untie Nephi. After these foreshadowing troubles, the ship landed in the promised land, which readers have interpreted as the Americas.[28]

This account of Nephite migration revived the legend of Israelites in the Americas, most commonly associated with the Lost Tribes of Israel myth. The Old Testament described twelve tribes of Israel, all originating with the sons of Jacob and divided between northern and southern kingdoms. Ten tribes lived in the northern kingdom until the Assyrian invasions of 732 and 721 BCE. The Assyrians exiled the northern tribes to Assyria and neighboring lands. Following this exile, the tribes disappeared from history and became an enduring myth.[29]

As Europeans explored beyond Europe and the Middle East, some theorists attempted to fit the earth's ethnic diversity into a biblical interpretation. The Lost Tribes were the ultimate placeless people, and Europeans "found" them everywhere. In North America, early missionaries, such as the millennialist Puritan missionary John Eliot, worked to convert the Indians, whom he viewed as a lost tribe of Israel. From the Book of Mormon, we learn that Lehi was a descendent of Joseph, "yea even that Joseph which was son of Jacob." The Book of Mormon emphasized biblical prophecy, such as that found in Isaiah 11:11–12, which foretold the reunion of dispersed Israelites from across the earth. The Book of Mormon stated that this reunion would occur during the Second Coming of Christ and included America's inhabitants.[30]

During the early American republic, Ethan Smith (no relation to Joseph), a Congregationalist minister in Poultney, Vermont, wrote the most thorough work that traced all Indians to the Lost Tribes of Israel. In 1823 Smith published his theories in *View of the Hebrews*, which documented linguistic and cultural similarities between the Indians and Jews. Regarding Indians, Ethan Smith observed, "Their language has a variety of dialects; but all are believed by some good judges to be the same radical language." He insisted that Indians in North and South America beat drums and praised their "Great Spirit": "Hal, hal, hal; then le, le, le; next lu, lu, lu; and then close yah, yah, yah," that is, Hallelujah! Noting that without books to preserve the language, he concluded that it was "a little less than miraculous" that traces of Hebrew had survived the centuries.[31]

In the Book of Mormon, the familial division between Laman and Nephi expanded into ancient America's central conflict, which explained in detail the lost but recoverable Christian culture of America. At first things went well. The new arrivals planted seeds brought from Jerusalem and found cattle, horses, and precious metals. Nephi discovered ore to craft his brass plates, containing prophecies and his family's history to be continued through subsequent generations. However, his elder brothers complained that Nephi wanted to be king and "it belongeth unto us which are the elder brethren to rule over this people." God again warned Nephi of his brothers' treachery, and

Nephi led his followers into the wilderness and established a settlement named Nephi. He taught his followers to build homes and work
with metals. They prospered and built temples. In contrast, Laman
and his followers turned against God's wishes, became a cursed people, and stalked prey in the wilderness. This split produced the Book
of Mormon's two rival peoples, the Lamanites and Nephites.[32]

The Book of Mormon described a dichotomous ancient America
of believers and nonbelievers, the civilized and the savage, and the
virtuous and the corrupt. At the heart of this cycle was ancient Christianity. Despite living centuries before Christ's birth, the Nephites
were actually proto-Christians. After arriving in America, a younger
brother of Nephi, Jacob, received a visit from an angel who foretold
of Christ's arrival and mission and confirmed earlier visions by Nephi
and his father, who knew of a redeemer but not his name. Throughout
the Nephites' subsequent history, Christianity's influence rose and fell
in cycles, reaching its peak during Christ's arrival in America following the resurrection. According to the Book of Mormon, while in the
Americas, Christ performed the Sermon on the Mount, administered
sacraments, and appointed twelve apostles before ascending to heaven.
His visit inaugurated an age of peace, but this peace did not last. As
had previously occurred, the wealthy and strong Nephites grew boast-
ful and forgot their beliefs, or at least its teachings. Internal strife left
the Nephites weakened against the more numerous Lamanites, who
waged brutal wars. At the Hill Cumorah, this cycle of violence ended
with the final victory of the Lamanites over the Nephites. In the years
following his discovery of the plates, Smith continued to receive revelations that pushed Mormonism to (or beyond) the margins of American Christianity. However, the Book of Mormon primarily expounded
the importance of Christian faith as revealed to its biblical prophets.[33]

Converts saw New York's Hill Cumorah as the great battlefield featured in the book. Describing the region between Manchester and
Canandaigua, Oliver Cowdery observed, "The soil is of the first quality for the country, and under a state of cultivation, which gives a
prospect at once imposing, when one reflects on the fact, that here,
between these hills, the entire power and national strength of both

the Jaredites and the Nephites were destroyed." To preserve the Nephites' history, a general named Mormon had buried plates in the Hill Cumorah prior to the great battle. Mormon gave other plates to his son Moroni, who later hid them "in the earth." Cowdery believed Smith had unearthed Moroni's plates. Cowdery's understanding fit well with earlier theories popularized by DeWitt Clinton, who had found evidence of cataclysmic warfare in Iroquoia's ruins.[34]

The location of additional ruins and locations from the Book of Mormon was less clear. Until the time of Mosiah I (ca. 130 BCE), the book primarily chronicled events near the land of Nephi. During a war against the Lamanites, the Nephite leader Mosiah received a commandment from God to take the Nephites north into the wilderness. Escaping the Lamanites, Mosiah and his followers discovered the land of Zarahemla, a great city founded by other Israelites who had fled Jerusalem when "Zedekiah, king of Judah, was carried away captive into Babylon." Mosiah became their king, which inaugurated Nephite history at Zarahemla. Few hints suggest this city's location. The River Sidon flowed past Zarahemla. Other rivers existed, but Sidon was the only named waterway. The Book of Mormon also mentioned an "East Sea" and a "West Sea," with a "small neck" or "narrow neck" of land leading between the waters—the only clue to the overall shape of the region. Cumorah stood north of the great city of Zarahemla. Mormon described Cumorah as "in a land of many waters, rivers, and fountains." None of the place-names correspond to any known locations. Consequently, readers could locate the events anywhere, and skeptics could never analyze unfindable locations.[35]

Nevertheless, Smith's followers could visualize how ruins found throughout their frontier had once been magnificent like the places mentioned in the Book of Mormon. When the early Lamanites rejected Christianity and attacked the Nephites, the residents of Nephi built fortifications. As decades passed and the Nephite settlements expanded, these too required fortifications against the continued Lamanite attacks. Moroni built "banks of earth" to protect his armies and "walls of stone" around cities and borders. After fourteen centuries of decline, perhaps these ruins had become nineteenth-century America's earthworks.[36]

On two occasions, the Nephite cities experienced mass destruction, leaving ruins across the land. Before Christ appeared in the Americas, great storms, fires, and earthquakes destroyed its settlements and roads. The city of Zarahemla burned, and the city of Moroni sank to the ocean's bottom. This destruction had been foreseen by Nephi before their migration to the New World, and it fulfilled a more recent prophecy of Samuel the Lamanite, who had warned the Nephites that their unrepentant wickedness would lead to their devastation. During a peaceful time after Christ's return to heaven, the Nephites rebuilt Zarahemla, but "many cities which had been sunk" remained underwater. Following the Lamanite victory at Cumorah, the cities experienced another round of destruction during the war's genocidal finale. As Nephite civilization collapsed, the Lamanites fought each other. Lacking writing, they left no accounts describing the centuries following the Book of Mormon's conclusion. Inclined to view Indians as wandering hunter-gatherers, nineteenth-century Americans would have concluded that the Nephite cities had been destroyed.[37]

Upon first glance, prior to their downfall, the Nephites resembled an ancient Eurasian society rather than an American Indian civilization. Cattle roamed their fields. The Nephites worked with iron and steel. They wielded swords and rode to battle in chariots pulled by horses. None of these plants, animals, or technologies existed in the Americas prior to 1492. However, nineteenth-century investigators assumed that at least some of these things had existed in America's ancient cities. In his speculations on Iroquoia's ruins, Clinton explained, "These numerous works could never have been supplied with provisions without the aid of agriculture. Nor could they have been constructed without the use of iron or copper." While some recent scholarship sees the chariot-riding Nephites as an example of the Book of Mormon's uniqueness, the civilization actually met early nineteenth-century expectations of what ancient America looked like.[38]

While the Nephites had obvious ancient counterparts—America's lost race—so too did the Lamanites. Smith and his early followers consistently linked all Indians to the Lamanites. Smith stated that Moroni "said the Indians were the literal descendent of Abraham,"

meaning that any pre-Columbian migrations to America had originated in the Middle East. In an 1842 account written for a Chicago
newspaper, Smith discussed the Lamanites' fate: "The remnant are
the Indians that now inhabit this country." Beginning in 1830, early
Mormon missionaries acted on their conviction that American Indians were the Lamanites and traveled west to convert them.[39]

Cursed by their fathers' actions, the Lamanites possessed characteristics that nineteenth-century Euro-Americans associated with savagery.
Most obviously, the Book of Mormon met Americans' expectations
that skin color reflected beauty, character, and innate potential. The
Book of Mormon explained the Lamanites' curse:

> Wherefore as they were white and exceedingly fair and delightsome,
> that they might not be enticing unto my people,
> therefore the Lord God did cause a skin of blackness to come upon
>   them.[40]

During the early American republic, biblical interpretations linked
a darker skin color to allegedly cursed people. Slaveholders had long
invoked the supposed "Curse of Ham" as a justification of African slavery. (After Ham had seen his father Noah naked, Noah cursed Ham's
son Canaan, whom slaveholders interpreted as the ancestor of Africans.) During the 1780s and 1790s some Christian converts among
the Oneida had asked their missionary Samuel Kirkland if Indians
too had been cursed because of the actions of their ancestors. This
question emerged from an internal debate over the limits of Christianity's universality. Kirkland assured the Oneida that they had not
been cursed. However, his Oneida converts struggled to reconcile
their adoption of Christianity with continuing rejection by American Christians and economic marginalization. The Lamanite curse
marked another aspect of the Book of Mormon that fit contemporary intellectual currents.[41]

In their appearance and beliefs, the Lamanites resembled popular
memories of Native Americans. In the book of Enos, the Lamanites
wandered the forest while the Nephites prospered as farmers. Idle and
violent, the Lamanites were also fond of drinking. On two occasions

captive Nephites escaped when their Lamanite guards became intox-
icated. The Lamanites' appearance befit their ferocity. They wore "a
short skirt girded about their loins" and had "their heads shaven."[42]

Having forgotten their ancient Christianity, some Lamanites nevertheless knew of a Great Spirit, spoken of by their fathers. "Great
Spirit" was the standard English rendition of American Indian concepts of a supreme deity. A king of the Lamanites asked a Nephite
missionary, "Is God that Great Spirit that brought our fathers out of
the land of Jerusalem?" In *View of the Hebrews*, Ethan Smith had also
collected travelers' accounts that described belief in the Great Spirit,
which he believed confirmed the ancient (but since degenerated) Juda-
ism of Native North America. He cited Meriwether Lewis and William Clark's discussion with the Mandan Indians, which contained
worries over God's rewards and punishment: "The whole religion of
the Mandans consists in a belief of one Great Spirit presiding over
their destinies. To propitiate whom, every attention is lavished, and
every personal consideration is sacrificed." Two centuries earlier, the
Jesuits of New France had looked for similar signs that North America's Indians had once known Christianity. In its brief treatment of the
Great Spirit, the Book of Mormon spoke to a long-standing Christian
endeavor of detecting traces of a presumably universal religion among
peoples who developed separately from Eurasia for more than 10,000
years—a still unfathomably ancient period for nineteenth-century
Euro-American understandings of world history.[43]

Faithful Nephites interpreted the Lamanites' attacks as divine punishment for disobedience. Grounded in the Old Testament, this interpretation also resembled (or foreshadowed) Puritanical views of Indian
warfare. Puritan minister Increase Mather believed that war was "the
greatest of all outward Judgments." Likewise, the Nephites understood that they would be "trodden under foot if we should fall into
transgression," which primarily meant unbelief. After this defeat happened at the Hill Cumorah, Moroni blamed the Nephites' tragedy on
their breaking of their covenant. Along the frontier during the American Revolution, as settlers once again experienced the devastation of
Indian wars, this emphasis on a covenant underwent a revival, recalled

in hymns borrowed from the Puritans and reprinted in Upstate New York's nineteenth-century local histories.[44]

Portrayed as savages—but also heirs to ancient American Christianity—the Lamanites offered a mixed legacy for their alleged nineteenth-century descendants. True, as some scholars have argued, the Lamanites were capable of great Christian devotion and honor. On one occasion, the Lamanites of Ammon converted to Christianity and became pacifists, and their children became Nephites. These new Nephites became great defenders of their country and demonstrated the ability of the Lamanites to redeem themselves. Moreover, on many other occasions over the centuries, the Nephites lost their way and suffered for their wickedness. Occasionally Lamanites and Nephites switched roles, with the Lamanites, such as the prophet Samuel, preaching goodness and warning the wicked Nephites that they would suffer punishment for their sins. However, the Book of Mormon also noted that the Lamanites who did not convert to Christianity "follow the wicked and abominable traditions of their fathers." This conclusion laid the groundwork for Mormon missionary activities to convert the still unredeemed "Lamanites" of the American West.[45]

The Book of Mormon established written history as superior to oral traditions, a view congruent with Euro-American beliefs that saw Indian traditions as inferior to the written word, especially regarding ancient America. In his study of New York's antiquities, Clinton declared, "If, in the course of thirty years, the Buccaneers of St. Domingo lost almost every trace of Christianity, what confidence can we repose in the oral history delivered to us by savages without the use of letters and continually engrossed in war or in the chase." The Book of Mormon indicated that the Nephite leaders carefully maintained their genealogy on the plates, which connected them to their history and religion, stretching back to Jerusalem. The Nephite King Benjamin noted that without written history, the Nephites would have forgotten their traditions and become unbelievers like the Lamanites. Enos, an early prophet, received a revelation which stated that if the Nephites "should fall into transgression and by any means be destroyed and the Lamanites should not be destroyed," then the plates would serve as a means of salvation for the future Lamanites. Enos's son, the prophet Jarom, agreed. Moroni, the last Nephite prophet, began his book by noting that he wrote for the Lamanites, who would learn the truth at some "future day." Moroni wrote while in hiding from the Lamanites, who exterminated any Nephite who would not renounce Christianity. Before beginning the final book, Moroni had foretold of a man, chosen by God, who would discover the plates, translate them, and spread the truth once again. Of course, this man was Joseph Smith, whom Moroni later visited as an angel.[46]

By salvaging this written history, Smith's "Golden Bible" offered physical proof of his abilities and beliefs to his followers, but outsiders perceived Smith and his book as frauds. An early reviewer claimed, "A viler imposition was never practiced. It is an evidence of fraud, blasphemy, and credulity, shocking to the Christian and moralist." The newspaper noted that Smith had convinced a "wealthy farmer," Martin Harris, to mortgage his farm to pay for printing the first edition. Harsh reviewers overlooked the book's impressive scope. With the exception of Constantine Rafinesque and his Lenape migration epic, the *Walum Olum*, no other American produced anything approaching the detail and sophistication found in the Book of Mormon's history.[47]

Smith's recent biographer, Richard Bushman, labels early nineteenth-century Iroquoia a "post-Indian environment." Earlier scholarship has also noted that Mormonism, and religious revivals in general, flourished in settled areas and drew followers from "longstanding neighborhoods" rather than from the frontier. From a demographic standpoint, Mormonism arose in a *relatively* "post-Indian environment." However, the Indians still exerted a cultural influence far greater than their small numbers in New York would have suggested. For decades, settlers had constructed their cultural identities by celebrating the conquest of the frontier, and the Indians were an inseparable part of this legacy. When cutting down trees or killing wolves, they thought of Indians, too. During the 1820s and 1830s, settlers looked back with nostalgia at frontiersmen heroes—Indian fighters—whom they then celebrated in local histories and in monuments. Finally, when scholars needed to explain where New York's ancient lost race had gone, they decided that the Indians had obviously killed them. As the Haudenosaunee's numbers reached a nadir, their place in popular culture climbed.[48]

While the Book of Mormon fulfilled religious needs, its alleged Indian history proved essential to its believability. In 1834 one Unitarian reviewer complained, "If you object to the historical accounts of their sacred books, they refer you to the mounds of the western country, as remains of ancient cities, and as proofs that this country was once inhabited by a race of people better acquainted with the arts of civilized life, than the present race of savages; and this, they contend, is satisfactory presumptive proof of the truth of their history." If North America had truly been a "virgin land," the Nephite civilization would have been impossible to believe. In short, Mormonism could not have emerged at another time or place other than the early American republic's newly conquered Native American homelands.[49]

Smith's discovery serves as a fitting conclusion of Iroquoia's story from the colonial period into the early American republic. Iroquoia's early white settlers had worked diligently to reshape the landscape to obliterate and deny native traces of possession. The "Burned-Over District" takes a new meaning in the context of the Haudenosaunee's history. During the Revolution, the Continental army had burned most of the Haudenosaunee's villages. To create farms, American settlers burned the forest. Only after these physical burnings did the revival "fires" thrive in the Burned-Over District. Yet white settlers remained haunted, indeed obsessed, by traces of the land's Indian history. From that haunting persistence emerged America's most famous "indigenous" religion. The Book of Mormon contained the fullest and most enduring narrative of the destruction of a high civilization by the ancestors of the American Indian.[50]

| Conclusion

Storied Monuments

During the early republic, contests over rights often centered on which people were allowed to move freely and live where they pleased. As the 1830s dawned, those groups who had cultivated the strongest attachment to Iroquoia's storied landscape had the greatest difficulty remaining in New York State. For a time, this removal and subsequent erasure seemed inevitable and permanent. Before the ink was even dry on the Book of Mormon's first edition, Joseph Smith's growing number of followers faced outright hostility from neighbors who viewed the book's author as a blasphemous fraud. But Smith's revelations also led the Latter-day Saints out of Iroquoia. In January 1831, at a Mormon conference in Fayette, New York, a revelation commanded the Latter-day Saints: "And that ye might escape the power of the enemy; and be gathered unto me a righteous people, without spot and blameless: Wherefore for this cause I gave unto you the commandant, that ye should go to the Ohio." Smith then led his family and followers to the town of Kirtland, Ohio, which served as the church's headquarters. Kirtland would only be the first stop in a long and difficult journey westward for the Mormon faithful, who carried a profound interest in place with them across the continent but would lose, for a time, residence in the land of their golden plates.[1]

During the heyday of America's Second Great Awakening, the

Mormons' millennialist neighbors often fixated on the timing of the Second Coming of Christ, but the early Mormons worried as much about the location where the faithful should properly await the millennium. Throughout the 1830s, Smith sought one particular location, Zion, where the Latter-day Saints would gather and build a temple of their "New Jerusalem." In 1830 Smith received a revelation that sent Oliver Cowdery to lead missionaries to Missouri to begin the process by converting the Indians. Smith's revelation had indicated that the New Jerusalem would be built "on the borders by the Lamanites," which contemporary geography suggested was Missouri, seemingly distant from Mormonism's roots in Iroquoia. Although the Haudenosaunee and other Native Americans still resided east of the Mississippi, their political power had declined so far that for many Americans, "Indian territory" meant west of the Mississippi River, a region where President Andrew Jackson and his vice president from New York State, Martin Van Buren, planned to move eastern America's Indians in what became one of America's great tragedies of unfree migrations, best remembered as the Cherokee's Trail of Tears but involving several Indian nations.[2]

With an outlook rooted in the Book of Mormon's stories of fallen (but redeemable) Lamanites, Mormons bound for Missouri continued to view Indians as essential to their religion's success. The presence of "Lamanites" in the American West suggested the reach of ancient American Christianity that the Mormons sought to restore. Not only did American Indians mark the place of the Second Coming but they would be instrumental in crafting its prerequisite sacred landscape, the city of Zion and its temple, as foretold in the Book of Mormon's prophecies. Supporting these beliefs, as Smith led a group of Mormon settlers to Missouri in 1831, he received a revelation confirming that Independence, Jackson County, Missouri, was Zion. Only a year after the Book of Mormon was published, the pieces were in place for significant developments in Mormon geography.[3]

In a fascinatingly fateful move, the Mormons' quest to Missouri took them near what had been the largest pre-Columbian settlement north of Mexico, Cahokia, east of present-day St. Louis. For years prior to Smith's departure from New York State, Americans and Smith's fellow New Yorkers had read of ancient mounds of an immense scale in the Mississippi Valley. These discoveries were the most significant find in the "Mound Builder" mystery that had attracted the attention of the famous DeWitt Clinton, the eccentric scholar C. S. Rafinesque, the innovative Haudenosaunee historian David Cusick, and finally the prophet Joseph Smith. We now know that beginning around the year 1050, what archaeologists have labeled Mississippian culture spread up and down the Mississippi and its tributaries. At the heart of this cultural development stood the city of Cahokia (its original name has been lost), which featured more than 120 earthwork pyramids, often called "mounds," and a central pyramid with a volume of 25 million cubic feet. Cahokians created a great fifty-acre plaza in front of the pyramid that suggested the active public life of its residents. From the top of this great pyramid, now known as Monk's Mound, an observer would have gained a sense of the immensity of the city, with 10,000 residents and another 20,000 to 30,000 in the surrounding hinterlands. Cahokia hid many secrets that archaeologists have only recently uncovered and deciphered: evidence of elaborate ceremonies linking this world and the next, human sacrifice, and hints of the origins of later Native American heroic mythological stories. Within the borders of the United States, the Cahokians came the closest to building a city of the scale found in the Book of Mormon.[4]

As the Mormon pioneers understood it, the Midwest's extensive Native American landscape revealed the continent's true Christian past: a centuries-old mystery that pointed to the place of the coming millennium, as foretold by Smith's prophecies. However, many Missourians saw Mormons as unwelcome fanatics rather than restorers of an ancient Christian homeland. In November 1833 Missourians expelled their Mormon neighbors from Jackson County, a move that threatened to disrupt the building of the New Jerusalem. In the summer of 1834, in the midst of this early instance of Mormon-Missourian conflict, Smith led a Mormon militia from Ohio to Missouri to aid the Jackson County residents. Known as Zion's Camp, Smith's militia completed the arduous journey to Missouri but never saw any

combat. (In June a revelation confirmed that Zion's camp should temporarily disband.) Along the way, Smith's party took time to examine the Mississippi watershed's ancient ruins, most notably a mound
just west of the Illinois River. Today archaeologists know this place
as the Naples 8 mound, constructed for burial purposes by people of
the Hopewell culture, perhaps a millennium prior to the rise of the
great city of Cahokia and approximately one hundred miles to its
south and east. Already ancient by America's Middle Ages, the prominent Naples 8 mound had long been visited by Native Americans who
left signs of their visits and undoubtedly had their own understanding of its meaning. Smith joined this long list of visitors but offered
an original interpretation: "During our travels we visited several of
the mounds which had been thrown up by the ancient inhabitants
of this country, Nephites, Lamanites, &c, and this morning I went
upon a high mound, over near the river, accompanied by the <sev-
eral> brethren." From the top, the party had a view of the surrounding landscape, which Smith described as "truly delightful." In a way,
this view of the landscape recast Smith and his followers as Christian
pilgrims into their own American holy land.[5]

These mysterious homelands possessed some power over the group,
reminiscent of the earlier enchantment that Upstate New York's hills
had upon Smith when he had entertained his family and friends with
detailed knowledge of ancient Americans, even prior to his claims of
discovery and translation of their history written on golden plates.
Climbing to the top of the Naples 8 mound, Smith and his companions discovered three ancient "altars." A member of the party began
digging with a shovel and unearthed a skeleton that had been buried
about a foot deep. Stuck between the skeleton's ribs, a "Lamanitish
arrow" suggested a violent death. According to Smith, the Midwest's
ancient ruins produced a mysterious effect on the party, causing them
to feel "peculiar sensations" prior to visions that they experienced.
Smith's account of his vision revealed a Christian history of the Mississippi watershed: "I discovered that the person whose Skeleton was
before us we had seen was a white Lamanite, a large thick-set man,
and a man of God." His lightened pigmentation indicated that the

Lamanites and their presumed descendants, the Indians, having been "cursed" with dark skin, could overcome their affliction by returning to their original faith. Smith described the man's history: "His name was Zelph. He was a warrior and Chieftain under the great prophet Onandagus, who was known from the ~~hill Cumorah, or~~ eastern sea, to the Rocky Mountains." Recalling a name that evoked the Onondaga, Smith linked Iroquoia's storied landscape and people to the American heartland as part of one extensive American story of Christianity.[6]

Through a combination of revelation and exploration, Smith and his followers reinvented the Midwest, and specifically Missouri, as a sacred place—the essential land where the Mormons had to gather to fulfill the promise of their Christian history. Expelled from Jackson County, and having temporarily avoided a full-scale conflict, the Mormons turned to another settlement, Far West. Located in Caldwell County, on the prairies of northwest Missouri, Far West served as headquarters of the church after Smith permanently left Kirtland, Ohio, in the spring of 1838. In May of that year Smith found additional evidence that Missouri's ancient landscape rivaled Christianity's sacred Middle East places in significance. In a search of land for additional Mormon settlements, the Prophet led a scouting party north into Daviess County. Near the Grand River, the party encountered the home of ferry operator Lyman Wright, who called a nearby hill Tower Hill on account of its ruins. Smith and his men climbed this landmark and examined "the remains of an old Nephitish Altar." As with the Zelph Mound and the quest for the golden plates, Smith and his followers found themselves drawn to mysterious hills, whose shapes could suggest the man-made, natural, or even supernatural. A revelation provided a more detailed history of nearby Spring Hill: "named by the mouth of [the] Lord and was called Adam Ondi Awmen [Adamondi-Ahman]" because it was the "place where Adam shall come to visit his people, or the Ancient of days shall sit as spoken of by Daniel the Prophet." Adam-ondi-Ahman apparently referenced the place where Adam lived following his expulsion from the Garden of Eden. Where the world had begun it would also end.[7]

This quest for Zion intensified divisions between Mormons and their

neighbors, more so than if the Latter-day Saints had simply sought the
time of the millennium rather than its location. Shortly before Smith
discovered Adam-ondi-Ahman, he had a revelation that called for the
Latter-day Saints to gather in Missouri. Consequently, from spring to
fall 1838, the state's Mormon population grew from between 3,000 to
more than 8,000, with another 2,000 immigrants on their way. Many
Mormons moved to the state's sparsely populated western counties,
four of which had small populations ranging from 1,800 to 4,500 inhabitants. Fearful of the potential power of what they saw as a Mormon
theocracy, Missourians grew alarmed at the gathering of Mormons en
masse near their designated Zion. Since their arrival in Missouri earlier in the decade, the Mormons had experienced robberies, attacks,
and destruction of their property, but they had backed down from full
retaliation, as evidenced by the disbanding of Zion's Camp in 1834.
However, by 1838 some Mormons were prepared to resist any persecu-
tions. In Far West, a secretive paramilitary organization known as the
"Danites" had formed to police internal dissent and defend against external threats. Already wary of the Danites, Missourians grew increasingly
concerned following a fiery Fourth of July speech by Smith's adviser
Sidney Rigdon, who asserted that the Mormons would defend themselves during a "war of extermination" instigated by their neighbors.
Problems began in August 1838, when residents of Gallatin tried to
prevent Mormons from voting and a brawl ensued. In October Mormon militias drove suspected hostile residents out of Daviess County
and confiscated their property. Violence between Mormons and their
neighbors eventually brought the full weight of the state against the
Latter-day Saints. Seemingly fulfilling Rigdon's Independence Day pre-
dictions, on October 27 Gov. Lilburn Boggs told Gen. John B. Clark,
"The Mormons must be treated as enemies and must be exterminated
or driven from the State if necessary for the public peace—their out-
rages are beyond all description." However, this extermination never
happened. On November 1 Joseph Smith and Far West surrendered.
In the aftermath of the violence, the Mormons sold their property in
Missouri for much less than market value. They then fled to Illinois,

where Smith established the city of Nauvoo. The name is Smith's angli-
cized Hebrew for "a beautiful place."[8]

Unable to remain in the sacred landscape of Missouri, the Mormons
needed a more flexible understanding of how, when, and perhaps where
Zion would be built, and Smith eventually received revelations that
accommodated contemporary political reality. Some early followers
later claimed that as early as the 1830s Smith had prophesied a Mormon exodus to the Rocky Mountains. Certainly by the 1840s Mormon
leaders were planning a move west. Other followers recalled an 1840
revelation, when Smith "said speaking of the Land of Zion, It Consists of all the N[orth] and S[outh] America but that any place where
the Saints gather is Zion which every righteous man will build up
for a place of safety for his children." In spirit, this definition echoed
Matthew 18:20, where Jesus stated, "For where two or three are gathered in my name, I am there among them." In March 1844, in one of
his last public pronouncements, Smith stated: "The whole of America is Zion itself from north to south, and is described by the Prophets, who declare that it is the Zion where the mountain of the Lord
should be, and that it should be in the center of the land." The Mormons would at the very least find a refuge in the American West, with
the hope that someday they would also return victoriously to Missouri.[9]

The Prophet never reached a western refuge. Smith's time in the
Midwest was marked by fear of capture, trial, and imprisonment. In
1839, following the Mormon War, he had escaped trial in Missouri,
where Smith feared he would fall victim to mob justice. Unfortunately, both internal dissent and external hostility followed the Mormons to Illinois. In 1844 a mob raided the jail in Carthage, Illinois,
where Smith, his brother Hyrum, and several other allies awaited
trial on charges of destroying a hostile Nauvoo newspaper that had
attacked the Mormons for Smith's doctrines. This dispute included
a growing scandal surrounding the practice of polygamy, which the
Prophet defended as a biblically sound practice. During the struggle
at the jail, the mob shot and killed Smith. The defendants were all
later acquitted.[10]

Following Smith's assassination, the Mormons sought a place where they could build cities without fear of vigilantes. The Latter-day Saints reached their western refuge by following a skilled planner, Brigham Young, who had emerged as Smith's successor. Young organized the migration of some 16,000 followers, divided into many groups. In April 1847 the first party, known as the "Pioneers," left the Mormon's winter camp in Nebraska for Utah. By the end of the year, 17,000 Mormons had made the journey across the Great Plains and Rocky Mountains to the valley of the Great Salt Lake, the home of the Ute people. Utah's arid landscape, red rocks, and snowcapped mountains looked radically different from the Eastern Woodlands. This relatively arid environment was more than symbolically distinct from eastern America, a region in many ways defined by its waterways: rivers, the Great Lakes, and, by the 1830s, canals. In contrast, the Mormons located their Great Salt Lake City at the eastern edge of America's Great Basin. Named by explorer John C. Frémont in 1844, the Great Basin is North America's largest endorheic watershed—that is, a region whose rivers fail to reach the ocean. In this isolated land of basins and ranges, the Mormons would begin anew their reinvention of the land and its history.[11]

This migration marked a new beginning for the Latter-day Saints, who may now be synonymous with the lands of Utah but long remembered for their religion's New York landscape. Only after decades of work on establishing economic stability and political legitimacy could residents of Utah finally turn their attention back to Mormonism's homelands. Beginning in the late nineteenth century, Mormons from Utah began visiting the Hill Cumorah, called the "Mormon Hill" by locals. Notable early visitors included church elders Orson Pratt and Joseph F. Smith, a future president of the church and the nephew of the prophet. A once arduous journey could now be made in relative comfort thanks to an extensive rail network. By 1911 groups of two hundred or more visitors traveled east to the Mormon homelands in Upstate New York, but non-Mormons still owned significant sites, namely, Cumorah and the Smith farm. In 1915 the church sent Willard Bean, an outgoing former boxer, to Palmyra to live on the Smith farm and to win over locals. Bean and his family faced hostility from still-skeptical neighbors, but Bean managed to develop good relations with James H. Inglis, a farmer who owned land that extended partially up the western side of Cumorah. In 1923 Inglis sold his farm to Bean, acting on behalf of the church. Bean had less success negotiating with wealthy banker Pliny T. Sexton, who owned much of the hill's remaining land. The two men became friends, but Sexton recognized the historical significance of Cumorah and asked as much as $100,000 for the sacred hill. Sexton died in 1924 without agreeing on a price that the Mormons would pay. After some negotiation with Sexton's heirs, in 1928 the church managed to buy the land for about half of the banker's asking price.[12]

Upon hearing of the purchase, sculptor and church member Torleif S. Knaphus proposed a monument to Smith's recovery of the plates and the subsequent restoration of ancient Christianity. The church approved and Knaphus spent five years working on a bronze and granite monument. In 1934 he visited the Hill Cumorah, where the monument would stand, and recalled the significance of the place "where heavenly beings had walked and talked to man in this modern time." On July 23, 1935, the church officially dedicated the new monument to a crowd reportedly numbering more than 2,000 people. The visitors glimpsed a ten-foot gold-plated statue of Moroni atop a thirty-foot granite base and pillar. Panels at the base depicted important historical moments, including Joseph Smith's receiving the plates directly from Moroni. Atop the pillar, the angel's statue holds the records in his left hand while his right hand points skyward. The monument still stands as a permanent reminder of the hill's Mormon past, one vision of the contested layers of history projected upon the lands of Iroquoia. Beyond that, it speaks to the transcontinental reach of stories of America's ancient landscape—at once local, but eventually enmeshed in a web of memories created by a people and a nation on the move.[13]

During the 1830s, as the Mormons struggled to find a new homeland, the Haudenosaunee faced pressure of a different kind as speculators and their political allies continued to press for additional land cessions, which they cast as part of a necessary and benevolent national project of "Indian removal." While anti-Mormon mobs feared that Mormon theocracy fostered communities hostile to a republic, proponents of

Indian removal expressed supposed pity for the Indians, who allegedly lacked the ability to integrate with American life and consequently faced extinction. Andrew Jackson's second annual address to Congress followed this reasoning for removal but also justified America's troubled history of Indian relations by recalling the continent's supposed pre-European landscape: "What good man would prefer a country covered with forests and ranged by a few thousand savages to our extensive Republic, studded with cities, towns, and prosperous farms embellished with all the improvements which art can devise or industry execute, occupied by more than 12,000,000 happy people, and filled with all the blessings of liberty, civilization, and religion?" The vast American West provided those in power with a solution for minority groups cast outside the boundaries of the dominant culture's definition of civilization—at least for a time, until additional conquests pushed America's borders to the Pacific Ocean.[14]

Jacksonian removal was the culmination of decades of erasing the native imprint upon the American landscape and imagining Indians as outsiders in their own homelands. Although Jackson rightly receives significant blame for the tragedy of removal, he built upon an idea born of colonial violence and implementable after the balance of power shifted decisively toward white Americans during the early republic. Years before the old gunfighter's presidency, New York land developers had pushed for the removal of the Haudenosaunee. In 1810 the Holland Land Company had sold its preemption right to the Seneca's eleven remaining reservations to David A. Odgen of the Odgen Land Company, who later served as a hardly impartial member of the House of Representatives. The Seneca still held almost 200,000 acres in western New York, most notably lands near Buffalo Creek. Near here, leading New Yorkers planned that the Erie Canal would eventually end at a well-developed harbor in the growing town of Buffalo. In 1819, complaining that the Seneca held too much prime land for their relatively small population, Congressman Odgen petitioned the secretary of war, John C. Calhoun, and President James Monroe to urge that the Seneca be removed from New York. With some help from Quaker allies, the Seneca refused to sell, and strong opposition to removal continued into the 1820s, with famous orators such as Red Jacket vehemently protesting any land cessions and relocation. With the Seneca resisting removal, advocates turned to the less powerful Oneida to the east.[15]

Numbering more than 600 people by the early nineteenth century, the Oneida struggled with internal cultural divisions and disputes that made them easier targets for removal. Advocacy for removal came from a seemingly unlikely source: a charismatic missionary of Mohawk-European descent named Eleazar Williams, who recognized the remaining divides between Christians and non-Christians that smoldered following the years of Samuel Kirkland's missionary work. In a time and place of colorful characters, Williams matched any of Iroquoia's residents in storytelling ability. At times exaggerating his status as a war hero during the War of 1812, Williams would eventually suggest that he was the lost dauphin of France, Louis XVII, who had died in 1795 but was rumored to have somehow escaped the turbulent years of the French Revolution by living abroad. For the time being, however, he focused on his work as an Episcopal missionary and employed his gifts of persuasion and self-promotion to lead the Oneida (and perhaps eventually the rest of the Six Nations) to a western refuge of their own, at least as he saw it. Beginning in 1816, Williams worked to convert the non-Christian chiefs while searching for land in the west. He received financial support from the federal government and agents of the Odgen Land Company to scout land in what is now Wisconsin. Odgen only had rights to buy Seneca land covered by the Holland Land Purchase, but if the Oneida established a distant reservation, those lands could also serve as a potential destination for other nations removed from New York State, namely, the Seneca. In 1822 Williams arranged for the controversial purchase—more precisely, the disputed agreement to hold a "right in common"—of millions of acres (eventually reduced to 65,426 acres in 1838) from the Menominee for approximately $3,000. By 1838, 654 Oneida people had followed Williams's lead and lived at what became known as the Duck Creek Reservation near Green Bay. Although the climate and ecology of Green Bay bore a strong resemblance to New York State, the land itself had no history for the Oneida, who struggled with leaving the homeland of their ancestors.[16]

Cloaked in language of benevolence, Indian removal actually entailed white Americans obtaining land through fraud and exploitation of divisions within Indian nations. In 1826 the Odgen Land Company conducted a controversial and immediately disputed negotiation with members of the Seneca, which resulted in the sale of all remaining Seneca land in the Genesee Valley. The Seneca alleged (and a later federal investigation confirmed) a mixture of corruption and coercion: agents in the pay of the land company, lies about potential removal if the Seneca failed to sell, and possible bribery of chiefs. In the infamous 1838 Treaty of Buffalo Creek, ratified during the Van Buren administration, the Haudenosaunee allegedly sold all remaining land in New York State to the Odgen Land Company, excluding the one-square mile Oil Spring Reservation, and were required to move to the Kansas Territory. At least sixteen Seneca chiefs had been bribed. Other signers later testified that they had been intimidated or that someone had forged their signatures. This corruption enabled Odgen to purchase land for $202,000, which had been appraised at $2 million. The Seneca and their Quaker allies pushed for a more equitable treaty, ratified by the U.S. Senate in 1842, which restored the Seneca's Cattaraugus and Allegany Reservations, the Tuscarora Reservation, and the Onondaga Reservation, while allowing the still traumatic sale of Buffalo Creek and Tonawanda.[17]

Cast as outsiders in their own homelands, the Haudenosaunee operated under conditions that were better than total dependence but lacking in the freedom awarded their white neighbors. In 1839, under the shadow of the Treaty of Buffalo Creek, a group of 242 Oneida sold their New York holdings to the state and then purchased land in London, Ontario, with the proceeds. This Canadian land had 410 Oneida residents by 1845. Combined with the earlier moves to Wisconsin, the migration to Canada left perhaps fewer than 200 Oneida living in New York State by the end of that decade. During the 1840s, other Haudenosaunee decided to try living in lands along the Marmaton River in the Kansas Territory. In 1846 215 left for these new lands, passing through the Mormons' sacred landscape of Missouri. The next year, as Mormon pioneers endeavored to establish a new home in Utah, 73 of the Haudenosaunee Indian pioneers returned to New York State. During their travels, they likely encountered other Americans on the move westward, a flood of migrants that increased in the coming years. By the late 1840s and 1850s, mineral rushes drew hundreds of thousands of Americans across the Great Plains and to the West in an unprecedented migration across the continent. In many ways the era came to be defined by mobility, eventually symbolized by dreams and then the reality of a transcontinental railroad. For the Haudenosaunee and many other Indian nations, however, mobility meant something less grand. Moves west, or into Canada, had occurred not for dreams of spectacular wealth but in an effort to maintain some autonomy and permanence in the face of fraudulent treaties and threats of removal. East of the Mississippi, in what had once been Indian country, Native peoples were but a small population in a sea of migrants.[18]

As waves of Euro-Americans pressed westward to make their own marks upon the land and history, many of them treated the Native American landscape with the same indifference that left much of Iroquoia destroyed, decaying, and underappreciated. Even spectacular Cahokia fared poorly. In 1813 an early American settler in Missouri, Henry Marie Brackenridge, wrote to Thomas Jefferson, and later published, an account that described relatively intact, numerous, and immense pyramids. Of the largest, he wrote, "I was struck by a degree of astonishment, not unlike that which is experienced in contemplating the Egyptian pyramids." By the 1860s Euro-Americans had destroyed at least twenty-four of those mounds. Over the next decades, farmers and developers leveled dozens more, greatly reducing the grandeur that Brackenridge had witnessed. By the 1960s one resident had even installed a swimming pool (since filled) at the base of the great pyramid. The Haudenosaunee would have recognized this callous treatment of the Native built environment. Everywhere that Euro-Americans expanded, they erased Native American history.[19]

Yet it would be a mistake to think of Native American history as totally lost, even in the aftermath of such destruction. Truly, European colonialism resulted in massive population losses among Native Americans, migrations, the reformation of group identities, and the loss of much of their landscapes. Before and after European colonization, social instability must have erased some knowledge of America's past. Notably, scholars have found frustratingly few clues of oral traditions that described Cahokia, a city that collapsed prior to European arrival but must have had descendants among peoples encountered during the colonial period. From the nineteenth century to the present, investigators have been disappointed by less-than-forthcoming Native accounts of America's "mounds," which often led Euro-American writers to conclude that this history was lost. To apply this standard to all times and places, however, is to believe the rationale of colonialism: as the landscape vanished, so too did Indians and their history, replaced by Euro-Americans.[20]

Returning to Iroquoia, we can see the dangers of this belief in the continued history of the Painted Post or, more accurately, posts. As the Mormons began thinking of a return presence in their homelands, which culminated in the building of a monument to the angel Moroni, residents of Painted Post considered a new monument of their own. In 1893 village residents had raised half of the $300 needed to build a new, more permanent statue of an Indian chief. Their fund-raising even caught the attention of the *New York Times*, which ran a story on the post's mysterious origins, its disappearance, and the search for the fate of the Montour brothers. The following year, a crowd reported at 5,000 people gathered to celebrate the unveiling of a new monument to John Montour. Constructed with a granite base, the twenty-foot tall monument was topped with a bronze statue of an Indian chief. With a number of notable locals scheduled to speak, such a public event required sorting out the meaning of the monument and its history.[21]

Some of the remembered history remained violent, but more than a story of heroics, the monument spoke to a community celebrating its origins and triumph on the frontier—in effect, the creation of the new American nation. By 1894 the legend of the Painted Post included details that the original had been painted with "Indians' blood," without clarifying the source. Newspaper announcements repeated the same lore of Montour's death, while some local historians suspected that Montour had been active after the battle of Fort Freeland. However, these clues had little influence on the ceremony's celebratory tone or overall message. Montour had passed from history and become a symbol of America's founding mythology on the frontier. Dead for a half century, early frontier heroes no longer needed Montour's defeat to build up their own legends. One of the featured speakers, John L. Sexton, described the land prior to the arrival of the "pale face," who "came from beyond the great ocean" to invade the lands of American Indians. He explained that these colonial wars left most of the "Red Men" dead, "dwelling with the Great Spirit in the happy hunting grounds of Eternity." Gesturing at the new monument, Sexton recalled the original Painted Post, perhaps erected for some "grand historical event," if not for Montour. Whatever the Painted Post's original meaning, by Sexton's reasoning the monument had become something more significant after the Revolution. The once-Indian post became "a beacon—an index, figuratively speaking, a landmark to attract, guide, and direct, the pale faces from all sections of this broad land, and from lands beyond the great ocean to this garden of the great confederation of the Six Nations, to the land of the Painted Post."[22]

As Sexton's briefly assumed Indian point of view toward the pale faces hinted, the dedication ceremony tapped into an American habit of appropriating Indian culture and identities for public events. From the era of the Revolution through the nineteenth century, many white Americans had played with Indian imagery to craft a uniquely American identity. This imagery appeared most prominently in fraternal organizations, complete with Indian names and membership titles, which gained popularity during the early republic. These societies included the New York Tammany Society (established 1786); the Society of Red Men, founded at the end of the War of 1812; and its successor, the Improved Order of Red Men (IORM), which grew in popularity from the mid-1830s onward. The IORM featured organization lodges named after famous Indians: Metamora (i.e., Metacom aka King Philip), Pocahontas, Powhatan, and James Fenimore Cooper's legendary "Mohican," Uncas. Members dressed in Indian regalia to perform Indian-inspired ceremonies in "wigwams," membership halls that could be decorated with artwork celebrating Indians and the frontier. At the same time, the organization's leadership claimed a patriotic history that connected to the earlier Tammany societies and America's most famous costumed "Indians," the Sons of Liberty, who had dressed as Mohawks when they dumped tea into Boston Harbor in 1773. The IORM operated under the contradictory impulses of celebrating America's revolution and the Indians whose land white Americans had taken during its aftermath.[23]

Sidestepping this contradiction, the IORM emphasized themes of noble but vanishing Indians who had honorable dealings with the nation's greatest founder, George Washington. Published a year before the dedication of the new Painted Post, *The Official History of the Improved Order of Red Men* stated that Indians believed that the Great Spirit had invited Washington to reside in a "celestial residence upon the plains of heaven, the only white man whose noble deeds had entitled him to this heavenly favor." This claim alluded to the visions of the Seneca prophet Handsome Lake, who, as he made his transcendent sky journey that led to the founding of the Longhouse religion some ninety years earlier, had glimpsed Washington and his dog sitting on a porch. As this vision recalled, in 1794 Washington (through his agent Timothy Pickering) had dealt honorably with the Seneca with the Treaty of Canandaigua, which had affirmed federal recognition of Haudenosaunee sovereignty over their remaining lands—an apparent permanence continually undermined by disputed treaties with New York State and the Odgen Land Company. The *Official History* described the Seneca's appreciation for Washington's fairness: a heavenly monument "more expressive" than the "proudest recitals on the obelisk [i.e., the Washington Monument], and more imperishable in its duration than the syenite which holds up the record to the gaze of centuries." But who would be left in this world to remember such a monument?[24]

The answer, of course, was members of the IORM, who believed that white Americans could learn the best aspects of Indian culture while avoiding the fate of noble savages in a civilized world. Honor, bravery,

and freedom ranked among the most desirable of Indian traits to emu-
late. The IORM categorized Native Americans as "the noblest type of
man in his natural state that has ever been discovered." This interpretation required a specific setting: the American continent itself,
with its wild landscape that produced free and noble men. Building
upon more than a century of Euro-American interest in Iroquoia as
the homeland of a great Indian empire, the IORM unsurprisingly identified the Haudenosaunee as the most noble of all Indian nations.
As this once proud people allegedly vanished, the IORM became the
guardians of their history. As the IORM's *Official History* noted, "Every
true, intelligent Red Man takes great delight in the fact that we are
the acknowledged conservators of the history, the customs, and the
virtues of the original American people." Fittingly, monuments and
objects figured in this process. The IORM's *Official History* stated that
its members would "take down the totem by which the primitive
Red Man distinguished his friend from his foe, and from them teach
object-lessons of the history of his country, and of Freedom, Friendship, and Charity to the coming young American." And so the final
speaker at the dedication of the Painted Post's monument was none
other than Martin Dunham, the "Deputy Sachem" of the Binghamton, New York, IORM.[25]

By the end of the nineteenth century, Euro-Americans had transformed Iroquoia's land and history to such a degree that it seemed
completely reasonable for a white man like Dunham to stand on Iroquoia's ground as a "red man" claiming to preserve its history. Standing before the crowd, Dunham apparently spoke without a prepared
speech that explained his order, according to the Reverend W. A.
Allen, who collected material from the day's events. Whatever Dunham said, Allen glowingly approved: "Can there be found anywhere a
scene more in harmony with the spirit of the organization of which a
branch had just been formed in our village? Think of it:—Indian traditions, Indian lore, an Indian monument; on a spot which had been
one of the great camping grounds of the Indian in the long ago! No
wonder the Red Men of '94 shouted until the circling hills echoed
the sound as it had done the war cry of the braves of other days." And

so in ceremonies like these, Iroquoia's story seems to reach its finale: white "Red Men" telling their history of the land and its people.[26]

Yet the IORM's boast of sole guardianship was premature. Hints of an alternative story were hidden in plain sight. In its report on the Painted Post, the *New York Times* mentioned yet another secondhand but telling account of the legend that local historians published during the early twentieth century. In 1833, hoping to discover the "correct version" of the Painted Post origin story, Capt. Samuel Adams visited Cornplanter on his reservation. Adams was a bit intimidated as he approached the legendary Seneca chief, who maintained a serious bearing befitting a man in his eighth decade of an eventful life. Reassured by Cornplanter's assistant that the chief was always "exceedingly formal" with visitors, Adams took a seat on a stool and explained the nature of his visit. Adams recalled that upon his mentioning the Painted Post, he witnessed a sparkle in Cornplanter's eyes as the chief produced the "faintest possible smile" before quickly resuming his more serious disposition. With his knife, Cornplanter drew a map of the Painted Post region and indicated the site of the deceased chief's alleged gravesite and then offered only vague details. In vain Adams prodded the distinguished chief to share specifics about the legendary landmark. Cornplanter was happy to talk about anything but the identity of the "chief" buried at the post. Changing the subject, Cornplanter entertained Adams by calculating his own age at more than 106 years, thereby indicating his own legendary history but leaving Adams without the actual legend that he desired to know. After he left, Adams guessed that the smile he had witnessed reflected the flash of a memory, "pleasant or savage," from a distant past, but the chief remained an enigmatic figure.[27]

Perhaps there was something more behind Cornplanter's smile that historians were not yet ready to understand. The late nineteenth-century historian who studied Adams's letter, Charles H. Erwin, commented, "For our purpose, it matters but little what reasons induced Cornplanter's silence regarding the name, and we cordially give to his memory thanks for the facts in his brief statement." By the time of Adams's visit, the landmark was already famous, having been appropriated (or stolen) and reinvented by locals as their place of victory

over John Montour. Possibly Cornplanter's smile indicated amuse-
ment and a bit of pride in his secret knowledge. When Cornplanter
met Adams, it had been more than three decades since the Seneca
leader had complained to John Adlum of the "great many lies" written
about Indians in history books. He had little reason to assume things
had changed. White Americans continued to spin stories about Iroquoia's storied landscape, and these stories portrayed the Indian landscape as a vanished land, the precursor of the fields and towns of New
York, eventually featuring their own lodges of "red men." Knowing
the correct identity of the chief would not have changed this narrative, which cared little for Cornplanter's "reasons." Whomever Cornplanter named would take his place in a story of settler victory as a
symbol of a bygone era.[28]

No longer believers in Mound Builders, and aware that American
Indians have not vanished, many Americans have yet to truly appreci-
ate their continent's actual Native American history—in part because
so much of its physical imprint has been destroyed or replaced with
tales of an invented past. That Americans have forgotten this history
is not surprising. Only recently have professional historians begun
to grasp the scope of devastation that accompanied European colonization of the Americas while recognizing the continued significance of Native Americans during the nation's founding and beyond.
Instead of appreciating its deep past, America's national culture cele-
brates (and occasionally laments) its youth: a new nation founded in
the wilderness of a so-called New World, lacking the antiquity—or
more precisely, the history—of Europe. Yet the Indians knew of an
Old World with an ancient and continuing history rooted in the land.
As Europeans pushed westward from the colonial period through the
nineteenth century, from the Painted Post to the Pacific Ocean, they
encountered Indians and their landscapes. Many of the subsequent
memories written on those lands are violent and tragic, but like the
storied landscape of Iroquoia, they are at the heart of the founding of
a nation built upon the homelands of others. As Cornplanter likely
knew, John Montour lived. The Haudenosaunee endured. And parts
of their storied history remained their own.[29]

| Notes

Introduction

1. For an analysis of imperial fictions in Canada, see Lennox, *Homelands and Empires*.

2. For more on Mitchell's map and the concept of settlement, see Chad Anderson, "Rediscovering Native North America." The lasting territorial control of Native Americans has been explored in several recent books, including Witgen, *An Infinity of Nations*.

3. For an introduction to the archaeology of the Haudenosaunee, see Engelbrecht, *Iroquoia*. The most complete summary of Haudenosaunee political history is Fenton, *The Great Law and the Longhouse*.

4. Spelling conventions and efforts at translation for Iroquoian words have varied widely both historically and professionally. Here I am following Engelbrecht, *Iroquoia*, 114–24. Throughout this book I have usually left eighteenth- and nineteenth-century phonetic spellings and translations as is. For the Oneida stone, see Belknap and Morse, "The Report of a Committee of the Board of Correspondents of the Scots Society for Propagating Christian Knowledge, who Visited the Oneida and Mohekunuh Indians in 1796," in Collections of the Massachusetts Historical Society for the Year 1798, 14. A good discussion of the stone can be found in Wonderley, *Oneida Iroquois Folklore, Myth, and History*, 24–25.

5. Jennings, *The Ambiguous Iroquois Empire*, 30–34; Taylor, *The Divided Ground*.

6. A useful, recent critical edition of Colden's work is *The History of the Five Nations*, 10–17.

7. "Conference between Governor Clinton and the Indians," in O'Callaghan, *Documents Relative to the Colonial History of the State of New-York*, 6:321; Governor Clinton to the Lords of Trade, July 17, 1751, in *Documents Relative*, 714; and Brandão and Starna, "'Some Things May Slip Out of Your Memory.'"

8. Jennings, *The Ambiguous Iroquois Empire*; Hämäläinen, "The Shapes of Power," in Barr and Countryman, *Contested Spaces of Early America*, 31–68; Fred Anderson, *Crucible of War*, 11–32.

9. The literature on the Haudenosaunee and European colonization is vast. See, for example, Brandão, *"Your Fyre Shall Burn No More"*; Richter, *The Ordeal of the Longhouse*; Richard White, *The Middle Ground*.

10. Hunn et al., *Čáw Pawá Láakni / They Are Not Forgotten*. See also Basso, *Wisdom Sits in Places*; Farmer, *On Zion's Mount*, 5–16.

11. For thoughts on the "woods," see Merrell, *Into the American Woods*, 25–26.

12. Although the Proclamation of 1763 is usually presented as a simple concept in early American history, the actual negotiations to create this imagined boundary line were much more complex: see Edelson, *The New Map of Empire*, chap. 4.

13. For a survey of memory, violence, and landscape, see Foote, *Shadowed Ground*. For gunfighters, see Slotkin, *Regeneration through Violence* and Slotkin, *Gunfighter Nation*.

14. DeWitt Clinton, "The Iroquois," in Campbell, *Life and Writings of DeWitt Clinton*, 265–66.

15. For the "Mound Builder" myth, see Kennedy, *Hidden Cities*.

16. For capitalism and the Second Great Awakening, the classic work is Paul Johnson, *A Shopkeeper's Millennium*. Although generally focused on a later period, an important study of Mormon history and landscape is Farmer's *On Zion's Mount*.

17. From the invented Plymouth Rock to the very real battlefields of the Civil War, foundational stories of the United States are written upon its landscape. See, for example, Seelye, *Memory's Nation*. Scholarship on the Hudson River School and sublime nature is vast. For an introduction to the paintings, see Ferber, *The Hudson River School*. For nature and the sublime, a classic work is Frazier Nash, *Wilderness and the American Mind*, 5th ed., 44–83.

1. Visions of the Great Island

1. The creation story's details vary across time and place. I have condensed the story, drawing upon the two earliest detailed accounts, which probably expressed the story as understood in the late eighteenth century. Klinck and Talman, *The Journal of Major John Norton, 1816*, 88–97; Dean, "Mythology of the Iroquois, or Six Nations of Indians," 157–62, reproduced in Elm and Antone, *The Oneida Creation Story*. For a useful discussion of the themes and variations in detail, see Wonderley, "The Iroquois Creation Story over Time," esp. 5–6, which suggest the common themes from Dean and Norton's texts (themes that I have followed above). Throughout this chapter, I have tried to follow other stories as recorded in the eighteenth and nineteenth centuries, which may differ from today's renditions—for example, muskrat instead of mink.

2. Beauchamp, *Moravian Journals Relating to Central New York, 1745–66*, 190.

3. Salisbury, "The Indians' Old World." For a biography of Zeisberger, see Olmstead, *David Zeisberger.*

4. Variations of America as a "New World" for its diverse inhabitants can be found in Calloway, *New Worlds for All;* Merrell, *The Indians' New World;* Breen, "Creative Adaptations," in Greene and Pole, *Colonial British America,* 195–232.

5. The theme of layered pasts is explored in Richter, *Before the Revolution,* 3–8.

6. For a much more detailed attempt to reconstruct the trail network, see L. H. Morgan, *League of the Ho-dé-no-sau-nee, Iroquois,* 412–43, and the included map. For corrections to Morgan's estimates in Beauchamp, *Perch Lake Mounds,* 33–47. For runners see Fenton, "The Journal of James Emlen," 296–97. Sharp Shin's achievement earned him enduring fame in scholarship on Native American running: Nabokov, *Indian Running,* 18. See also messengers mentioned in Beauchamp, *Moravian Journals,* 45, 114.

7. ("principle Sachims") John Riggs et al. to Peter Schuyler, September 14, 1720, in O'Callaghan, *Documents Relative to the Colonial History of the State of New York,* 5:570–71; ("reached an Old Indian settlement") Beauchamp, *Moravian Journals,* 68; ("anaye") Pilkington, *Journals of Samuel Kirkland,* 140; also 151n44. For the archaeology of this site, see K. A. Jordan, "Seneca Iroquois Settlement Pattern," 36–37. For a list of synonyms and references to primary sources, see Hodge, *Handbook of American Indians North of Mexico,* 2:121–22.

8. Starna, "Aboriginal Title and Traditional Iroquois Land Use," 43. For trees, see Richard Smith, *A Tour of Four Great Rivers,* 29, 38–39. For land use patterns, see Taylor, "The Great Change Begins," 267–68. For the broader use of fire, see C. C. Mann, *1491: New Revelations of the Americas before Columbus,* 282–88.

9. For the archaeology of the Mohawk villages, see Snow, *Mohawk Valley Archaeology,* 485–95. For the Cayuga settlements, see Journal of Thomas Grant, 143, and for Genesee Castle, see Major Gen. Sullivan's Official Report, 301; Journal of Lt. Erkuries Beatty, 32; Journal of Lt. Thomas Blake, 40; Journal of Maj. John Burrows, 48; Journal of Lt. Col. Henry Dearborn, 75; Journal of Sgt. Maj. George Grant, 112; Journal of Lt. Col. Adam Hubley, 162–63; for Kanadesaga, see Journal of Lt. William Barton, 10; Journal of Lt. Erkuries Beatty, 30; Journal of Major John Burrows, 46; Journal of Dr. Jabez Campfield, 58; Journal of Lt. Henry Dearborn, 74—all in Cook, *Journals of the Military Expedition.* For the Oneida villages, see Taylor, *Divided Ground,* 54, overall population on 108.

10. Hart, "New Dates from Classic New York Sites," 1–22; Bartram, *Observations,* 40–41.

11. Journal of Lt. Erkuries Beatty, 23, and Journal of Major John Burrows, 47, in Cook, *Journals of the Military Expedition.* Chad Anderson, "The Built Landscape and the Conquest of Iroquoia," 266–74. For geographic variability, see K. A.

Jordan, "Regional Diversity and Colonialism in Eighteenth-Century Iroquoia." Jordan stresses tradition over adoption of European forms. For building material, see Jordan, "An Eighteenth-Century Seneca Iroquois Short Longhouse."

12. For these metaphors see, for example, Sir William Johnson's 1753 conference with the Six Nations in O'Callaghan, *Documents Relative to the Colonial History of the State of New York*, 6:810–11. See also Jennings et al., *The History and Culture of Iroquois Diplomacy*, 121–24. For warfare outside of the league, see Taylor, *American Colonies*, 104; Richter, *The Ordeal of the Longhouse*, chap. 3.

13. Klinck and Talman, *Journal of Major John Norton*, 98.

14. Klinck and Talman, *Journal of Major John Norton*, 98. For discussion of the possible origins of the place-name Cataraqui, see MacKenzie, "Cataraqui," 142–46.

15. Klinck and Talman, *Journal of Major John Norton*, 98. Norton left Ondat-shaigh untranslated but provided the basic context of the word. His writing, however, presents problems for translation. I believe he was probably trying to write something along the lines of "They argue." See Zeisberger, *Zeisberger's Indian Dictionary*, 152; Woodbury, *Onondaga-English / English-Onondaga Dictionary*, 996. I am grateful to Hanni Woodbury for her thoughts on translating the term. She notes that the word should be *dehonsadatsha?ih* and that Norton's rendition is off in too many ways to determine its meaning with certainty.

16. Klinck and Talman, *Journal of Major John Norton*, 99–102, also 99n2. There are several good attempts to synthesize the various accounts of the League's origins: A. F. C. Wallace, "The Dekanawideth Myth Analyzed," 118–30; Fenton, "The Lore of the Longhouse"; Vecsey, "The Story and Structure of the Iroquois Confederacy," 76–106.

17. Klinck and Talman, *Journal of Major John Norton*, 100. For the common theme of tragedies, see Wallace, "The Dekanawideth Myth," 121, and Vecsey, "The Story and Structure of the Iroquois Confederacy," 85. For an example of geographic variability in the details of the story, see William Fenton's analysis of John Gibson's late nineteenth-/early twentieth-century account: Fenton, *The Great Law and the Longhouse*, 92–93.

18. Klinck and Talman, *Journal of Major John Norton*, 104–5; Cusick, *Sketches of Ancient History of the Six Nations*, 17.

19. Kirkland, "Extracts from the Journal of the Rev. Mr. Kirkland," 95. See also Pilkington, *Journals of Samuel Kirkland*, 140–41. In the Pilkington edition, Kirkland notes a battle occurred 270 years prior (i.e., approximately 1518 CE); however, this detail does not appear in the *European Magazine* publication of Kirkland's journal. While the details of the journal differ, the overall point remained the same: the Seneca inhabited the forts before European contact. "Swift Running Water" is translated by William Beauchamp, *Aboriginal Place Names*

of New York, 257; Engelbrecht, *Iroquoia*, 98–99; Neusius et al., "Fortified Village or Mortuary Site?" 202–30. Most of these sites were destroyed during the nineteenth century, and therefore we know very little about them. The most complete catalog of earthworks in New York is Squier, *Antiquities of the State of New York*, 15–85; Parker, *The Archaeological History of New York*, 559–62; M. E. White, *Iroquois Culture History in the Niagara Frontier Area of New York State*, 52–54; M. E. White, "Ethnic Identification and Iroquois Groups in Western New York and Ontario," 25–27; J. V. Wright, *The Ontario Iroquois Tradition*, 83–84, 87–90, 101; Niemczycki, *The Origin and Development of the Seneca and Cayuga Tribes of New York State*, 10–13, 111.

20. Richter, *Ordeal of the Longhouse*, 62–66, "foreigners" quote on 65; Joseph Brant to Timothy Pickering, December 30, 1794, reproduced in Stone, *The Life and Times of Red Jacket, or So-Go-Ye-wat-Ha*, 475. By "another nation," Brant probably meant the Susquehannock.

21. ("We came to a place") Beauchamp, *Moravian Journals*, 30, 36. Translation of Tehotitachse and Gahontoto from Speck, "Siouan Tribes of the Carolinas as Known from Catawba, Tutelo, and Documentary Sources," 210. Scholars have had trouble translating Tehotitachse: see Sorg, "Lost Tribes of the Susquehanna," 68. Frank G. Speck relied upon Gladys Tantaquidgeon, who had a Cayuga translator, Alexander J. General. Speck offered the Tutelo as a candidate for the Tehotitachse. Beauchamp translates Gahontoto as "To Lift the Canoe," in reference to falls in the river: *Aboriginal Place Names of New York*, 262. Translation of Aquanoschioni from John Heckewelder, *History, Manners, and Customs*, 98.

22. For firearms dating, see Snow, *The Iroquois*, 113–14. For seventeenth-century Iroquois warfare, see Richter, "War and Culture."

23. For the lack of archaeological evidence, see Kent, *Susquehanna's Indians*, 33–34. More than any other searcher, John S. Clark believed in the existence of Carantouan. See Murray, *Selected Manuscripts of General John S. Clark*, 3–47. Recently only one scholar has attempted to revive Clark's search. See Sorg, "Lost Tribes," 64, for a discussion of Carantouan. For the war between the Haudenosaunee and Susquehannock and its unclear ending, see Jennings, "'Pennsylvania Indians' and the Iroquois," 76–80; Tooker, "Demise of the Susquehannocks"; Richter, *Ordeal of the Longhouse*, 136, 337n6.

24. Pauketat, *Cahokia*, 27; Taylor, *American Colonies*, 74. One scholar has proposed another candidate for a lost Iroquoian nation in western New York in the region of the Neutral, Erie, and Wenro; Pendergast, "The Kakouagoga or Kahkwas." Because the evidence is not definitive, this possible nation has not generally been included in scholarship on the Iroquois nations. For a more skeptical

take on American Indian knowledge of ancient places, see Bradley T. Lepper, "Early Historic American Indian Testimony," 1–14.

25. Klinck and Talman, *Journal of Major John Norton*, 110; Cusick, *Sketches*, 11–12; Boyce, "'As the Wind Scatters the Smoke'" ("kinsmen"), quoted on 155.

26. For the "invention of tradition," the classic is Hobsbawm and Ranger, *The Invention of Tradition*, 12. For thoughts on the evolution of Iroquoian languages, see Mithun, "The Proto-Iroquoians"; Whyte, "Proto-Iroquoian Divergence in the Late Archaic–Early Woodland Period Transition of the Appalachian Highlands."

27. Richter, *Ordeal of the Longhouse*, 144–89; White, *The Middle Ground*, 32–49; McDonnell, *Masters of Empire*, 65–68.

28. ("We came to a place") Beauchamp, *Moravian Journals*, 115; see also 67 and 111; Richter, *Ordeal of the Longhouse*, 186. John Norton wrote an extensive history of the war with the French. His account mixes Iroquois traditions with secondary readings. Klinck and Talman, *Journal of Major John Norton*, 222–56, quote on 233.

29. ("When the great warriors") Beauchamp, *Moravian Journals*, 41; see also 11, 46; ("All Indian nations") Heckewelder, *History*, 130. Other scholars have described Hahotschaunquas's monument. See Shoemaker, *A Strange Likeness*, 28–29; Levy, *Fellow Travelers*, 64.

30. Beauchamp, *Moravian Journals*, 68. "Zisagechrohne" is a synonym in Hodge, *Handbook of American Indians North of Mexico*, 2:909–10.

31. Joseph Brant to Timothy Pickering, December 30, 1794, in Stone, *Life and Times of Red Jacket*, 475. For European versus Indian concepts of landownership, see Shoemaker, *A Strange Likeness*, 13–34.

32. Pilkington, *Journal of Samuel Kirkland*, 33–34.

33. Cusick, *Sketches*, 15–16. In the eastern colonies, the earliest recorded accounts of giants date from the seventeenth century. See Simmons, *Spirit of the New England Tribes*, 172–74. For twentieth-century accounts of the stone giants, see Beauchamp, *Iroquois Folklore*, 40–41; Cornplanter, *Legends of the Longhouse*, 58–66. The earliest recorded accounts of giants in Iroquoia date from the discovery of a mastodon in the Hudson Valley in 1705, though it is not certain that the Haudenosaunee were present at the excavation. Stanford, "The Giant Bones of Claverack, New York, 1705"; Semonin, *American Monster*, 15–40; Mayor, *Fossil Legends of the First Americans*, 34–50; Levin, "Giants in the Earth," 751–70.

34. Heckewelder, *History*, 47, 49–51, quotes on 47, 50; Heckewelder, "Names which the Lenni Lenape or Delaware Indians, who once inhabited this country, had given to Rivers, Streams, Places &c. &c.," 367; Steiner, "Account of Some Old Indian Works." Some earthworks in this part of Ohio date from 1000 to 600 BCE, while others were much more recent. For early inhabitation, see Stothers

and Abel, "Early Woodland Prehistory (1000–1 BC)," 81–83, 87. For protohistoric sites, see Brose, "Penumbral Protohistory on Lake Erie's South Shore."

35. Kirkland, "Extracts from the Journal of the Rev. Mr. Kirkland," 96; Hart, Brumbach, and Lusteck, "Extending the Phytolith Evidence for Early Maize." I have used the more conservative dates in their calibrated range. See also Thompson et al., "Phytolith Evidence"; Hart, Thompson, and Brumbach, "Phytolith Evidence for Early Maize (*Zea mays*) in the Northern Finger Lakes Region of New York"; Hart and Scarry, "The Age of Common Beans." The recent debate on what scholars call *in situ* vs. migration theories can be found in two articles by Snow, "Migration in Prehistory" and "More on Migration in Prehistory." Refutation of Snow's position and criticism of Iroquois prehistory periodization can be found in Hart and Brumbach, "The Death of Owasco," 67–90.

36. Pilkington, *Journal of Samuel Kirkland*, 139; Journal of Lt. Erkuries Beatty in Cook, *Journals of the Military Expedition of Major General John Sullivan*, 27; Tooker, "Women in Iroquois Society."

37. Klinck and Talman, *Journal of John Norton*, 96; James Dean, "Mythology of the Iroquois, or Six Nations of Indians," in Elm and Antone, *The Oneida Creation Story*, 160; Bartram, *Observations on the Inhabitants*, 37. This hill is also discussed in Weiser, "Narrative of a Journey, Made in the Year 1737," 19, and Shoemaker, *A Strange Likeness*, 24. There are no Mohawk, Seneca, Cayuga, or Tuscarora creation myths written in the same period as Dean and Norton. The next closest is David Cusick's Tuscarora version, published in 1825. For the broader importance of agriculture, see Richter, *Before the Revolution*, 35.

38. Pilkington, ed. *Journals of Samuel Kirkland*, 141; Hamell, "Strawberries, Floating Islands, and Rabbit Captains," 78; Hamell, "The Panther in Huron-Wyandot and Seneca Myth, Ritual, and Material Culture," 258, 264, 270; Curtin and Hewitt, *Seneca Fiction, Legends, and Myths*, 797n135; Hewitt, "Kaahastinens or the Fire-dragon," 384.

39. Frisch, "The Divers Lake Quarry Site"; ("Arriving within") Thwaites, *The Jesuit Relations and Allied Documents*, 51:181–83. For a summary of the Little People, see Wonderley, *Oneida Iroquois Folklore*, 88–91.

40. Cusick, *Sketches*, 18; Beauchamp, "The Great Mosquito," 284; Beauchamp, *Aboriginal Place Names in New York*, 144–45.

41. Winterbotham, *An Historical, Geographical, Commercial, and Philosophical View*, 140.

42. "An Indian Conference," September 8–10, 1762, 505–6; Wallace, *The Death and Rebirth of the Seneca*, 114–21; Richter, *Facing East from Indian Country*, 191–201; White, *Middle Ground*, 269–314. For management of expansion, see Taylor, *Divided Ground*, 10. For the fossils, see also Mayor, *Fossil Legends of the First Americans*, 1–31.

43. Beauchamp, *Moravian Journals,* ("We went on") and ("long ago"), 35–37, ("David's Castle"), 29, ("Rose Meadow"), 31, ("Senneka Mail Station"), 68. For the idea of imagination and feeling, see Basso, *Wisdom Sits in Places,* 5.

2. Predators of the Vanishing Landscape

1. For some perceptive counterfactual thoughts about the significance of American Indians, see Axtell, "Colonial America without the Indians." See also Sleeper-Smith et al., *Why You Can't Teach United States History without American Indians*; Jefferson quoted in Richter, *Facing East from Indian Country,* 217.

2. Turner, *Pioneer Settlement of Phelps & Gorham's Purchase,* 134. Poetry from O'Reilly, *Settlement in the West,* front matter. See also Cronon, *Changes in the Land,* 159–70; Gross, *The Minutemen and Their World,* 79–83, 85–88, 177.

3. Taylor, *Divided Ground.*

4. Taylor, "The Great Change Begins," 265–68; Early, "Place Your Bets," 79–105.

5. For the destruction of Onondaga, see Graymont, *The Iroquois in the American Revolution,* 196. For a concise summary of the campaign, see Taylor, *The Divided Ground,* 98. For a detailed account of the military operations in Iroquoia, see Mintz, *The Seeds of Empire.*

6. Adler, *Chainbreaker's War,* 72. For Kanadesaga, see Journal of Lt. William Barton, 10; for Genesee Castle, see Journal of Lt. Colonial Henry Dearborn, 75; Maj. Gen. John Sullivan's Official Report, 303, all in Cook, *Journals of the Military Expedition.*

7. The U.S. government and the State of New York continually pressured the Haudenosaunee for more land sales. Thus these reservations do not exist today. Most notably, the Treaty of Buffalo Creek (1838) eliminated the Buffalo Creek Reservation. A good map that summarizes these land losses can be found in Hauptman, *A Conspiracy of Interests,* 93.

8. Turner, *Pioneer Settlement of Phelps and Gorham's Purchase,* 163–64; Schein, "Urban Origin and Form in Central New York."

9. Munro, "A Description of the Genesee Country, in the State of New York," 2:691; Wyckoff, *The Developer's Frontier,* 80–81. See also Clark, *Onondaga,* 2:187.

10. Coventry, *Memoirs of an Emigrant,* 2:665. Turner, *Pioneer Settlement of Phelps and Gorham's Purchase,* 168, 190, 247, 435, Durfee quoted on 383. See also O'Reilly, *Settlement in the West,* 249, and Turner, *Pioneer History of the Holland Land Purchase,* 386.

11. Coates, *Onnaghee,* 10–12. Background on Wyckoff can be found in John Franklin Meginness, *Otzinachson,* rev. ed, 1:541–43. The sentiment of victory is alluded to in Turner, *Pioneer Settlement of Phelps & Gorham's Purchase,* 133–34.

12. Cooper, *A Guide in the Wilderness*, 7; Taylor, "The Great Change Begins," 279–82; Wyckoff, *Developer's Frontier*, 62, 158. Statistics adapted from Brooks, "Overrun with Bushes," 22.

13. Maude, *Visit to the Falls of Niagara in 1800*, 45; Cooper, *Guide in the Wilderness*, 15; Lincklaen, *Travels in the Years 1791 and 1792*, 67.

14. Turner, *Pioneer History of the Holland Land Purchase*, 494. The words are Turner's, who interviewed Morrison. For other encounters with wolves, see also Turner, *Holland Purchase*, 488, 495; Turner, *Pioneer Settlement of Phelps & Gorham's Purchase*, 203, 209, 211, 359, 395, 400, 552; Clark, *Onondaga*, 1:184–85; Beardsley, *Reminiscences*, 21–22; Goodwin, *Pioneer History*, 307–17.

15. Sperry quoted in Turner, *Pioneer Settlement of Phelps & Gorham's Purchase*, 191; Beardsley, *Reminiscences*, 21–22; Goodwin, *Pioneer History*, 307.

16. For colonial precedents, see New York State, *The Colonial Laws of New York*, 744; New York State, *Laws of the Colony of New York, Passed in the Years 1774 and 1775. Fourteenth and Fifteenth George III*, 131–32. For the 1797 act, see New York State, *Laws of the State of New York, Passed at the Session of the Legislature Held in the Years 1797, 1798, 1799, and 1800, inclusive, being the Twentieth, Twenty-First, Twenty-Second, and Twenty-Third Sessions*, 133–34.

17. Humphreys, *An Essay on the Life of the Honorable Major-General Israel Putnam*, 21–25; *Otsego Herald*, June 9, 1803; Coleman, *Vicious*, 106–9.

18. *Otsego Herald*, September 19, 1799; Henry C. Goodwin, *Pioneer History*, 307.

19. Maude, *Visit to the Falls of Niagara*, 77; "RATS," *Otsego Herald*, January 19, 1804, and subsequent weeks; "Indian Scent," *Otsego Herald*, April 26, 1804, and subsequent weeks.

20. Goodwin, *Pioneer History*, 316.

21. *Ithaca Journal*, December 23, 1823. For information on Drake, see Selkgreg, *Landmarks of Tompkins County*, 115–19, 127, 147. For another recollection of a wolf hunt, see Clark, *Onondaga*, 1:175. For the popularity and communal spirit of these hunts, see Coleman, *Vicious*, 114–16.

22. *Ithaca Journal*, December 23, 1823.

23. *Otsego Herald*, April 1, 1822; *Otsego Herald*, December 18, 1820; *Ithaca Journal*, May 5, 1830.

24. Beauchamp, *Aboriginal Place Names of New York*, 69, 88–89; De Kay, *Zoology of New-York*, 47–49.

25. *Otsego Herald*, October 5, 1797; Taylor, "The Great Change Begins," 273–74. For discussion of horned serpents, see Wonderley, *At the Font of the Marvelous*, chap. 3. For some scientific reviews of Seneca Guns, see the U.S. Geological Survey article "Earthquakes Booms, Seneca Guns, and Other Sounds." http://earthquake.usgs.gov/learn/topics/booms.php, accessed September 17, 2018.

26. For an announcement of this museum, see *Otsego Herald*, January 14, 1802. See also DeWitt Clinton, "Introductory Discourse delivered before the Society on 4th of May, 1814 by DeWitt Clinton, LL. D.," in *Transactions of the Literary and Philosophical Society of New York* 1 (1814): 106; Sylvanus Miller to DeWitt Clinton, October 1814, in *Transactions of the Literary and Philosophical Society of New York* 1 (1814): 112.

27. Semonin, *American Monster*, 115, 356; Clinton, "Introductory Discourse," 107.

28. Harris, "New York's First Scientific Body."

29. Spafford, *A Gazetteer of the State of New York*, 161; "Description of a Remarkable Tooth, in the Possession of Mr. Peale." The origins of the name "Chemung" are indeed unclear; see Beauchamp, *Aboriginal Place Names in New York*, 43.

30. *Otsego Herald*, January 14, 1802; Clinton, "Introductory Discourse," 100.

31. *Otsego Herald*, June 12, 1817; J. H. Mather and Brockett, *A Geographical History of the State of New York*, 39. For another list of assumed mastodon finds within New York State, see De Kay, *Zoology of New-York*, 103–4. For a settler digging up fossils in Rochester, see O'Reilly, *Settlement in the West*, 78.

32. Silvanus Miller to DeWitt Clinton, October 1814, in *Transactions of the Literary and Philosophical Society of New-York*, 1:113. For a variation, see Williamson, *Observations on the Climate*, 110–11.

33. Berkhofer, *The White Man's Indian*, 38–43, quote on 41–42; Sheehan, *Seeds of Extinction*, 15–44; Clinton, "Introductory Discourse"; Jordan, *White over Black*, chap. 14. The first two decades of the nineteenth century marked the end of this kind of environmental understanding of race. See Sweet, *Bodies Politic*, 271–311.

34. Williamson, *Observations on the Climate*, quotation on 115, 96, 101, 102, 117, 119. For more on declension, see also James Madison, "Address to the Agricultural Society of Ablemarle," May 12, 1818, in *The National Archives, Founders Online*.

35. DeWitt Clinton, "The Iroquois," address delivered before the New-York Historical Society, December 6, 1811, in Campbell, *Life and Writings of DeWitt Clinton*, 211, 220; Williamson, *Observations*, 123.

36. For a good summary of the development of the idea of progress in history, see Pittock, "Historiography," 258–79. For the importance of the theory to the early American republic, see Wood, *Empire of Liberty*, 42–43. For an example of the influence and persistence of enlightenment ideas in nineteenth-century America, see Adams, "Society and Civilization," quote on 81. See also *Watch-tower*, June 29, 1829.

37. Turner, *Pioneer History of the Holland Land Purchase*, 566; Chad Anderson, "The Built Landscape and the Conquest of Iroquoia," 279–82.

38. Quoted in Turner, *Pioneer Settlement of Phelps and Gorham's Purchase*, 552.

39. For uses of this hymn, see Kelsey, *The Lives and Reminiscences of the Pioneers of Rochester and Western New York*, 49; and Goodwin, *Pioneer History*, 385. For American reproductions of Watts's hymn, see Worcester, *Christian Psalmody in Four Parts*, 59–60; Winchell, *An Arrangement of the Psalms*, 582; Watts, *Psalms Carefully Suited to the Christian Worship*, 206. The hymn was also well known on the later frontier of the Illinois Prairie: Faragher, *Sugar Creek*, 169.

40. George Washington to James Duane, September 7, 1783, in Fitzpatrick, *Writings of George Washington from the Original Manuscript Sources*, vol. 27.

41. Marbois, "Journey to the Oneidas," 305; Engelbrecht, *Iroquoia*, 157–58; Taylor, *The Divided Ground*, 146.

42. Belknap and Morse, "The Report of a Committee of the Board of Correspondents," 19–22, quote on 22; La Rochefoucauld-Liancourt, *Travels through the United States*, 1:175.

43. Abler, *Cornplanter*, 137–40; Wallace, *The Death and Rebirth of the Seneca*, 221–28, 272–84, 310–14.

44. Quoted in Taylor, *The Divided Ground*, 240; White, *The Middle Ground*, 469–517. For the broader relationship between the federal government and Indians, see Nichols, *Red Gentlemen & White Savages*.

45. Quoted in Wallace, *Death and Rebirth of the Seneca*, 281.

46. Hopkins, "Visit of Gerald T. Hopkins," 221; Norton to Unknown, 277–78; Tiro, "'We Wish to Do You Good,'" 374–75.

47. Clinton, "The Iroquois," *in Life and Writings of DeWitt Clinton*, ed. W. Campbell, 241, 252. For an analysis of the mischaracterization of Indians as hunters, see Richter, "'Believing That Many of the Red People Suffer,'" 601–28.

48. Cooper, *Guide in the Wilderness*, 7; *Otsego Herald*, April 1, 1822.

49. *Cherry Valley Gazette*, May 11, 1819.

50. *New-York Statesman*, July 18, 1820. *Rochester Telegraph*, July 11, 1820. *Cherry-Valley Gazette*, July 18, 1820; Hosack, *Memoir of DeWitt Clinton*, 456–57; Clark, *Onondaga*, 2:98.

51. *Palmyra Register*, July 19, 1820.

52. For some thoughts on the long-term development of Indian removal, see Richter, *Facing East from Indian Country*, 235–36.

3. The Many Deaths of John Montour

1. *Albany Centinel*, December 1, 1797.

2. *Albany Centinel*, December 5, 1797.

3. Farmer, *On Zion's Mount*, esp. 283–327.

4. Taylor, *William Cooper's Town*, 60.

5. Kent and Deardorff, "John Adlum on the Allegheny," 459.

6. See the account of taking of Fort Freeland and the Wyoming Massacre. For examples of the nineteenth-century New York histories, see the works of Turner, McMaster, Gould, and Clark.

7. Turner, *Pioneer Settlement of Phelps & Gorham's Purchase*, 359n.

8. Belknap, "Dr. Belknap's Tour to Oneida, 1796," 354–55. The rocks still receive local attention today. See Bob Cudmore's article "Rufus Grinder and the Painted Rocks," in the July 5, 2010, issue of the Schenectady *Daily Gazette*. There are only two known pictographs (rock drawings) within Iroquoia. In the early twentieth century, Arthur Parker documented one at Black Lake in St. Lawrence County. See Lenik, *Picture Rocks*, 195–201.

9. DeWitt Clinton, "Private Canal Journal," in Campbell, *Life and Writings of DeWitt Clinton*, 35.

10. Priest, *The Deeply Interesting Story of General Patchin of Schoharie County*, 14; Chad Anderson, "The Built Landscape and the Conquest of Iroquoia," 282–88.

11. McMaster, *History of the Settlement of Steuben County*, 34n. For repeats of this version, see Child, *Gazetteer and Business Directory of Steuben County, N.Y. for 1868*, 96; Erwin, *Early History of Painted Post and the Town of Erwin*, 61.

12. Mary V. Derickson to [Samuel Hazard?], December 17, 1855, in Hazard, *Pennsylvania Archives*, 12:364–66.

13. Erwin, *Early History of Painted Post*, 19–21; Cowan, *Charles Williamson*, 62–63. Cowan has mistaken Catharine Montour for Isabel Montour, as many historians tend to do.

14. Report of the committee on claims, on the claim Benjamin Patterson, a soldier of the revolutionary war, March 14, 1829, Revolutionary War Pension and Bounty—Land Warrant Application Files, Publication Number M804, Catalog ID 300022, RG15, Pension Number R8010, National Archives, Washington DC; Resch, *Suffering Soldiers*, 89–90, 258–59n84.

15. For the lack of information on Taggart, see Severance, ed. *Publications of the Buffalo Historical Society*, 9:297. Severance incorrectly assumes that Taggart referred to Roland Montour, who had not yet died—once again illustrating the confusion historians have dealt with when writing about the Montour family. Arthur Taggart can be found in "Muster Rolls and Papers Relating to the Associators and Militia of the County of Northumberland," in Egle, ed. *Pennsylvania Archives 2nd ser.*, vol. 14, 333. For the list of casualties, see Col. Matthew Smith to Pres. Reed, August 3, 1779, in Hazard, ed. *Pennsylvania Archives*, vol. 7, 610. For Watt's serving under Taggart, see Jordan, ed. *Colonial and Revolutionary Families of Pennsylvania*, 381. Patterson's marriages can be found in, W. W. Clayton, *History of Steuben County, New York* (Philadelphia: Lewis, Peck, & Co., 1879), 286.

16. Sexton, *An Outline History of Tioga and Bradford Counties*, 175. French, *Gazetteer of the State of New York*, 624n6; Revolutionary War Pension and Bounty—Land Warrant Application Files. Petition of John Knox, July 18, 1826, Publication Number M804, Catalog ID 300022, RG15, Pension Number R8010, National Archives.

17. Merrell, *Into the American Woods*, 54–55; Most researchers have stated that Margaret was Andrew's sister, but James Merrell's research suggests she may have been a niece of Isabel Montour, making her Andrew's cousin. See Merrell, "'The Cast of His Countenance,'" 16, note 5. For Catharine as Margaret's daughter, see Nathaniel Holland to the Governor, September 17, 1760, in Pennsylvania State, *Minutes of the Provincial Council of Pennsylvania, from the Organization to the Termination of the Proprietary Government*, 8:499. While it is certain that John and Roland were related to Catharine, proof that she was their mother relies almost solely on the statements of antiquarian historians, who often fail to offer evidence. For doubts that John and Roland Montour were Catharine's children, see Murray, *A History of Old Tioga Point and Early Athens Pennsylvania*, 109. For identification of Edward Pollard as Roland, John, and Belle Montour's father, see Francis Goring to Edward Pollard, September 12, 1779, in Ketchum, *An Authentic and Comprehensive History of Buffalo*, vol. 2, 345. For Pollard's career, see Wilson, "The Struggle for Wealth and Power at Fort Niagara, 1775–1783," 144.

18. Journal of Lt. William Barton, in Cook, *Journals of the Military Expedition of Major General John Sullivan*, 9.

19. Kelly, "John Montour,"; William Crawford to George Washington, November 14, 1774; John Montour to George Washington, May 27, 1782; Washington to Benjamin Lincoln, May 28, 1782, Washington Papers, Library of Congress, Manuscripts Division. [Collection available online: http://memory.loc.gov/ammem/gwhtml/gwhome.html]; ("faithful Indian")

20. The most complete roster of Butler's Rangers is Smy, *An Annotated Nominal Roll of Butler's Rangers 1777–1784*. The Montours do not appear on this roster.

21. Stone, *The Poetry and History of Wyoming*, iv; Silver, *Our Savage Neighbors*, 53–54; Young, *The Shoemaker and the Tea Party*, 135–36, 239n7.

22. Zebulon Butler to the Board of War, July 10, 1778, in Dawson, *Battles of the United States*, 1:429–30. Articles of capitulation reprinted in Harvey, *A History of Wilkes-Barré*, 2:1033–34.

23. "Contemporary Account of Attack on Wyoming," in University of the State of New York, Divisions of Archives and History, *The Sullivan-Clinton Campaign in 1779*, 66; Willard, *History of the United States*, 215. Although full of contempt for "savages," the best summary of the early published accounts and historiography of the battle of Wyoming can be found in Harvey, *A History of Wilkes-Barré*, 2:1060–72. For the continued significance of the Wyoming Massacre in

nineteenth-century local histories and memoirs, see Turner, *Pioneer History of the Holland Purchase of Western New York*, 274–75; Simms, *History of Schoharie County*, 281–82; Beardsley, *Reminiscences*, 470. For examples of claims that Brant was there, see Chapman, *A Sketch of the History of Wyoming*, 126. Chapman does not mention the Montours.

24. John Butler to Mason Bolton, July 8, 1778, in Davies, *Documents of the American Revolution*, 15:165–66, quote on 166; Zebulon Butler to the Board of War, July 10, 1778, Dawson, *Battles of the United States*, 1:430.

25. Campbell, *Gertrude of Wyoming*, 57; Taylor, *The Divided Ground*, 93.

26. William L. Stone, *Life of Joseph Brant—Thayendanega: Including the Border Wars of the American Revolution, and Sketches of the Indian Campaigns of Generals Hamar, St. Clair, and Wayne*, vol. 1 (New York: Alexander V. Blake, 1838), 339; ("When a lad of fourteen") Eleazer Carey to Charles Miner, July 24, 1843, reprinted in Miner, *History of Wyoming*, 233.

27. Miner, *History of Wyoming*, [appendix] 23.

28. Miner, *History of Wyoming*, 226; Skinner, *A History of the Revolutionary War between Great Britain and the United States in Verse*, 153; Journal of William Rogers, 248, 251; also Journal of Sergeant Nathaniel Webb, 287, both in Cook, *Journals of the Military Expedition of Major General John Sullivan*; Lossing, *The Pictorial Field-Book of the Revolution*, 1:357–58. At the dedication of the Wyoming memorial, James May also only cited an unnamed captive, almost certainly Elliot, as the source of the story about Esther Montour: *Hazard's Register of Pennsylvania*, 39–42.

29. Miner, *History of Wyoming*, 232–33; "Blacksnake Conversations," Draper Manuscripts, University of Wisconsin, 4-s-28–29; Abler, ed. *Chainbreaker*, 137. Abler believes Blacksnake referred to Wyoming in these statements, though we cannot be certain. When Draper interviewed Blacksnake, he clearly asked about the myths of Wyoming.

30. Address of Col. Hartley to Congress, October 8, 1778, in Hazard, ed. *Pennsylvania Archives*, 7:5–9, quote on 5; Day, *Historical Collections of the State of Pennsylvania*, 144.

31. Revolutionary War Pension and Bounty—Land Warrant Application Files. Petition of Robert Covenhoven, January 27, 1826. Publication Number M804, Catalog ID 300022, RG15. Pension Number R8010. National Archives, Washington DC; Meginness, *Otzinachson*, 1:615–16. Covenhoven's career is discussed in his own pension application: RG 15. Pension Number S12574. Boone is mentioned in Address of Col. Hartley to Congress, October 8, 1778, in Hazard, ed., *Pennsylvania Archives*, 7:7.

32. Walter Butler to Mason Bolton, November 17, 1778, in Davies, *Documents of the American Revolution*, 15:262. For accurate civilian counts see, for example, *Pennsylvania Packet*, December 19, 1778.

33. Cruikshank, *The Story of Butler's Rangers and the Settlement of Niagara*, 54, 58.

34. James Clinton to Walter Butler, January 1, 1779, in Hugh Hastings, *Public Papers of George Clinton*, 4:457–59. Quotations from William Campbell, *Annals of Tryon County*, 119, 181. For the story reprinted, see Stone, *Life of Joseph Brant*, 391; Ketchum, *History of Buffalo*, 1:325; W. Reid, *The Mohawk Valley*, 218.

35. McMaster, *History of the Settlement of Steuben County*, 28.

36. Meginness, *Otzinachson*, 251–52.

37. Meginness, *Otzinachson*, 254–55.

38. Meginness, *Otzinachson*, 130n255. Derickson gives her birthdate as May 20, 1779, in Mary V. Derickson to [Samuel Hazard?], December 17, 1855, in Hazard, ed. *Pennsylvania Archives*, 12:364–66.

39. Col. Samuel Hunter to William Maclay, July 19, 1779, in Harzard, *Pennsylvania Archives*, 12:590. Recently historian Max Mintz asserted twenty-four British and Indians were killed: *Seeds of Empire*, 120. Given that he has cited McDonnel's letter, this count is puzzling. He also cites and repeats Meginness's version, which has no basis in firsthand sources. John Buyers to Wm. Maclay, July 29, 1779, in Hazard, *Pennsylvania Archives*, 7:591. Buyers became justice of the peace the following year. Supreme Executive Council, minutes September 28, 1780, in Hazard, ed. *Pennsylvania Archives*, 12:491.

40. Meginness, *Otzinachson*, 1:593–94; Rupp, *History and Topography*, 144.

41. John McDonnell to John Butler, August 5, 1779, in USNY, *The Sullivan-Clinton Campaign in 1779*, 115. McMaster, *Steuben County*, 43. The Seneca chief Blacksnake also recalled Montour's wound as superficial, but he forgot Montour's name: "Blacksnake Conversations," Draper Manuscripts, University of Wisconsin, 4-s-34.

42. Gould, *History of Delaware County and Border Wars of New York*, 2:30–38; "Roster of Officers in Sullivan's Expedition, 1779" in Cook, *Journals of the Military Expedition of Major General John Sullivan*, 326.

43. Journal of Sergeant Major George Grant, 109, Journal of Ensign Daniel Gookin, 131–32, in Cook, *Journals of the Military Expedition of Major General John Sullivan*, 103–4; John Butler to Mason Bolton, August 26, 1779, in *the Sullivan-Clinton Campaign in 1779*; Mintz, *Seeds of Empire*, 107–8.

44. James Clinton to George Clinton, 132–33, John Butler to Mason Bolton, August 31, 1779, 135–38, in *The Sullivan-Clinton Campaign in 1779*; Graymont, *Iroquois in the American Revolution*, 209–15; Mintz, *Seeds of Empire*, 122, 126–29. For the Newtown "Hog Back," see Journal of Lt. John L. Hardenbergh, in Cook,

Journals of the Military Expedition of Major General John Sullivan against the Six Nations of Indians in 1779, 127, footnote.

45. John Butler to Mason Bolton, August 31, 1779, in *The Sullivan-Clinton Campaign in 1779,* 135–38; James Clinton to George Clinton, August 30, 1779, in *The Sullivan-Clinton Campaign in 1779,* 132–33, quote on 133.

46. Butler to Bolton, August 31, 1779, in *The Sullivan-Clinton Campaign in 1779,* 135–38; Journal of Lt. John Jenkins, 173; Journal of Major James Norris, 233; Major Gen. John Sullivan's Official Report, 299 in Cook, *Journals of the Military Expedition of Major General John Sullivan Against the Six Nations of Indians.*

47. Swetland, *A Very Remarkable Narrative of Luke Swetland,* 15. Haldimand quoted in Graymont, *Iroquois in the American Revolution,* 159.

48. Francis Goring to Edward Pollard, September 12, 1779, in Ketchum, *History of Buffalo,* 345; John Butler to Mason Bolton, August 26, 1779, in *The Sullivan-Clinton Campaign in 1779,* 131.

49. Graymont, *Iroquois in the American Revolution,* 229, 240.

50. Walton, *A Narrative of the Captivity and Sufferings of Benjamin Gilbert and His Family,* 6–7. *Pennsylvania Packet,* May 6, 1780; *Connecticut Courant,* May 16, 1780; *American Journal,* May 17, 1780; *Connecticut Journal,* May 18, 1780.

51. For two later examples of Roland buried at the Painted Post, see Ketchum, *History of Buffalo,* 2:5; F. C. Johnson, "A Monument of the Old Indian Wars," 60.

52. McMaster, *History of the Settlement of Steuben County,* 34n; Spafford, *A Gazetteer of the State of New York,* 268–69; F. Hall, *Travels in Canada and the United States, in 1816 and 1817,* 253.

53. Clinton, "Private Canal Journal," in Campbell, *Life and Writings of DeWitt Clinton,* 150, 154; *Watch-tower,* July 20, 1829.

54. Faragher, *Daniel Boone,* 323, 351–52, Boone quoted on 39.

55. Meginness, *Otzinachson,* 254; Herman, "The Other Daniel Boone." For the broader significance of this transformation in American views of wilderness, the best recent work is Powell, *Vanishing America,* esp. chap. 1.

56. Thomas Maxwell to Henry Rowe Schoolcraft, September 10, 1853, in Schoolcraft, *Information Respecting the History,* 5:670; Erwin, *Early History of Painted Post and the Town of Erwin,* 22–23.

57. Macleod, *Harper's New York and Erie Railroad Guide Book,* 159; T. F. Minier, "Historical Address," in Erwin, *Early History of Painted Post,* 62.

58. For DeWitt's cartography, see Mano, "Unmapping the Iroquois," 171–96.

59. D. H. Bisell to Lyman Draper, [May?] 21, 1877, Draper Manuscripts, University of Wisconsin, 17-F, 1–2. So far as I know, no primary sources exist to support the story of poisoning. Hints of Indian suspicions of British goodwill at Niagara can be found in Mason Bolton to Frederick Haldimand, November 11,

1779, in E. A. Cruikshank, ed. *Records of Niagara: A Collection of Documents Related to the First Settlement, 1778–1783* (Niagara-on-the-Lake, Ontario: Niagara Historical Society, 1927), 15–16. Discussions about lack of provisions for Indians, and plans for supplying flour, can be found in Captain Matthews to John Butler, May 19, 1782, and Frederick Haldimand to H. Watson Powell, May 31, 1782, in Cruikshank, ed. *Records of Niagara*, 37–38. The Seneca oral history is mentioned in Barbara Alice Mann, *George Washington's War on Native America* (Westport CT: Praeger, 2005), 107, 219n618.

60. Doty, *A History of Livingston County, New York*, 124–25.

61. Angel quoted in G. H. Harris, *The Life of Horatio Jones*, Publications of the Buffalo Historical Society, vol. 6 (Buffalo NY: Buffalo Historical Society, 1906), 513. Dennis, *Seneca Possessed*, 1–3, 95–114. See also Wallace, *The Death and Rebirth of the Seneca*, 254–62.

62. Hall, *Travels in Canada and the United States*, 253; Deloria, *Playing Indian*, chap. 1.

63. McMaster, *History of Settlement of Steuben County*, 51.

64. *Western Recorder*, September 12, 1826; May's address reproduced in *Hazard's Register of Pennsylvania*, July 21,1832; DeWitt Clinton, "The Iroquois," Address Delivered before the New-York Historical Society, December 6, 1811, in Campbell ed., *The Life and Writings of DeWitt Clinton*, 251.

65. Addition monuments, "last" Indians, and their graves are discussed in O'Brien, *Firsting and Lasting*.

66. William Lyman to Lyman Draper, August 28, 1879, in Draper Manuscripts, University of Wisconsin, 17-F-3-4.

4. The Decline and Fall of the Romans of the West

1. Watson, *Men and Times of the Revolution*, 291–92; "Observations on the State of New York," *New York Magazine, or Literary Repository*, March 1791, 136–40. For their involvement in speculation, see Hauptman, *Conspiracy of Interests*, 13, 15, 226n29.

2. Watson, *Men and Times*, 300, 303–4.

3. Watson, *Men and Times*, 297.

4. [Livingston], "Newly Discovered Indian Fortifications."

5. [Livingston], "Newly Discovered Indian Fortifications."

6. Cornog, *Birth of Empire*, 12–19.

7. Cornog, *Birth of Empire*, 22; Taylor, *Divided Ground*, 165, 184–85, 201.

8. Cornog, *Birth of Empire*, 34, 45, 54, 96, 97, 135–44.

9. Cornog, *Birth of Empire*, 62–68; Clinton, "Introductory Discourse Delivered before the Society," 1:19.

10. *Albany Chronicle,* October 10, 1796; New-York Historical Society, *Collections of the New-York Historical Society, for the Year 1809,* 13.

11. DeWitt Clinton, "Private Canal Journal," in Campbell, *Life and Writings of DeWitt Clinton,* 172–73.

12. Clinton, "Private Canal Journal."

13. Heart, "Account of Some Remains," 425; Pauketat, *Cahokia,* 16–17; Hart, "New Dates from Classic New York Sites," 1–22.

14. Jefferson, *Notes on the State of Virginia,* 156.

15. Wallace, *Jefferson and the Indians,* 131–60.

16. Webster, "Antiquity. Letter III," 147; Adair, *History of the American Indians,* 377–78.

17. Webster, "Antiquity," "Antiquity. Letter II," "Antiquity. Letter III." For Webster's source, see Roberts, *An Account of the First Discovery,* 33–79. Webster later retracted his theory, but Clinton still felt the need to engage it in "The Iroquois," in Campbell, *Life and Writings of DeWitt Clinton,* 258–259. For de Soto, see Hudson, *Knights of Spain,* 44, map of route on 430; Weber, *The Spanish Frontier in North America,* 50.

18. "American Chronology. Containing, An Accurate and Comprehensive Account of the Most remarkable Events and memorable Occurrences of the New York, From its first Discovery to the present Times, most particularly as to what respects the United States; Interspersed with such Foreign Transactions as appear most interesting in the History of the World." See also "Proofs to Ascertain That America Was First Discovered by the Ancient Britons." Scholars know little about the Doeg, who probably spoke an Algonquian language that has since become extinct. For brief mentions, see Christian F. Feest, "Nanticoke and Neighboring Tribes," in *Handbook of North American Indians,* 2:240; and Feest, "Virginia Algonquians," in *Handbook of North American Indians,* 2:256. For the Doeg in Bacon's Rebellion, see Morgan, *American Slavery, American Freedom,* 250–51. The Welsh tales were especially popular in Kentucky: Imlay, *A Topographical Description,* 91–93; Owen, "Discovery of the Madawgwys."

19. Clinton, "The Iroquois," 260–61. There is a mistake in this version of Clinton's discourse that reads "action or modern times." Belknap, *American Biography,* 194.

20. King, "Notes on a Visit to Western New York in 1810."

21. "Consequences of the Discovery of America and the Indies," 584; Pennant, *Arctic Zoology,* 1:161,

22. Clinton, "The Iroquois," 251–52; Pennant, *Arctic Zoology,* 1:164.

23. William Smith, *The History of the Province of New-York,* 53; Clinton, "The Iroquois," 238. For a nineteenth-century repetition, see Campbell, *Border Warfare of New York,* 17.

24. Clinton, "The Iroquois," 210, 212–13, 224.

25. Carver, *Three Years Travels*, 106; Clinton, "The Iroquois," 262–64, quote on 264.

26. [Livingston], "Newly Discovered Indian Fortifications."

27. Clinton, "The Iroquois," 265–66.

28. See, for example, Kennedy, *Hidden Cities*. Clark is quoted in Pauketat, *Cahokia*, 27.

29. Petition of Nicholas Cusick, Revolutionary War Pension and Bounty—Land Warrant Application Files; Taylor, *Divided Ground*, 172–73; Abler, *Cornplanter*, 23–25; Hauptman, *Seven Generations of Iroquois Leadership*, 105–6. For examples of Cusick's heroism, see Elias Johnson, *Legends, Traditions, and Laws*, 165–66. Elias Johnson was a Tuscarora historian.

30. Taylor, *Divided Ground*, 46–52; Jefferson, *Notes on the State of Virginia*, 229; Samuel Kirkland, "Journal," in Ibbotson, *Documentary History of Hamilton College*, 26. Kirkland to Reverend [?], January 14, 1803. David is also mentioned in Kirkland to Reverend Thacher, November 6, 1799, Kirkland Papers, Hamilton College Archives. For possible common ground with Indian leaders, see Nichols, *Red Gentlemen and White Savages*.

31. Cusick to Samuel Kirkland Jr., March 22, 1800, Kirkland Papers, Hamilton College Archives; Taylor, *Divided Ground*, 369.

32. *Albany Centinel*, July 11, 1797; Caines, *New-York Term Reports of Cases*, 2:188–98; James Cusick to Millard Filmore, October 8, 1850; Petition of Nicholas Cusick, Revolutionary War Pension and Bounty—Land Warrant Application Files. .

33. Duncan, *Travels through Part of the United States and Canada*, 2:75–81, quotes on 75, 77; for improvement, see also Clinton, "Private Journal," in Campbell, *Life and Writings*, 122; Stansbury, *A Pedestrian Tour*, 98.

34. John Wheelock to Samuel Kirkland, November 28, 1787, Kirkland Papers, Hamilton College Archives; Kirkland, "Extracts from the Journal of the Rev. Mr. Kirkland, 96.

35. Joseph Brant to Samuel Kirkland, March 8, 1791, Kirkland Papers, Hamilton College Archives.

36. Samuel Miller, "Annual Report of the Directors," 204.

37. [Gray], "Extract of a Letter," 107; Cusick, *Sketches*, 1.

38. Cusick, *Sketches*, 19; "Tuscarora Indians," *Boston Recorder*, July 8, 1820.

39. Bullock, "Sketch of a Journey through the Western States," 19:149–50; Sturtevant, "Early Iroquois Realist Painting and Identity Marking"; Brydon, "Ingenuity in Art"; Keating, *Iroquois Art, Power, and History*, 138–51.

40. Cusick, *Sketches*, 1.

41. Cusick, *Sketches*, 4n.

42. Cusick, *Sketches*, 10–11.

43. Cusick, *Sketches*, 11–13.

44. Cusick, *Sketches*, 17.

45. See chap. 1.

46. Cusick, *Sketches*, 27–28; Clinton, "Private Canal Journal," in Campbell, *Life and Writings of DeWitt Clinton*, 122.

47. Cusick, *Sketches*, 31–34.

48. Noble, "Historic Neutral Iroquois Settlement Patterns," 18, 19; White, *Iroquois Culture History*, 28–31, 54–56; White, "Neutral and Wenro," 15:407–11; Warrick, *A Population History of the Huron-Petun*, 225; Rotstein, "The Mystery of the Neutral Indians," Champlain quoted on 12. The Neutral primarily lived to the west of the Niagara River, and consequently the Wenro possibly occupied Kienuka. We know even less about the Wenro than the Neutral. The Wenro were another Iroquoian group dispersed by the Five Nations during the mid-seventeenth-century wars. A smaller nation, the Wenro were closely associated with the Neutral. For the Peace Queen, see Wallace and Holler, "Reviving the Peace Queen." Wallace and Holler argue, "The Tuscarora had no independent version of the founding story because they were separated from their 'cousins' of the northern Iroquois nations well before the Confederacy was organized. Cusick does not mention Dekanawidah, Hiawatha, or Jiconsaseh at all (95)." Wallace and Holler are correct in arguing that Cusick does not include the story of Hiawatha, or any variation of the story with the Peace Queen. However, he clearly includes a story of Jiconsaseh (called Yagowanea in his account) similar to the stories of wars in the west collected by Morgan.

49. Cusick, *Sketches*, 38; Richter, "War and Culture."

50. Cusick, *Sketches*, 38. Variations of the "War in the West" are expertly discussed in Anthony Wonderley, *At the Font of the Marvelous*, chap. 2. For the early settlement near Kauhanauka, see Johnson, *Legends, Traditions, and Laws*, 72–73.

51. Constantine Samuel Rafinesque to James Barbour, August 27, 1826; Rafinesque to George Clinton, October 30, 1827, in Boewe, *Correspondence of C. S. Rafinesque*, 1241, 1283; "Indian Literature," *Boston Lyceum* 2, no. 1 (July 15, 1827): 46; *Western Recorder*, July 10, 1827.

52. Boewe, *The Life of C. S. Rafinesque*, 1–102.

53. [Mitchill], "The Original Inhabitants of America" ; Boewe, *Life of C. S. Rafinesque*, 102–3.

54. Boewe, *Life of C. S. Rafinesque*, 109–10; Rafinesque's definitive statement on oral traditions can be found in his *American Nations*, 58.

55. Boewe, *John D. Clifford's Indian Antiquities*, 27.

56. C. S. Rafinesque, "Alleghawee Antiquities of Fayette County, KY," to the American Antiquarian Society, 88–98, and "Enumeration of the Sites of Ancient

Towns and Monuments of Kentucky, &c.," 117–28 in Boewe, ed. *Clifford's Indian Antiquities.*

57. Rafinesque, *Ancient History or Annals of Kentucky*, 12–13, quote on 23.

58. Nigel Leask, "Francis Wilford," 216.

59. Rafinesque, *Annals of Kentucky*, 13–14; Wilford, "An Essay on the Sacred Isles in the West," 8:272, 373, and plates 1 and 4.

60. C. S. Rafinesque to Elias Boudinot, April 5, 1828, 1295–1313, quote on 1296, and Rafinesque to J. M. McCulloh, *Saturday Evening Post*, July 19, 1828, 1329–34, quote on 1331, in Boewe, *Correspondence of C. S. Rafinesque.*

61. Rafinesque, *American Nations*, 125–44.

62. The definitive debunking of Rafinesque is Oestreicher, "Unmasking the *Walum Olum*"; Boewe, *Life of C. S. Rafinesque*, 363. Some scholarship has examined Tuscarora migration myths, collected during the twentieth century, which described a crossing of ice, see Wallace and Reyburn, "Crossing the Ice," 42–47.

63. Rafinesque, *American Nations*, 1:28, quote on 30; Rafinesque, *American Nations*, 2:234–35; American Sunday School Union, *History of the Delaware and Iroquois Indians*, 5–6.

64. Rafinesque, *American Nations*, 2:10–13, 237, 228–29.

65. Rafinesque, *American Nations*, 190–93.

66. *Hudson River Chronicle*, November 24, 1840; Final Payment Voucher for Nicholas Cusick, Catalog ID 2733385, RG 217, Records of the Accounting Officers of the Department of the Treasury, 1775–1978, National Archives, Washington DC. For Cusick's death prior to 1846, see James Cusick quoted in Schoolcraft, *Notes on the Iroquois*, 475.

67. *Albany Chronicle*, October 10, 1796.

68. Turner, *Pioneer History of the Holland Purchase of Western New York*, 18–26, quotes on 18, 26; Salisbury, "The Indians' Old World"; Galloway, *New Worlds for All.*

69. Thomas, *Report on the Mound Explorations of the Bureau of Ethnology.*

5. The Burned-Over District

1. Sheriff, *The Artificial River*, 36 and chap. 2; Howe, *What Hath God Wrought*, chap. 6, figures on 217; Taylor, *The Transportation Revolution*. Historians have written extensively about the development of capitalism and the middle class in the early nineteenth century, and central and western New York has been a significant area of study. Among other works, for example, see Ryan, *Cradle of the Middle Class*; Wyckoff, *The Developer's Frontier*. Canal progress reports were featured prominently in New York's newspapers. For example, see *Palmyra Register*, February 25, 1818; *Palmyra Register*, March 4, 1818; *Palmyra Register*, March 11, 1818; *Palmyra Register*, February 24, 1819; *Palmyra Register*, March 10, 1819.

2. Cross, *The Burned-Over District*, vii, 3, 28–29, 75–76; Brooke, *The Refiner's Fire*, xiv–xvi, 59. For capitalism and religion, see Paul Johnson, *A Shopkeeper's Millennium*; Howe, *What Hath God Wrought*, chap. 5, Finney quoted on 172.

3. Taylor, "The Early Republic's Supernatural Economy," 10–13.

4. Similar arguments are most thoroughly explored in Vogel, *Indian Origins of the Book of Mormon*. Kennedy noted Mormonism's origins in American archaeology in *Hidden Cities*, 228–31. Evan Cornog briefly examines connections between Smith, DeWitt Clinton's theories, and the Erie Canal in *The Birth of Empire*, 121, 166. Professional and amateur historians have produced an immense amount of work on Mormonism's origins. As many writers have been motivated by a desire to discredit or, alternatively, confirm Smith's revelations, their work can be divisive. For the state of the field, see Shipps, "Richard Lyman Bush, the Story of Joseph Smith and Mormonism, and the New Mormon History."

5. Bushman, *Joseph Smith, Rough Stone Rolling*, 18–19, 31–32.

6. Turner, *History of the Pioneer Settlement of Phelps & Gorham's Purchase*, 213–14. While dismissive of Smith, Turner believed in Clinton's Mound Builder theories. See Turner, *Pioneer History of the Holland Purchase of Western New York*, 18–26.

7. ("From these") *Palmyra Register*, May 26, 1819. See also *Otsego Herald*, May 17, 1819; Clinton, *A Memoir on the Antiquities*. For an announcement of Clinton's publication, see *Otsego Herald*, November 16, 1818.

8. *Palmyra Register*, June 2, 1818; *Palmyra Register*, August 20, 1820; O'Connor, *Chronicles of Eri*, ix.

9. ("We feel") *Palmyra Register*, March 24, 1818; ("Renouncing") *Palmyra Register*, July 7, 1818.

10. Smith, "History Draft, 1839," in Vogel, *Early Mormon Documents*, 1:59; Smith, "History, 1832," in Jessee, *Personal Writings of Joseph Smith*, 5; Dennis, *Seneca Possessed*, 57, Red Jacket quoted on 59.

11. Smith, "History, 1832," 6; ("I was answered") Smith, "History, 1838," in Jessee, *Personal Writings*, 200; Bushman, *Joseph Smith*, 39–41; Shipps, *Mormonism*, 1–3, 9, 32–33; Brooke, *Refiner's Fire*, 62; See also the sarcastic announcement of a new age of revelations in *Palmyra Reflector*, June 30, 1830, reprinted in Vogel, *Early Mormon Documents*, 2:235.

12. Joseph Smith, "History, 1838," 202–4; Shipps, *Mormonism*, 32–33; "Martin Harris Interview with Joel Tiffany, 1859," in Vogel, *Early Mormon Documents*, 2:304.

13. Smith, "History, 1832," 7. Descriptions from Oliver Cowdery to W. W. Phelps, July 1835, 448; James Gordon Bennett, "Mormonism—Religious Fanaticism—Church and State Party," August 31, 1831, in Vogel, *Early Mormon Documents*, 3:286.

14. Lucy Mack Smith, *Biographical Sketches of Joseph Smith the Prophet, and His Progenitor for Many Generations* [1853], reprinted in Vogel, *Early Mormon Documents*, 1:296.

15. *The Watch-tower*, August 12, 1822. The most detailed survey of Smith's digging can be found in Dan Vogel, "The Locations of Joseph Smith's Early Treasure Quests."

16. Quinn, *Early Mormonism and the Magic World View*, 41–42.

17. Taylor, "Early Republic's Supernatural Economy," 26–26; Washington Irvin [Geoffrey Crayon], *Tales of a Traveler*, 252–81. For Webster, see chapter 4.

18. Bushman, *Joseph Smith*, 51–52, 574nn90 and 91; Brooke, *Refiner's Fire*, 154; Vogel, "The Locations of Joseph Smith's Early Treasure Quests," 219; Fayette Lapham, "Interview with the Father of Joseph Smith, the Mormon Prophet, Forty Years Ago. His Account of the Finding of the Sacred Plates," in Vogel, *Early Mormon Documents*, 1:461; Joseph Smith, "History, 1838," 207; "Bainbridge (NY) Court Record," March 20, 1826, in Vogel, *Early Mormon Documents*, 4:248–56, and Vogel's editorial note regarding the missing original documents, 239–48.

19. Taylor, "Early Republic's Supernatural Economy," 16–19.

20. "Roswell Nichols Statement," December 1, 1833, in Vogel, *Early Mormon Documents*, 2:37; Martin Harris, "Interview with Joel Tiffany," 1859, reprinted in Vogel, *Early Mormon Documents*, 2:303.

21. "Peter Ingersoll, Statement," December 2, 1833, in Vogel, *Early Mormon Documents*, 2:41–42.

22. D. Michael Quinn, *Early Mormonism and the Magical World View*, 41; Clinton, *Memoir on the Antiquities*, 14. New Yorkers' long-standing interest in giants would reach its peak—and nadir—with the ten-foot Cardiff Giant, a spectacular hoax unearthed in 1869. See Rose, "When Giants Roamed the Earth."

23. "A History of the Divining Rod; with the Adventures of an Old Rodsman," 317–20; Brooke, *Refiner's Fire*, 53, 333n75. For authentic Adena stone tablets, see Power, *Early Art of the Southeastern Indians*, 25–26. Locals excavated (or looted) the mound in 1838, allegedly finding a small sandstone tablet, called the "Grave Creek Stone," which featured twenty-four strange characters. Henry Rowe Schoolcraft lent credibility to the stone by identifying its writing as Phoenician, Celtiberian, Old British, and other European characters. David Oestreicher, debunker of the *Walum Olum* hoax, convincingly argues the Grave Creek stone was a hoax, copied from an eighteenth-century book as part of a plan to sell access to the mound. Oestreicher's paper remains unpublished. For an accessible summary, see Feder, *Encyclopedia of Dubious Archaeology*, 123–27.

24. Clinton, "Private Canal Journal," in Campbell, *Life and Writings of DeWitt Clinton*, 172; Hasenstab, "Aboriginal Settlement Patterns in Late Woodland

Upper New York State"; Clinton, *Memoir on the Antiquities*, 6. Ephraim Squier mentioned relics taken from near Auburn in *Antiques of the State of New York*, 49.

25. Brooke, *Refiner's Fire*, 163 and 366n49, which suggests comparing photographs of the Whitmer stone in Quinn, *Early Mormonism and the Magic World View* with artifacts in Ritchie, *The Archaeology of New York State*, 181, 219, 222, 224, 249.

26. ("money diggers") Lorenzo Saunders to Thomas Gregg, January 28, 1885, in Vogel, ed. *Early Mormon Documents*, 3:186; Pomeroy Tucker, *Origin, Rise and Progress of Mormonism*, reprinted in Vogel, *Early Mormon Documents*, 3:104; Smith, "History, 1832," 7; Bushman, *Joseph Smith*, 61–62.

27. All citations to the Book of Mormon are from Skousen, *The Book of Mormon: The Earliest Text*. I have used biblical-style citations but, for convenience, added page numbers to Skousen's edition. "Reformed Egyptian" mentioned in Mormon 9:32–34, 672. For the only presumed surviving example of "Reformed Egyptian," see the "Anthon Transcript," transcript from 1828, which Martin Harris brought to Columbia professor Charles Anthon: Vogel, *Early Mormon Documents*, 4:414–17. My summary of the translation process is derived from Bushman, *Joseph Smith*, 61–83. See also Brooke, *Refiner's Fire*, 142, 361n42.

28. 1 Nephi 1:13, 6–7; quote from 1 Nephi 18:2, 56.

29. Parfitt, *The Lost Tribes of Israel*, 3; Benite, *The Ten Lost Tribes*, 8–11.

30. Parfitt, *Lost Tribes*, 1–6; Brooke, *Refiner's Fire*, 35; Benite, *The Ten Lost Tribes*, 174–75; 1 Nephi 5:14, 17; 3 Nephi 17:4, 609. For prophecy and the Lost Tribes, see Parfitt, *Lost Tribes*, 4.

31. Ethan Smith, *View of the Hebrews*, 85, 86 (quotes), 88–92.

32. 1 Nephi 18:24–15; Nephi 19:1, 59–60; 2 Nephi 5:7–25, 89–90.

33. 2 Nephi 10:1–10, 104–5; Alma 4:1–10, 288–89; Helaman 4:2–13, 517–18; 3 Nephi 1:4–30, 565–75; 3 Nephi 11:1–26:21, 593–633; Brooke, *Refiner's Fire*, 4; Shipps, *Mormonism*, ix–x.

34. Oliver Cowdery to W. W. Phelps, July 1835, in Vogel, *Early Mormon Documents*, 2:449. For Clinton, see chapter 4.

35. ("Zedekiah") Omni 1:12–19, 187–88, quote on 187; ("small neck") Alma 22:32–33, 362–63. quote on 363; ("narrow neck") Ether 10:20, 700; ("many waters") Mormon 6:4, 660; Mormon 8:4, 664. Interested parties have devoted considerable time to locating the places described in the book, especially Zarahemla. Unsurprisingly, these debates are also contentious and unresolvable. Michael de Groote, "The Fight over Book of Mormon Geography," *Deseret News*, May 27, 2010. Researchers associated with the Foundation for Apologetic and Information Research (FAIR) have placed the Book of Mormon's events near the Isthmus of Panama. This twentieth-century view sees the Hill Cumorah as different from the battlefield described on the plates. For a summary and their bibliography, see

http://www.fairlds.org/wp-content/uploads/2011/12/ash-Where_Did_the_Book_of_Mormon_Take_Place.pdf, accessed September 14, 2018].

36. Jacob 7:25, 179; Jarom 1:7, 184; quotes from Alma 48:8, 449.

37. 1 Nephi 12:4, 31; 3 Nephi 8:5–23, 586–87; 4 Nephi 1:8–9, 643.

38. 1 Nephi 18:24–25, 59; Jarom 1:8, 184; Alma 43:18, 429; 3 Nephi 3:22, 572; Clinton, "Address on the Iroquois," in Campbell, *Life and Writings of DeWitt Clinton*, 264. For the non-Indian nature of the Book of Mormon, see Bushman, *Joseph Smith*, 97. For the development of agriculture, the domestication of animals, and associated technological advancements, see Diamond, *Guns, Germs, and Steel*, charts on 100, 126–27, 167, 362–63.

39. Joseph Smith, "Recital to Robert Matthews, 9 November 1835," in Vogel, *Early Mormon Documents*, 1:44; Smith, "Historical Sketch, March 1, 1842," in Jessee, *Personal Writings of Joseph Smith*, 215.

40. 2 Nephi 5, 90.

41. Fox-Genovese and Genovese, *Mind of the Master Class*, 522; James H. Sweet, "The Iberian Roots of American Racist Thought"; Silverman, "The Curse of God."

42. Enos 1:20, 182; Mosiah 22:6–11, 253.

43. Ethan Smith, *View of the Hebrews*, 93–104, quote on 103; Greer, *The Jesuit Relations*, 28–29, 41–42; Alma 17:3–5, 343; Alma 22:8–11, 359. See, for example, Clinton, "The Iroquois," in Campbell, *Life and Writings*, 217. Indian speeches also contained this phrase: "Substance of the Speech of Good Peter to Governor Clinton and the Commissioners of Indian Affairs, at Albany, on the occasion referred to in the discourse," in Campbell, ed. *Life and Writings*, 379. For Palmyra, see *Palmyra Register* July 19, 1820.

44. ("trodden under foot") Alma 46:22, 442; Helaman 4:20–26, 519–20; Helaman 7:17–24, 532–33. See the discussion of Isaac Watts's "Hymn for New England" in chapter 2. For Puritan New England's view of Indian warfare as God's punishment, see Jill Lepore, *The Name of War*, 97–105, Mather quoted on 99.

45. Bushman, *Joseph Smith*, 98; Alma 53:2–20, 470–71; Helman 13:4–12, 550–51; Helman 15:7, 559.

46. Clinton, *Memoir on the Antiquities*, 1; Enos 1:13, 181; Mosiah 1:5, 192; Jarom 1:2, 183–84; Alma 37:9; Moroni 1:4, 717; Mormon 8:15–16, 665. For significant, nuanced scholarship on Native Americans and writing, see Shoemaker, *A Strange Likeness*, chap. 3; Lisa Brooks, *The Common Pot*.

47. *Ithaca Journal*, April 28, 1830.

48. Bushman, *Joseph Smith*, 95; Cross, *The Burned-Over District*, 146.

49. Jason Whitman, "The Book of Mormon," *Christian Intelligencer and Eastern Chronicle* January 24, 1834.

50. Dennis, *Seneca Possessed*, 54–55. See chapter 2 for clearing the land. For a differing conclusion about the Book of Mormon's Indian narrative, see Bushman, *Joseph Smith*, 98.

Conclusion

1. Smith, *A Book of Commandments*, 48:27–28.

2. Farmer, *On Zion's Mount*, 36–38. For an introduction to the vast literature on the Trail of Tears and removal, see Perdue and Green, *The Cherokee Nation and the Trail of Tears*.

3. Smith, *The Doctrine and Covenants of the Church*, 28:8–9, 42, 57:3, 89.

4. For Cahokia, see Pauketat, *Cahokia*. The origins, scale, and collapse of Cahokia remain a subject of debate. See also Pauketat, *Ancient Cahokia and the Mississippians*; Milner, *The Cahokia Chiefdom*; Fowler, *Cahokia*; Koepke, *Envisioning Cahokia*. For knowledge of Cahokia in Upstate New York, see, for example, *Watch-tower*, August 30, 1830.

5. Smith, *History, 1838–1856*, vol. A-1, 482–83, Smith Papers. The document has been edited, and I have included original phrases that were later crossed out. For more detail on Zion's Camp, see Bushman, *Joseph Smith*, 235–47.

6. Smith, *History, 1838–1856*, vol. A-1, 483, Smith Papers. The Book of Mormon also contains the suggestive but less geographically specific name of "Onidah": Alma 32:4 and Alma 47:5. For a survey of the Naples 8 mound, see Farnsworth, "Lamanitish Arrows and Eagles with Lead Eyes."

7. Bushman, *Joseph Smith*, 342–46; Gentry, "Adam-ondi-Ahman"; quotation from Smith, "The Scriptory Book—of Joseph Smith Jr.—President of the Church of Jesus Christ, of Latterday Saints In all the World," Journal, March–September 1838, 43–44, Smith Papers.

8. LeSueur, *The 1838 Mormon War in Missouri*, 29, 38–53, 58–64, 177–79, 219–44, Rigdon quoted on 50; Bushman, *Joseph Smith*, 355–72, Boggs quoted on 365.

9. Christian, "Mormon Foreknowledge of the West," 404–5; Jessee, "Joseph Smith's 19 July 1840 Discourse," 392; Matthew 18:20 from Coogan, *New Oxford Annotated Bible*, 1772; Smith's 1844 pronouncement quoted in Farmer, *On Zion's Mount*, 37.

10. Bushman, *Joseph Smith*, 539–50.

11. Howe, *What Hath God Wrought*, 727–31; Farmer, *On Zion's Mount*, 20–24.

12. Packer, "Acquiring Cumorah," 29–50

13. Gerritsen, "The Hill Cumorah Monument," 125–35, quote on 132. For the historic site, see http://www.hillcumorah.org.

14. Andrew Jackson, "Transcript of President Andrew Jackson's Message to Congress 'On Indian Removal'" (1830), http://www.ourdocuments.gov/doc.php?-flash=true&doc=25&page=transcript, accessed September 17, 2018.

15. Richter, *Facing East from Indian Country*, 189–236; Hauptman, *Conspiracy of Interests*, 114–20.

16. Tiro, *The People of the Standing Stone*, 133–56; Oberg, *Professional Indian*, 1–14, 45, 62–69, 77–106; Campisi, "Oneida," 485; Horsman, "The Origins of Oneida Removal to Wisconsin"; Cornelius et al., "Contemporary Oneida Perspectives of Oneida History," 127–33.

17. Hauptman, *Conspiracy of Interests*, 154–61; Blau, Campisi, and Tooker, "Onondaga"; White, Engelbrecht, and Tooker, "Cayuga," 502–3; Abler and Tooker, "Seneca," 511; Landy, "Tuscarora among the Iroquois."

18. Tiro, *People of the Standing Stone*, 97, 163–67, 193; Campisi, "Oneida," 485; West, *Contested Plains*.

19. Pauketat, *Cahokia*, 2–3, 25–29; Brackenridge, *Views of Louisiana*, 187.

20. Lepper, "Early Historic American Indian Testimony." Perhaps the more egalitarian descendants of the Mississippians deliberately forgot Cahokia. See Pauketat, *Cahokia*, 159–60.

21. *Rochester Democrat and Chronicle*, June 20 and 22, 1894.

22. *New York Times*, June 23, 1894. For the evidence of Montour's activities, see *New York Times*, August 13, 1893. The *Times* correctly noted that Montour could not have been buried at the post, but based this conclusion on the continued Revolutionary War activity of the Patriot-allied John Montour—that is, the wrong Montour." Address of John L. Sexton," in Erwin, *Early History of Painted Post*, 71–72.

23. Deloria, *Playing Indian*, 38–70; Miller, *The New Four Winds Guide to American Indian Artifacts*, 147–92; Powell, *Vanishing America*, 121–24.

24. Litchman, *Official History of the Improved Order of Red Men*, 49; Wallace, *Death and Rebirth of the Seneca*, 244; Campisi and Starna, "On the Road to Canandaigua."

25. Litchmen, ed., *Official History*, 11, 12, 15; Allen, "Conclusion," 84.

26. Allen, "Conclusion," 84.

27. Erwin, *Early History of Painted Post*, 6–7.

28. Erwin, *Early History of Painted Post*, 7.

29. For an example of the stakes surrounding America's ancient past, see the ongoing debate about the population of the Americas in 1492, summarized in Mann, *1491*, 110–51. For thoughtful studies that address violence, place, and memory, see Brooks, *Our Beloved Kin*; Brooks, *Mesa of Sorrows*; DeLucia, *Memory Lands*; Kelman, *A Misplaced Massacre*.

| Bibliography

Archival Material

Covenhoven, Robert. Revolutionary War Pension and Bounty—Land Warrant Application Files. Publication Number M804, Catalog ID 30022. RG15. Pension Number S. 12574. National Archives.

Cusick, Nicholas. Revolutionary War Pension and Bounty—Land Warrant Application Files. Publication Number M804, Catalog ID 300022. RG15. Pension Number S. 18788. National Archives.

Draper Manuscripts. State Historical Society of Wisconsin.

Evans, Lewis. *A General Map of the Middle British Colonies in North America* (1755). Library of Congress, Geography and Maps Division.

Johnson, Guy. *Map of the Country of the Six Nations Proper* (1771; reprint 1851), New York Public Library.

King, William. "Notes on a Visit to Western New York in 1810." Mss. A00–256. Buffalo and Erie County Historical Society Archives.

Kirkland, Samuel. Papers. Hamilton College Archives.

Mitchell, John. *A Map of the British and French Dominions in North America* (1755). Library of Congress, Geography and Maps Division.

Petterson, Benjamin. Revolutionary War Pension and Bounty—Land Warrant Application Files. Publication Number M804, Catalog ID 30022. RG15. Pension Number R. 8010. National Archives.

Smith, Joseph. Papers. https://www.josephsmithpapers.org/.

Published Works

Abler, Thomas S., ed. *Chainbreaker: The Revolutionary War Memoirs of Governor Blacksnake*. Lincoln: University of Nebraska Press, 1989.

———. *Cornplanter: Chief Warrior of the Allegany Senecas*. Syracuse NY: Syracuse University Press, 2007.

Abler, Thomas S., and Elisabeth Tooker. "Seneca." In *Northeast*, vol. 15 of *Handbook of North American Indians*, edited by Bruce G. Trigger, 505–17. Washington DC: Smithsonian Institution, 1978.

Adair, James. *The History of the American Indians; particularly Those Nations adjoining to the Missisippi, East and West Florida, Georgia, South and North Carolina, and Virginia.* London: Edward and Charles Dilly, 1775.

Adams, John Quincy. "Society and Civilization." *American Whig Review* 2, no. 1 (July 1845): 80–90.

Adler, Jeanne Winston, ed. *Chainbreaker's War: A Seneca Chief Remembers the American Revolution.* Hensonville NY: Black Dome, 2002.

Allen, W. A. Conclusion. In *Early History of Painted Post and the Town of Erwin*, edited by Charles E. Erwin, 84–85. Painted Post NY: Automatic, 1917.

"American Chronology. Containing, An Accurate and Comprehensive Account of the Most remarkable Events and memorable Occurrences of the New York, From its first Discovery to the present Times, most particularly as to what respects the United States; Interspersed with such Foreign Transactions as appear most interesting in the History of the World." *New York Magazine, or Literary Repository* 1, no. 12 (December 1790): 1.

American Sunday School Union. *History of the Delaware and Iroquois Indians, formerly Inhabiting the Middle States with Various Anecdotes, Illustrating Their Manners and Customs.* Philadelphia: American Sunday School Union, 1832.

Anderson, Chad. "The Built Landscape and the Conquest of Iroquoia, 1750–1820." In *Investing in the Early Modern Built Environment: Europeans, Asians, Settlers, and Indigenous Societies*, edited by Carole Shammas, 265–94. Leiden: Brill, 2012.

———. "Rediscovering Native North America: Settlements, Maps, and Empires in the Eastern Woodlands." *Early American Studies: An Interdisciplinary Journal* 14, no. 3 (Summer 2016): 478–505.

Anderson, Fred. *Crucible of War: The Seven Years' War and the Fate of Empire in British North America, 1754–1766.* New York: Vintage, 2001.

Anderson, Lisa M. "Vine Valley Revisited." In *Golden Chronograph for Robert E. Funk*, edited by Chris Lindner and Edward V. Curtis, 155–61. Occasional Publications in Northeast Anthropology, no. 15. Bethlehem CT: Archaeological Services, 1996.

Axtell, James. "Colonial America without the Indians: Counterfactual Reflections." *Journal of American History* 73, no. 4 (March 1987): 981–96.

Barr, Juliana, and Edward Countryman, eds. *Contested Spaces of Early America.* Philadelphia: University of Pennsylvania Press, 2014.

Bartram, John. *Observations on the Inhabitants, Climate, Soil, Rivers, Productions, Animals, and other matters worthy of Notice. Made by John Bartram, in his Travels from Pensilvania to Onondaga, Oswego and the Lake Ontario in Canada.* London: J. Whiston and B. White, 1751.

Basso, Keith. *Wisdom Sits in Places: Landscape and Language among the Western Apache.* Albuquerque: University of New Mexico Press, 1996.

Beauchamp, William M. *Aboriginal Place Names of New York.* Albany: New York State Education Department, 1907.

———. "The Great Mosquito." *Journal of American Folklore* 2, no. 7 (October–December 1889): 284.

———. *Iroquois Folk Lore.* Syracuse NY: Dehler, 1922. Reprinted New York: AMS, 1976.

———, ed. *Moravian Journals Relating to Central New York, 1745–66.* Syracuse: Dehler, 1916. Reprinted New York: AMS, 1976.

———. *Perch Lake Mounds, with Notes on Other New York Mounds, and Some Accounts of Indian Trails.* Albany: New York State Education Department, Bulletin 87, Archaeology 10 (1905). Reprinted New York: AMS, 1976.

Beardsley, Levi. *Reminiscences; Personal and Other Incidents; Early Settlement of Otsego County; Notices and Anecdotes of Public Men; Judicial, Legal and Legislative Matters; Field Sports; Dissertations and Discussions.* New York: Charles Vinten, 1852.

Belknap, Jeremy. *American Biography; or, An historical account of those persons who have been distinguished in America, as adventurers, statesmen, philosophers, divines, warriors, authors and other remarkable characters.* Boston: Isaiah Thomas and Ebenezer T. Andrews, 1794.

———. "Dr. Belknap's Tour to Oneida, 1796." In *In Mohawk Country: Early Narratives about a Native People*, edited by Dean R. Snow, Charles T. Gehring, and William A. Starna, 354–55. Syracuse NY: Syracuse University Press, 1996.

Belknap, Jeremy, and Jedidiah Morse. "The Report of a Committee of the Board of Correspondents of the Scots Society for Propagating Christian Knowledge, who Visited the Oneida and Mohekunuh Indians in 1796." In Collections of the Massachusetts Historical Society for the Year 1798. Boston: Samuel Hall, 1798. Reprinted Boston: John H. Eastburn, 1835.

Benite, Zvi Ben-Dor. *The Ten Lost Tribes: A World History.* New York: Oxford University Press, 2009.

Berkhofer, Robert F., Jr. *The White Man's Indian: Images of the American Indian from Columbus to the Present.* New York: Vintage, 1978.

Bierhorst, John. *Mythology of the Lenape: Guide and Texts.* Tucson: University of Arizona Press, 1996.

Blau, Harold, Jack Campisi, and Elisabeth Tooker. "Onondaga." In *Northeast*, vol. 15 of *Handbook of North American Indians*, edited by Bruce G. Trigger, 496. Washington DC: Smithsonian Institution, 1978.

Boewe, Charles, ed. *The Correspondence of C. S. Rafinesque.* Philadelphia: American Philosophical Society, 2011, CD-ROM.

———. *John D. Clifford's Indian Antiquities: Related Materials by C. S. Rafinesque.* Knoxville: University of Tennessee Press, 2000,

———. *Life of C. S. Rafinesque: A Man of Uncommon Zeal.* Philadelphia: American Philosophical Society, 2011.

Boyce, Douglas W. "'As the Wind Scatters the Smoke': The Tuscaroras in the Eighteenth Century." In *Beyond the Covenant Chain: The Iroquois and Their Neighbors in Indian North America, 1600–1800,* edited by Daniel K. Richter and James Merrell, 153–61. University Park: Pennsylvania State University Press, 2003.

Brackenridge, H. M. *Views of Louisiana: Together with a Journal of a Voyage up the Missouri River, in 1811.* Pittsburgh: Cramer, Spear and Eichbaum, 1814.

Brandão, José António. *"Your Fyre Shall Burn No More": Iroquois Policy toward New France and Its Native Allies to 1701.* 1997. Lincoln: University of Nebraska Press, 2000.

Brandão, José António, and William A. Starna. "'Some Things May Slip Out of Your Memory and Be Forgott': The 1701 Deed and Map of Iroquois Hunting Territory Revisited." *New York History* 86, no. 4 (Fall 2005): 417–33.

Breen, T. H. "Creative Adaptations: Peoples and Cultures." In *Colonial British America: Essays in the New History of the Early Modern Era,* edited by Jack P. Greene and J. R. Pole, 195–232. Baltimore: Johns Hopkins University Press, 1984.

Broadie, Alexander, ed. *The Cambridge Companion to the Scottish Enlightenment.* Cambridge: Cambridge University Press, 2003.

Brooke, John L. *The Refiner's Fire: The Making of Mormon Cosmology, 1644–1844.* New York: Cambridge University Press, 1994.

Brooks, Charles E. "Overrun with Bushes: Frontier Land Development and the Forest History of the Holland Land Purchase." *Forest and Conservation History* 39, no. 1 (January 1995): 17–26.

Brooks, James F. *Mesa of Sorrows: A History of the Awat'ovi Massacre.* New York: W. W. Norton, 2016.

Brooks, Lisa. *The Common Pot: The Recovery of Native Space in the Northeast.* Minneapolis: University of Minnesota Press, 2008.

———. *Our Beloved Kin: A New History of King Philip's War.* New Haven CT: Yale University Press, 2018.

Brose, David S. "Penumbral Protohistory on Lake Erie's South Shore." In *Societies in Eclipse: Archaeology of the Eastern Woodlands Indians, A.D. 1400–1700,* edited by David S. Brose et al., 49–65. Washington DC: Smithsonian Institution Press, 2001.

Brydon, Sherry. "Ingenuity in Art: The Early 19th-Century Works of David and Dennis Cusick." *American Indian Art* 20, no. 2 (Spring 1995): 60–69.

Bullock, William. "Sketch of a Journey through the Western States of North America, from New Orleans, by the Mississippi, Ohio, City of Cincinnati and Falls of Niagara, to New York, in 1827." In *Early Western Travels, 1748–1846,* edited by Reuben Gold Thwaites, 19: 119–58. Cleveland: Arthur H. Clark, 1905.

Bushman, Richard Lyman. *Joseph Smith, Rough Stone Rolling: A Cultural Biography of Mormonism's Founder.* New York: Vintage, 2005.

———. *The Refinement of America: Persons, Houses, Cities.* New York: Knopf, 1992.

Caines, George. *New-York Term Reports of Cases Argued and Determined in the Supreme Court of That State.* Vol. 2. New York: Isaac Riley, 1805.

Calloway, Colin G. *New Worlds for All: Indians, Europeans, and the Remaking of Early America.* Baltimore: Johns Hopkins University Press, 1997.

Campbell, Thomas. *Gertrude of Wyoming; A Pennsylvania Tale.* London: Longman, Hurst, Rees, and Orme, 1809.

Campbell, William W. *Annals of Tryon County; or the Border Warfare of New-York during the Revolution.* New York: J. & J. Harper, 1831.

———. *The Border Warfare of New York, during the Revolution; or, The Annals of Tryon County.* New York: Baker and Scribner, 1849.

———. *The Life and Writings of DeWitt Clinton.* New York: Baker and Scribner, 1849.

Campisi, Jack. "Oneida." In *Northeast,* vol. 15 of *Handbook of North American Indians,* edited by Bruce G. Trigger, 481–90. Washington DC: Smithsonian Institution, 1978.

Campisi, Jack, and William A. Starna. "On the Road to Canandaigua: The Treaty of 1794." *American Indian Quarterly* 19, no. 4 (Autumn 1995): 467–90.

Carver, Jonathan. *Three Years Travels throughout the Interior Parts of North America.* Boston: Samuel Etheridge, 1803.

Chapman, Isaac. *A Sketch of the History of Wyoming.* Wilkes-Barre PA: Sharp D. Lewis, 1830.

Child, Hamilton. *Gazetteer and Business Directory of Steuben County, N.Y. for 1868.* Syracuse NY: Journal Office, 1868.

Christian, Lewis Clark. "Mormon Foreknowledge of the West." *Brigham Young Studies* 21 (Fall 1981): 403–15.

Clark, Joshua Victor Hopkins. *Onondaga; or, Reminiscences of Earlier and Later Times; Being a Series of Historical Sketches Relative to Onondaga; with Notes on the Several Towns in the County, and Oswego.* 2 vols. Syracuse NY: Stoddard and Babcock, 1849.

Clinton, DeWitt. "Introductory Discourse Delivered before the Society on 4th of May, 1814, by DeWitt Clinton, LL. D. President of the Literary and

Philosophical Society of New York, Fellow of the American Philosophical Society, of the American Antiquarian Society; President of the American Academy of Arts, &c." In *Transactions of the Literary and Philosophical Society of New York* I (1814): 19–184. New York: Van Winkle and Wiley, 1815.

———. "The Iroquois." In *The Life and Writings of DeWitt Clinton*, edited by William W. Campbell, 205–66. New York: Baker and Scribner, 1849.

———. *A Memoir on the Antiquities of the Western Parts of the State of New-York: Read before the Literary and Philosophical Society of New-York.* Albany: I. W. Clark, 1818.

Coates, Irving W. *Onnaghee. A Visit to the Site of the Ancient Seneca Village, or Castle of "Onnaghee" and Its Burial Place, Situated on Fall Brook, on Lot No. 20, in Western Part of Town of Hopewell, Ontario County, N.Y. August 8, 1882.* Canandaigua NY: privately printed, 1892; reprinted from *Ontario County Times.*

Colden, Cadwallader. *The History of the Five Nations Depending on the Province of New York in America and are the Barrier between the English and French in that Part of the World.* Edited by John M. Dixon and Karim M. Tiro. Ithaca: Cornell University Press, 2016.

Coleman, Jon T. *Vicious: Wolves and Men in America.* New Haven CT: Yale University Press, 2004.

"Consequences of the Discovery of America and the Indies." *New York Magazine, or Literary Repository*, October 1793, 579–84.

Coogan, Michael D., ed. *The New Oxford Annotated Bible: New Revised Standard Version with the Apocrypha.* 4th ed. New York: Oxford University Press, 2010.

Cook, Frederick, ed. *Journals of the Military Expedition of Major General John Sullivan against the Six Nations of Indians in 1779 with Records of Centennial Celebrations.* Auburn NY: Knapp, Peck & Thomson, 1887.

Cooper, William. *A Guide in the Wilderness; or, The History of the First Settlement in the Western Counties of New York, with Useful Instructions to Future Settlers.* Dublin: Gilbert & Hodges, 1810. Reprinted Cooperstown NY: Freeman's Journal, 1936.

Cornelius, Amelia, et al. "Contemporary Oneida Perspectives of Oneida History." In *The Oneida Indian Journey: From New York to Wisconsin, 1784–1860*, edited by Laurence M. Hauptman and L. Gordon McLester III, 126–44. Madison: University of Wisconsin Press, 1999.

Cornplanter, Jesse J. *Legends of the Longhouse.*1938. Port Washington NY: Ira J. Friedman, 1963.

Cornog, Evan. *The Birth of Empire: DeWitt Clinton and the American Experience.* New York: Oxford University Press, 1998.

Coventry, Alexander. *Memoirs of an Emigrant: The Journal of Alexander Coventry, M.D.*, vol. 2. Albany NY: Albany Institute, 1978.

Cowan, Helen I. *Charles Williamson: Genesee Promoter, Friend of Anglo-American Rapprochement.* Rochester NY: Rochester Historical Society, 1941. Reprinted Clifton NJ: Augustus M. Kelley, 1973.

Cronon, William. *Changes in the Land: Indians, Colonists, and the Ecology of New England.* New York: Hill and Wang, 1983.

Cross, Whitney. *The Burned-Over District: The Social and Intellectual History of Enthusiastic Religion in Western New York, 1800–1850.* Ithaca NY: Cornell University Press, 1950.

Cruikshank, Ernest Alexander, ed. *Records of Niagara: A Collection of Documents Related to the First Settlement, 1778–1783.* Niagara-on-the-Lake ON: Niagara Historical Society, 1927.

———. *The Story of Butler's Rangers and the Settlement of Niagara.* Welland ON: Tribune, 1893.

Curtin, Jeremiah, and John Napoleon Brinton Hewitt. *Seneca Fiction, Legends, Myths.* Thirty-Second Annual Report of the Bureau of American Ethnology. Washington DC: Smithsonian Institute, 1918.

Cusick, David. *Sketches of Ancient History of the Six Nations.* In *The Iroquois Trail*, edited by William Beauchamp. Fayetteville NY: H. C. Beauchamp, 1892. Reprinted New York: AMS, 1976.

Davies, K. G., ed. *Documents of the American Revolution*, vol. 15. Dublin: Irish Academy Press, 1976.

Dawson, Henry B. *Battles of the United States, by Sea and Land.* 2 vols. New York: Johnson, Fry, 1858.

Day, Sherman. *Historical Collections of the State of Pennsylvania; Containing a Copious Selection of the Most Interesting Facts, Traditions, Biographical Sketches, Anecdotes, etc., Relating to the History and Antiquities, Both General and Local, with Topographical Descriptions of Every County and All the Larger Towns in the State.* Philadelphia: George W. Gorton, 1843.

De Kay, James E. *Zoology of New-York, the New-York Fauna; Comprising Detailed Descriptions of All the Animals Hitherto Observed within the State of New-York.* Albany: W. and A. White & J. Visscher, 1842.

Dean, James. "Mythology of the Iroquois, or Six Nations of Indians." In *The Oneida Creation Story*, translated and edited by Floyd G. Lounsbury and Bryan Gick, 157–62. Lincoln: University of Nebraska Press, 2000.

Deloria, Phillip J. *Playing Indian.* New Haven CT: Yale University Press, 1999.

DeLucia, Christine M. *Memory Lands: King Philip's War and the Place of Violence in the Northeast.* New Haven CT: Yale University Press, 2018.

Dennis, Matthew. *Seneca Possessed: Indians, Witchcraft, and Power in the Early American Republic.* Philadelphia: University of Pennsylvania Press, 2010.

"Description of a Remarkable Tooth, in the Possession of Mr. Peale." *Columbian Magazine* 1, no. 13 (September 1787): 655.

Diamond, Jared. *Guns, Germs, and Steel: The Fates of Human Societies.* New York: W. W. Norton, 1997.

Doty, Lockwood L. *A History of Livingston County, New York: From Its Earliest Traditions to Its Part in the War for the Union.* Genesso NY: Edward E. Doty, 1876.

Duncan, John Morison. *Travels through Part of the United States and Canada in 1818 and 1819.* 2 vols. New York: W. B. Gilley, 1823.

Early, Carville. "Place Your Bets: Rates of Frontier Expansion in American History, 1650–1890." In *Cultural Encounters with the Environment: Enduring and Evolving Geographic Themes,* edited by Alexander B. Murphy and Douglas L. Johnson with Viola Haarmann, 79–105. Lanham MD: Rowman & Littlefield, 2000.

Edelson, S. Max. *The New Map of Empire: How Britain Imagined America before Independence.* Cambridge MA: Harvard University Press, 2017.

Egle, William H., ed. *Pennsylvania Archives,* 2nd ser., vol. 14. Harrisburg: State of Pennsylvania, 1888.

Elm, Demus, and Harvey Antone. *The Oneida Creation Story.* Translated and edited by Floyd G. Lounsbury and Bryan Gick. Lincoln: University of Nebraska Press, 2000.

Engelbrecht, William. *Iroquoia: The Development of a Native World.* Syracuse NY: Syracuse University Press, 2003.

Erwin, Charles E. *Early History of Painted Post and the Town of Erwin: Containing an Authentic Record of Its Traditions, Divisions, Important Events and Statistics, from 1779 to 1874 and Several Brief Sketches of Some of the Most Prominent Pioneers.* Painted Post NY: Automatic, 1917.

Faragher, John Mack. *Daniel Boone: The Life and the Legend of an American Pioneer.* New York: Henry Holt, 1992.

———. *Sugar Creek: Life on the Illinois Prairie.* New Haven CT: Yale University Press, 1986.

Farmer, Jared. *On Zion's Mount: Mormons, Indians, and the American Landscape.* Cambridge MA: Harvard University Press, 2008.

Farnsworth, Kenneth B. "Lamanitish Arrows and Eagles with Lead Eyes: Tales of the First Recorded Explorations in an Illinois Valley Hopewell Mound." *Illinois Archaeology* 22, no. 1 (2010): 25–48.

Feder, Kenneth L. *Encyclopedia of Dubious Archaeology: From Atlantis to the Walum Olum.* Santa Barbara CA: Greenwood, 2010.

Feest, Christian F. "Nanticoke and Neighboring Tribes." In *Handbook of North American Indians*, edited by Bruce G. Trigger, 2:240. Washington DC: Smithsonian Institution, 1978.

———. "Virginia Algonquians." In *Handbook of North American Indians*, edited by Bruce G. Trigger, 2:256. Washington DC: Smithsonian Institution, 1978.

Fenton, William N. *The Great Law and the Longhouse: A Political History of the Iroquois Confederacy*. Norman: University of Oklahoma Press, 1998.

———. "The Journal of James Emlen Kept on a Trip to Canandaigua, New York." *Ethnohistory* 12, no. 4 (Autumn 1965): 279–342.

———. "The Lore of the Longhouse: Myth, Ritual, and Red Power." *Anthropology Quarterly* 48, no. 3 (July 1975): 131–47.

Ferber, Linda S. *The Hudson River School: Nature and the American Vision*. New York: Skira Rizzoli, 2009.

Fitzpatrick, James C., ed. *The Writings of George Washington from the Original Manuscript Sources*, vol. 27. Available online, Washington Resources at the University of Virginia Library: http://etext.virginia.edu/toc/modeng/public/WasFi27.html, accessed September 17, 2018.

Fitzpatrick, T. J. *Rafinesque: A Sketch of His Life with Bibliography*. Des Moines: Historical Department of Iowa, 1911.

Foote, Kenneth E. *Shadowed Ground: America's Landscapes of Violence and Tragedy*. Austin: University of Texas Press, 2003.

Fowler, Melvin. *Cahokia: The Great American Metropolis*. Urbana: University of Illinois Press, 2001.

Fox-Genovese, Elizabeth, and Eugene Genovese. *The Mind of the Master Class: History and Faith in the Southern Slaveholders' Worldview*. New York: Cambridge University Press, 2005.

Frazier Nash, Roderick. *Wilderness and the American Mind*. 5th ed. New Haven CT: Yale University Press, 2014.

French, John Horner. *Gazetteer of the State of New York: Embracing a Comprehensive View of the Geography, Geology, and General History of the State, and a Complete History and Description of Every County, City, Town, Village, and Locality*. Syracuse NY: R. Pearsall Smith, 1860.

Frisch, Betty Coit. "The Divers Lake Quarry Site—Genesee County, New York." *New York State Archaeological Association Bulletin* 66 (March 1976): 8–18.

Gentry, Leland H. "Adam-ondi-Ahman: A Brief Historical Survey." *BYU Studies* 13, no. 4 (1973): 553–76.

Gerritsen, Allen P. "The Hill Cumorah Monument: An Inspired Creation of Torleif S. Knaphus." *Journal of Book of Mormon Studies* 13, no. 1–2 (2004): 125–35, 173.

Goodwin, H. C. *Pioneer History; or Cortland County and the Border Wars of New York. From the Earliest Period to the Present Time.* New York: A. B. Burdick, 1859.

Gould, Jay. *History of Delaware County and Border Wars of New York.* Roxbury NY: Kenny & Gould, 1856.

Gray, Andrew. "Extract of a Letter from the Rev. Andrew Gray, Missionary among the Tuscaroras; dated Tuscarora Village, Dec. 8, 1809." *Christian's Magazine: Designed to Promote Knowledge and Influence of Evangelical Truth and Order* 3, no. 2 (February 1, 1810): 105–9.

Graymont, Barbara. *The Iroquois in the American Revolution.* Syracuse NY: Syracuse University Press, 1972.

Greer, Allan, ed. *The Jesuit Relations: Natives and Missionaries in Seventeenth-Century North America.* New York: Bedford/St. Martin's, 2000.

Gross, Robert. *The Minutemen and Their World.* 1976. Reprinted New York: Hill and Wang, 2001.

Haas, Marilyn. *The Seneca and Tuscarora Indians: An Annotated Bibliography.* Native American Bibliography Series no. 17. Metuchen NJ: Scarecrow, 1994.

Hall, Francis. *Travels in Canada and the United States, in 1816 and 1817.* London: Longman, Hurst, Rees, Orme, & Brown, 1818.

Hall, Roger, William Westfall, and Laurel Sefton MacDowell, eds. *Patterns of the Past: Interpreting Ontario's History.* Toronto: Dundurn, 1988.

Hamell, George R. "The Panther in Huron-Wyandot and Seneca Myth, Ritual, and Material Culture." In *Icons of Power: Feline Symbolism in the Americas,* edited by Nicholas J. Saunders, 258–87. New York: Routledge, 1998.

———. "Strawberries, Floating Islands, and Rabbit Captains: Mythical Realities and European Contact in the Northeast during the Sixteenth and Seventeenth Centuries." *Journal of Canadian Studies* 21, no. 4 (Winter 1986–87): 72–94.

Harris, George H. *The Life of Horatio Jones.* Publications of the Buffalo Historical Society, vol. 6. Buffalo NY: Buffalo Historical Society, 1906.

Harris, Jonathan. "New York's First Scientific Body: The Literary and Philosophical Society, 1814–1834." *Annals of the New York Academy of Sciences* 196 (December 1972): 329–37.

Hart, John P. "New Dates from Classic New York Sites: Just How Old Are Those Longhouses?" *Northeast Anthropology* 60 (Fall 2000): 1–22.

Hart, John P. and Hetty Jo Brumbach. "The Death of Owasco." *American Antiquity* 68, no. 4 (October 2003): 737–52.

Hart, John P., Hetty Jo Brumbach, and Robert Lusteck. "Extending the Phytolith Evidence for Early Maize (*Zea mays* ssp. *mays*) and Squash (*Cucurbita sp.*) in Central New York." *American Antiquity* 72, no. 3 (July 2007): 563–83.

Hart, John P., and C. Margaret Scarry. "The Age of Common Beans (*Phaseolus vulgaris*) in the Northeastern United States." *American Antiquity* 64, no. 4 (October 1999): 653–58.

Hart, John P., Robert G. Thompson, and Hetty Jo Brumbach. "Phytolith Evidence for Early Maize (*Zea mays*) in the Northern Finger Lakes Region of New York." In *Archaeology of the Iroquois: Selected Readings and Research Sources*, edited by Jordan E. Kerber, 93–123. Syracuse NY: Syracuse University Press, 2007.

Harvey, Oscar Jewell. *A History of Wilkes-Barré, Luzerne County, Pennsylvania.* 2 vols. Wilkes-Barre PA, 1909.

Hasenstab, Robert J. "Aboriginal Settlement Patterns in Late Woodland Upper New York State." In *Archaeology of the Iroquois: Selected Readings and Research Sources*, edited by Jordan E. Kerber, 164–73. Syracuse NY: Syracuse University Press, 2007.

Hastings, Hugh, ed. *Public Papers of George Clinton, First Governor of New York, 1777–1795.* Vol. 4. Albany NY: James B. Lyon, 1900.

Hauptman, Laurence M. *Conspiracy of Interests: Iroquois Dispossession and the Rise of New York State.* Syracuse NY: Syracuse University Press, 1999.

———. *Seven Generations of Iroquois Leadership: The Six Nations since 1800.* Syracuse NY: Syracuse University Press, 2008.

Hauptman, Laurence M., and L. Gordon McLester III, eds. *The Oneida Indian Journey: From New York to Wisconsin, 1784–1860.* Madison: University of Wisconsin Press, 1999.

Hazard, Samuel. *Hazard's Register of Pennsylvania*, vol. 9, *January to July 1832.* Philadelphia: Wm. F. Geddes, [1832].

———, ed. *Pennsylvania Archives.* 12 vols. Philadelphia: Joseph Severns, 1856.

Heart, Jonathan. "Account of Some Remains of Ancient Works, on the Muskingum, with a Plan of These Works," *Columbian Magazine* 1, no. 9 (May 1787): 425–27.

Heckewelder, John. *History, Manners, and Customs of the Indian Nations Who Once Inhabited Pennsylvania and the Neighboring States.* 1876. Reprinted Salem NH: Ayer, 1991.

———. "Names which the Lenni Lenape or Delaware Indians, who once inhabited this country, had given to Rivers, Streams, Places &c. &c. within the now States of Pennsylvania, New Jersey, Maryland, and Virginia." *Transactions of the American Philosophical Society*, n.s., 4 (1834): 351–96.

———. "Narrative of John Heckewelder's Journey to the Wabash in 1792." *Pennsylvania Magazine of History and Biography* 11, no. 4 (January 1888): 466–75.

———. "Narrative of John Heckewelder's Journey to the Wabash in 1792 (continued)." *Pennsylvania Magazine of History and Biography* 12, no. 1 (April 1888): 34–54.

———. "Narrative of John Heckewelder's Journey to the Wabash in 1792 (concluded)." *Pennsylvania Magazine of History and Biography* 12, no. 2 (July 1888): 165–84.

———. *Narrative of the Mission of the United Brethren among the Delaware and Mohegan Indians.* Philadelphia: McCarty & Davis, 1820. Reprinted New York: Arno, 1971.

Herman, Daniel J. "The Other Daniel Boone: The Nascence of a Middle-Class Hunter Hero, 1784–1860." *Journal of the Early Republic* 18, no. 3 (Autumn 1998): 429–57.

Hewitt, John Napoleon Brinton. "Kaahastinens or the Fire-dragon." *American Anthropologist* 4 (1891): 384.

"A History of the Divining Rod; with the Adventures of an Old Rodsman." *United States Magazine and Democratic Review* 26 (1850): 218–25, 317–26.

Hobsbawm, Eric, and Terence Ranger, eds. *The Invention of Tradition.* Cambridge, UK: Cambridge University Press, 1983, 2003.

Hodge, Frederick Webb, ed. *Handbook of American Indians North of Mexico.* Vol. 2. Washington DC: Government Printing Office, 1912.

Hoffman, Ronald, Mechal Sobel, and Frederika J. Teute, eds. *Through a Glass Darkly: Reflections on Personal Identity in Early America.* Chapel Hill: University of North Carolina Press, 1997.

Holly, Donald J. "Places of the Living, Places of the Dead: Situating a Sacred Geography." *Northeast Anthropology* 66 (Fall 2003): 57–76.

Hopkins, Gerald T. "Visit of Gerald T. Hopkins: A Quaker Ambassador to the Indians Who Visited Buffalo in 1804." In *Publications of the Buffalo Historical Society*, edited by Frank H. Severance, 6:217–22. Buffalo NY, 1906.

Horsman, Reginald. "The Origins of Oneida Removal to Wisconsin, 1815–1822." In *The Oneida Indian Journey: From New York to Wisconsin, 1784–1860*, edited by Laurence M. Hauptman and L. Gordon McLester III, 53–69. Madison: University of Wisconsin Press, 1999.

Hosack, David. *Memoir of DeWitt Clinton.* New York: J. Seymour, 1829.

Hovey, Edmund Otis, ed. *Annals of the New York Academy of Sciences*, vol. 58. New York: New York Academy of Sciences, 1908.

Howe, Daniel Walker. *What Hath God Wrought: The Transformation of America, 1815–1848.* New York: Oxford University Press, 2007.

Hudson, Charles. *Knights of Spain, Warriors of the Sun: Hernando de Soto and the South's Ancient Chiefdoms.* Athens: University of Georgia Press, 1997.

Hulbert, Archer B., and William N. Schwarze, eds. *The Moravian Records II.* Ohio Archaeological and Historical Publications 21. Columbus: Ohio State Archaeological and Historical Society, 1912.

Humphreys, David. *An Essay on the Life of the Honorable Major-General Israel Putnam: Addressed to the State Society of Cincinnati in Connecticut.* Hartford: Hudson and Goodwin, 1788.

Hunn, Eugene S., et al. *Čáw Pawá Láakni / They Are Not Forgotten: Sahaptian Place Names Atlas of the Cayuse, Umatilla, and Walla Walla.* Pendleton OR: Tamástslikt Cultural Institute, 2015.

Ibbotson, Joseph D., ed. *Documentary History of Hamilton College.* Clinton NY: Hamilton College, 1922.

Imlay, Gilbert. *A Topographical Description of the Western Territory of North America; Containing a Succinct Account of its Climate, Natural History, Population, Agriculture, Manners and Customs, with an Ample Description of the Several Divisions into which that Country is Divided.* New York: Samuel Campbell, 1793.

"An Indian Conference," September 8–10, 1762. In *The Papers of Sir William Johnson,* vol. 10, edited by Milton W. Hamilton, 505–6. Albany: University of the State of New York, 1951.

Irving, Washington. *Tales of a Traveler.* Vol. 2. London: John Murray, 1824.

Jefferson, Thomas. *Notes on the State of Virginia.* London: John Stockdale, 1787.

Jennings, Francis. *The Ambiguous Iroquois Empire.* New York: Norton, 1984.

———. "'Pennsylvania Indians' and the Iroquois." In *Beyond the Covenant Chain: The Iroquois and Their Neighbors in Indian North America, 1600–1800,* edited by Daniel K. Richter and James H. Merrell, 75–91. University Park: Pennsylvania State University Press, 2003.

Jennings, Francis, et al., eds. *The History and Culture of Iroquois Diplomacy: An Interdisciplinary Guide to the Treaties of the Six Nations and Their League.* Syracuse NY: Syracuse University Press, 1985.

Jessee, Dean C., ed. "Joseph Smith's 19 July 1840 Discourse." *BYU Studies* 19, no. 3 (1979): 390–94.

———. *The Personal Writings of Joseph Smith.* Salt Lake City: Deseret, 1984.

Johnson, Elias. *Legends, Traditions, and Laws, of the Iroquois Six Nations, and History of the Tuscarora Indians.* Lockport NY: Union Printing and Publishing, 1881.

Johnson, Paul. *A Shopkeeper's Millennium: Society and Revivals in Rochester, New York, 1815–1837.* New York: Hill and Wang, 1978, 2004.

Jordan, John W., ed. *Colonial and Revolutionary Families of Pennsylvania,* vol. 1. New York: Lewis, 1911. Reprinted Baltimore: Clearfield, 2004.

Jordan, Kurt A. "An Eighteenth-Century Seneca Iroquois Short Longhouse from the Townley-Read Site, ca. AD 1715–1754." In *Archaeology of the Iroquois: Selected*

Readings and Research Sources, edited by Jordan E. Kerber, 234–50. Syracuse
NY: Syracuse University Press, 2007.

———. "Regional Diversity and Colonialism in Eighteenth-Century Iroquoia."
In *Iroquoian Archaeology and Analytic Scale,* edited by Laurie E. Miroff and
Timothy D. Knapp, 215–30. Knoxville: University of Tennessee Press, 2009.

———. "Seneca Iroquois Settlement Pattern, Community Structure, and Housing, 1677–1779." *Northeast Anthropology* 67 (Spring 2004): 23–60.

———. *The Seneca Restoration, 1715–1754: An Iroquois Local Political Economy.*
Gainesville: University of Florida Press, 2009.

Jordan, Winthrop D. *White over Black: Attitudes toward the Negro, 1550–1812.* 2nd
ed. Chapel Hill: University of North Carolina Press, 2012.

Judkins, Russell A., ed. *Iroquois Studies: A Guide to Documentary and Ethnograph-
ic Resources from Western New York and the Genesee Valley.* Geneseo NY: Department of Anthropology, State University of New York and the Geneseo
Foundation, 1987.

Johnson, F. C., ed. "A Monument of the Old Indian Wars." *The Historical Record: A Quarterly Publication Devoted Principally to the Early History of Wyoming Valley* 6 (1905): 60.

Keating, Neal B. *Iroquois Art, Power, and History.* Norman: University of Oklahoma Press, 2012.

Kelly, Kevin P. "John Montour: Life of a Cultural Go-Between." *Colonial Wil-
liamsburg Interpreter* 21, no. 4 (2000–2001).

Kelman, Ari. *A Misplaced Massacre: Struggling over the Memory of Sand Creek.*
Cambridge MA: Harvard University Press, 2013.

Kelsey, John. *The Lives and Reminiscences of the Pioneers of Rochester and Western
New York.* Rochester NY: J. Kelsey, 1854.

Kennedy, Roger G. *Hidden Cities: The Discovery and Loss of Ancient North American Civilization.* New York: Free Press, 1994.

Kent, Barry C. *Susquehanna's Indians.* Anthropological Series, no. 6. Harrisburg:
Pennsylvania Historical and Museum Commission, 1984.

Kent, Donald H., and Merle K. Deardorff, eds. "John Adlum on the Allegheny:
Memoirs for the Year 1794." *Pennsylvania Magazine of History and Biography*
84, no. 4 (October 1960): 435–80.

Kerber, Jordan, ed. *Archaeology of the Iroquois: Selected Readings and Research Sources.* Syracuse NY: Syracuse University Press, 2007.

Ketchum, William. *An Authentic and Comprehensive History of Buffalo, with Some
Accounts Its Early Inhabitants, Both Savage and Civilized.* 2 vols. Buffalo: Rock-
well, Baker & Hill, 1865.

Kirkland, Samuel. "Extracts from the Journal of the Rev. Mr. Kirkland, Missionary to the Six Indian Nations." *European Magazine*, August 1790, 94–96.

Klinck, Carl F., and James J. Talman, eds. *The Journal of Major John Norton, 1816*. Toronto: Champlain Society, 1970.

Koepke, John A. *Envisioning Cahokia: A Landscape Perspective*. DeKalb: Northern Illinois University Press, 2003.

La Rochefoucauld-Liancourt, François-Alexandre-Frédéric, duc de la. *Travels through the United States of North America, the country of the Iroquois, and Upper Canada, in the years 1795, 1796, and 1797; with an authentic account of Lower Canada*. 2 vols. London: R. Phillips, 1799.

Lady, David. "Tuscarora among the Iroquois." In *Northeast*, vol. 15 of *Handbook of North American Indians*, edited by Bruce G. Trigger, 518–24. Washington DC: Smithsonian Institution, 1978.

Landy, David. "Tuscarora among the Iroquois." In *Northeast*, vol. 15 of *Handbook of North American Indians*, edited by Bruce G. Trigger, 522. Washington DC: Smithsonian Institution, 1978.

Leask, Nigel. "Francis Wilford and the Colonial Construction of Hindu Geography, 1799–1822." In *Romantic Geographies: Discourses of Travel, 1775–1844*, edited by Amanda Gilroy, 204–22. Manchester: Manchester University Press, 2000.

Lenik, Edward J. *Picture Rocks: American Indian Rock Art in the Northeast Woodlands*. Hanover NH: University Press of New England, 2002.

Lennox, Jefferson. *Homelands and Empires: Indigenous Spaces, Imperial Fictions, and Competition for Territory in Northeastern North America, 1690–1763*. Toronto: University of Toronto Press, 2017.

Lepore, Jill. *The Name of War: King Philips's War and the Origins of American Identity*. New York: Knopf, 1998.

Lepper, Bradley T. "Early Historic American Indian Testimony Concerning the Ancient Earthworks of Eastern North America." *Journal of Ohio Archaeology* 3 (2014): 1–11.

LeSueur, Stephen C. *The 1838 Mormon War in Missouri*. Columbia: University of Missouri Press, 1987.

Levin, David. "Giants in the Earth: Science and the Occult in Cotton Mather's Letters to the Royal Society." *William and Mary Quarterly*, 3rd. ser., 45, no. 4 (October 1988): 751–70.

Levy, Philip. *Fellow Travelers: Indians and Europeans Contesting the Early American Trail*. Gainesville: University Press of Florida, 2007.

Lewin, Howard. "A Frontier Diplomat: Andrew Montour." *Pennsylvania History* 23, no. 2 (April 1966): 153–86.

Lincklaen, John. *Travels in the Years 1791 and 1792 in Pennsylvania, New York, and Vermont.* Edited by Helen Lincklaen Fairchild. New York: G. P. Putnam's Sons, 1897.

Lindner, Chris, and Edward V. Curtis, eds. *A Golden Chronograph for Robert E. Funk.* Occasional Publications in Northeast Anthropology, no. 15. Bethlehem CT: Archaeological Services, 1996,

Litchman, Charles H., ed. *Official History of the Improved Order of Red Men.* Boston: Fraternity, 1893.

[Livingston, Henry.] "Newly Discovered Indian Fortifications." *New-York Magazine; or, Literary Repository* 4, no. 1 (January 1793): 23–24.

Lossing, Benson J. *The Pictorial Field-Book of the Revolution; or, Illustrations, by Pen and Pencil, of the History, Biography, Scenery, Relics, and Traditions of the War for Independence.* 2 vols. New York: Harper & Brothers, 1860.

MacKenzie, Charles. "Cataraqui." *Ontario Historical Society Papers and Records* 8 (1907): 142–46.

Macleod, William. *Harper's New York and Erie Railroad Guide Book: Containing a Description of the Scenery, River Towns, Villages, and Most Important Works on the Road.* New York: Harper & Brothers, 1851.

Madison, James. "Address to the Agricultural Society of Ablemarle," May 12, 1818. National Archives, Founders Online, https://founders.archives.gov/documents/Madison/04-01-02-0244, accessed September 1, 2019.

Mann, Barbara Alice. *George Washington's War on Native America.* Westport CT: Praeger, 2005.

Mann, Charles C. *1491: New Revelations of the Americas before Columbus.* 2nd ed. New York: Vintage, 2011.

Mano, Jo Margaret. "Unmapping the Iroquois: New York State Cartography, 1792–1845." In *The Oneida Journey: From New York to Wisconsin,* edited by Laurence M. Hauptman and L. Gordon McLester III, 171–96. Madison: University of Wisconsin Press, 1999.

Marbois, François. "Journey to the Oneidas." In *In Mohawk Country: Early Narratives about a Native People,* edited by Dean R. Snow, Charles T. Gehring, and William A. Starna, 300–317. Syracuse NY: Syracuse University Press, 1996.

Mather, J. H., and L. P. Brockett. *A Geographical History of the State of New York: Embracing Its History, Government, Physical Features, Climate, Geology, Mineralogy, Botany, Zoology, Education, Internal Improvements, &c.* Utica NY: John W. Fuller, 1853.

Maude, John. *Visit to the Falls of Niagara in 1800.* London: Longman, 1826.

Mayor, Adrienne. *Fossil Legends of the First Americans.* Princeton NJ: Princeton University Press, 2005.

McCoy, Drew R. *The Elusive Republic: Political Economy in Jeffersonian America.* Chapel Hill: University of North Carolina Press, 1980.

McDonnell, Michael A. *Masters of Empire: Great Lakes Indians and the Making of America.* New York: Hill and Wang, 2015.

McMaster, Guy Humphrey. *History of the Settlement of Steuben County, N.Y.* Bath NY: R. S. Underhill, 1853.

Meginness, John Franklin. *Otzinachson: A History of the West Branch of the Susquehanna.* Philadelphia: Henry B. Ashmead, 1857.

———. *Otzinachson: A History of the West Branch of the Susquehanna*, vol. 1. Rev. ed. Williamsport PA: Gazette and Bulletin Printing House, 1889.

Merrell, James H. "'The Cast of His Countenance': Reading Andrew Montour." In *Through a Glass Darkly: Reflections on Personal Identity in Early America*, edited by Ronald Hoffman, Mechal Sobel, and Frederika J. Teute, 13–39. Chapel Hill: University of North Carolina Press, 1997.

———. *The Indians' New World: Catawbas and Their Neighbors from European Contact through the Era of Removal.* Chapel Hill: University of North Carolina Press, 1989.

———. *Into the American Woods: Negotiations on the Pennsylvania Frontier.* New York: W. W. Norton, 1999.

———. "Some Thoughts on Colonial Historians and American Indians." *William and Mary Quarterly*, 3rd. ser., 45, no. 1 (January1989): 94–119.

[Mitchill, Samuel Latham]. "The Original Inhabitants of America consisted of the same Races with the Malays of Australasia, and the Tartars of the North." In *The Medical Repository of Original Essays and Intelligence*, ed. Felix Pascalis Mitchill and Samuel Akerly, 187–89. New York: T. and J. Sword, 1817.

Miller, Preston. *The New Four Winds Guide to American Indian Artifacts.* Atglen PA: Schiffer, 2006.

Miller, Samuel. "Annual Report of the Directors." *New-York Missionary Magazine, and Repository of Religious Intelligence*, January 6, 1802, 202–9.

Milner, George R. *The Cahokia Chiefdom: The Archaeology of a Mississippian Society.* Washington DC: Smithsonian Institution Press, 1998

Miner, Charles. *History of Wyoming, in a Series of Letters, from Charles Miner, to His Son, William Penn Miner, Esq.* Philadelphia: J. Crissy, 1845.

Mintz, Max. *The Seeds of Empire: The American Revolutionary Conquest of the Iroquois.* New York: New York University Press, 2002.

Miroff, Laurie E., and Timothy D. Knapp, eds. *Iroquoian Archaeology and Analytic Scale.* Knoxville: University of Tennessee Press, 2009.

Mithun, Marianne. "The Proto-Iroquoians: Cultural Reconstructions from Lexical Materials." In *Extending the Rafters: Interdisciplinary Approaches to Iroquoian*

Studies, ed. Michael K. Foster, Jack Campisi, and Marianne Mithun, 259–82. Albany: State University of New York Press, 1984.

Morgan, Edmund S. *American Slavery, American Freedom*. New York: W. W. Norton, 1975, 2003.

Morgan, Lewis Henry. *League of the Ho-dé-no-sau-nee, Iroquois*. Rochester NY: Sage & Brother, 1851. Reprinted New York: Corinth, 1962.

Mt. Pleasant, Alyssa. "After the Whirlwind: Maintaining a Haudenosaunee Place at Buffalo Creek, 1780–1825." PhD diss., Cornell University, 2008.

Munro, Robert. "A Description of the Genesee Country, in the State of New York." In *The Documentary History of the State of New York*, edited by E. B. O'Callaghan, 2:691. Albany NY: Weed, Parsons, 1849–51.

Murray, Louise Welles. *A History of Old Tioga Point and Early Athens Pennsylvania*. Wilkes-Barre PA: Raeder, 1908.

———, ed. *Selected Manuscripts of General John S. Clark Relating to the Aboriginal History of the Susquehanna*. Athens: Society for Pennsylvania Archaeology, 1931.

Nabokov, Peter. *Indian Running: Native American History and Tradition*. Santa Fe NM: Ancient City, 1987.

Nichols, David Andrew. *Red Gentlemen & White Savages: Indians, Federalists, and the Search for Order on the American Frontier*. Charlottesville: University of Virginia Press, 2008.

Niemczycki, Mary Ann Palmer. *The Origin and Development of the Seneca and Cayuga Tribes of New York State*. Research Records 17. Rochester NY: Rochester Museum and Science Center, 1984.

Noble, William C. "Historic Neutral Iroquois Settlement Patterns." *Canadian Journal of Archaeology* 8, no. 1 (1984): 3–27.

Norton, John, to Unknown. In *The Valley of the Six Nations: A Collection of Documents on the Indian Lands of the Grand River*, edited by Charles M. Johnston, 277–78. Toronto: Champlain Society, 1964.

Nostrand, Richard L., and Lawrence E. Estaville, eds. *Homelands: A Geography of Culture and Place across America*. Baltimore: Johns Hopkins University Press, 2001.

Oberg, Michael Leroy. *Professional Indian: The American Odyssey of Eleazer Williams*. Philadelphia: University of Pennsylvania Press, 2015.

O'Brien, Jean M. *Firsting and Lasting: Writing Indians out of Existence in New England*. Minneapolis: University of Minnesota Press, 2010.

O'Callaghan, E. B., ed. *Documents Relative to the Colonial History of the State of New York*. 15 vols. Albany NY: Weed, Parsons, 1853–87.

O'Connor, Roger. *Chronicles of Eri; being the History of the Gaal Sciot Iber; or, the Irish People; Translated from the Original Manuscripts in the Phoenician Dialect of the Scythian Language.* London: Sir Richard Phillips, 1822.

Oestreicher, David M. "Unmasking the *Walum Olum*: A 19th-Century Hoax." *Bulletin of the Archaeological Society of New Jersey* 49 (1994): 1–44

Olmstead, Earl P. *David Zeisberger: A Life among the Indians.* Kent OH: Kent State University Press, 1997.

O'Reilly, Henry. *Settlement in the West: Sketches of Rochester; with Incidental Notices in Western New York.* Rochester: William Alling, 1838.

Owen, William. "Discovery of the Madawgwys." *Gentlemen's Magazine* 61, no. 3, pt. 2 (September 1791): 795–96.

Packer, Cameron J. "Acquiring Cumorah." *Religious Educator* 6, no. 2 (2005): 29–50.

Parfitt, Tudor. *The Lost Tribes of Israel: The History of a Myth.* London: Weidenfeld & Nicolson, 2002.

Parker, Arthur C. *The Archaeological History of New York.* New York State Museum Bulletin, no. 237–38 (1920).

Pauketat, Timothy. *Ancient Cahokia and the Mississippians.* New York: Cambridge University Press, 2004.

———. *Cahokia: Ancient America's Great City on the Mississippi.* New York: Penguin, 2009.

Pendergast, James F. "The Kakouagoga or Kahkwas: An Iroquoian Nation Destroyed in the Niagara Region." *Proceedings of the American Philosophical Society* 138, no. 1 (March 1994): 96–144.

Pennant, Thomas. *Arctic Zoology*, vol. 1. London: Henry Hughs, 1784.

Pennsylvania State. *Minutes of the Provincial Council of Pennsylvania, from the Organization to the Termination of the Proprietary Government*, vol. 8. Harrisburg PA: Theo. Fenn, 1852.

Perdue, Theda, and Michael D. Green. *The Cherokee Nation and the Trail of Tears.* New York: Penguin, 2007.

Pilkington, Walter, ed. *The Journals of Samuel Kirkland, 1764–1807.* Clinton NY: Hamilton College, 1980.

Pittock, Murray G. H. "Historiography." In *The Cambridge Companion to the Scottish Enlightenment*, edited by Alexander Broadie, 258–79. Cambridge: Cambridge University Press, 2003.

Powell, Miles A. *Vanishing America: Species Extinction, Racial Peril, and the Origins of Conservation.* Cambridge MA: Harvard University Press, 2016.

Power, Susan C. *Early Art of the Southeastern Indians: Feathered Serpents & Winged Beings.* Athens: University of Georgia Press, 2004.

Priest, Josiah. *The Deeply Interesting Story of General Patchin of Schoharie County, Stolen When a Lad by Brant and His Indians.* Lansingburgh [NY]: W. Harkness, 1840. Reprinted Tarrytown NY: William Abbatt, 1918.

Prisch, Betty Coit. "The Divers Lake Quarry Site—Genesee County, New York." *New York State Archaeological Association Bulletin* 66 (March 1976): 8–18.

"Proofs to Ascertain That America Was First Discovered by the Ancient Britons." *American Magazine* II, no. 4 (April 1792): 152–56.

Quinn, D. Michael. *Early Mormonism and the Magic World View.* Rev. ed. Salt Lake City: Signature, 1998.

Rafinesque, Constantine Samuel. *The American Nations; or, Outlines of a National History of the Ancient and Modern Nations of North and South America.* 2 vols. Philadelphia: self-published, 1836.

———. *Ancient History or Annals of Kentucky; with a Survey of the Ancient Monuments of North America, and a Tabular View of the Principal Languages and Primitive Nations of the Whole Earth.* Frankfort KY: self-published, 1824.

———. *A Life of Travels and Researches in North America and South Europe.* Philadelphia: F. Turner, 1836.

Reid, Max W. *The Mohawk Valley: Its Legends and Its History.* New York: G. P. Putnam's Sons, 1904.

Resch, John P. *Suffering Soldiers: Revolutionary War Veterans, Moral Sentiment, and Political Culture in the Early Republic.* Amherst: University of Massachusetts Press, 1999.

Richter, Daniel K. *Before the Revolution: America's Ancient Pasts.* Cambridge MA: Belknap Press of Harvard University Press, 2011.

———. "'Believing That Many of the Red People Suffer Much for the Want of Food': Hunting, Agriculture, and a Quaker Construction of Indianness in the Early Republic." *Journal of the Early Republic* 19, no. 4 (Winter 1999): 601–28.

———. *Facing East from Indian Country: A Native History of Early America.* Cambridge MA: Harvard University Press, 2001.

———. *The Ordeal of the Longhouse: The Peoples of Iroquois League in the Era of European Colonization.* Chapel Hill: University of North Carolina Press, 1992.

———. "War and Culture: The Iroquois Experience." *William and Mary Quarterly* 3rd ser., 40, no. 4 (October 1983): 528–59.

Richter, Daniel K., and James H. Merrell, eds. *Beyond the Covenant Chain: The Iroquois and Their Neighbors in Indian North America, 1600–1800.* University Park: Pennsylvania State University Press, 2003.

Ritchie, William A. *The Archaeology of New York State.* Garden City NY: Natural History, 1965.

Roberts, William. *An Account of the First Discovery and Natural History of Florida, with a Particular Detail of the Several Expeditions and Descents Made on That
Coast.* London: T. Jefferey's, 1763.

Rose, Mark. "When Giants Roamed the Earth." *Archaeology* 58, no. 6 (November-
December 2005). http://www.archaeology.org/0511/etc/giants.html, accessed
September 15, 2018.

Rotstein, Abraham. "The Mystery of the Neutral Indians." In *Patterns of the Past:
Interpreting Ontario's History,* edited by Roger Hall, William Westfall, and Laurel Sefton MacDowell, 11–36. Toronto: Dundurn, 1988.

Rupp, Israel Daniel. *History and Topography of Northumberland, Huntingdon, Mif-
flin Centre, Union, Columbia, Juniata, and Clinton Counties, Pa.* Lancaster City
PA: Gilbert Hills, 1846.

Ryan, Mary. *Cradle of the Middle Class: The Family in Oneida County, New York,
1790–1850.* New York: Cambridge University Press, 1983.

Salisbury, Neal. "The Indians' Old World: Native Americans and the Coming of
Europeans." *William and Mary Quarterly,* 3rd ser., 53, no. 3 (July 1996): 435–58.

Saunders, Nicholas J., ed. *Icons of Power: Feline Symbolism in the Americas.* New
York: Routledge, 1998.

Sayre, Gordon M. "The Mound Builders and the Imagination of American Antiquity in Jefferson, Bartram, and Chateaubriand." *Early American Literature*
33, no. 3 (1998): 225–49.

Schein, Richard H. "Urban Origin and Form in Central New York." *Geographical Review* 81, no. 1 (January 1991): 52–69.

Schoolcraft, Henry Rowe. *Information Respecting the History, Conditions, and Pros-
pects of the Indian Tribes of the United States: Collected and Prepared under the
Direction of the Bureau of Indian Affairs per Act of Congress of March 3rd 1847.*
Vol. 5. Philadelphia: J. B. Lippincourt, 1856.

——— . *Notes on the Iroquois; or, Contributions to American History, Antiquities,
and General Ethnology.* Albany: Erastus H. Pease, 1847.

Seelye, John. *Memory's Nation: The Place of Plymouth Rock.* Chapel Hill: University of North Carolina Press, 1998.

Selkgreg, John H., ed. *Landmarks of Tompkins County, New York.* Syracuse NY:
D. Mason, 1894.

Semonin, Paul. *American Monster: How the Nation's First Prehistoric Creature Became a Symbol of National Identity.* New York: New York University Press, 2000.

Severance, Frank H., ed. *Publications of the Buffalo Historical Society.* Vol. 6. Buffalo: Buffalo Historical Society, 1903.

——— . *Publications of the Buffalo Historical Society.* Vol. 9. Buffalo: Buffalo Historical Society, 1906.

Sexton, John L. *An Outline History of Tioga and Bradford Counties in Pennsylvania, Chemung, Steuben, Tioga, Tompkins, and Schuyler in New York, by Townships, Villages, Boro's and Cities*. Elmira NY: Gazette, 1885.

Shammas, Carole, ed. *Investing in the Early Modern Built Environment: Europeans, Asians, Settlers, and Indigenous Societies*. Leiden: Brill, 2012.

Sheehan, Bernard W. *Seeds of Extinction: Jeffersonian Philanthropy and the American Indian*. Chapel Hill: University of North Carolina Press, 1973.

Sheriff, Carol. *The Artificial River: The Erie Canal and the Paradox of Progress, 1817–1862*. New York: Hill and Wang, 1996.

Shipps, Jan. *Mormonism: The Story of a New Religious Tradition*. Urbana: University of Illinois Press, 1985.

——. "Richard Lyman Bush, the Story of Joseph Smith and Mormonism, and the New Mormon History." Review of Richard Lyman Bushman, *Rough Stone Rolling*, *Journal of American History* 94, no. 2 (September 2007): 498–516.

Shoemaker, Nancy. *A Strange Likeness: Becoming Red and White in Eighteenth-Century North America*. New York: Oxford University Press, 2004.

Silver, Peter. *Our Savage Neighbors: How Indian War Transformed Early America*. New York: W. W. Norton, 2008.

Silverman, David J. "The Curse of God: An Idea and Its Origins among the Indians of New York's Revolutionary Frontier." *William and Mary Quarterly* 3rd ser., 66, no. 3 (July 2009): 495–534.

Simmons, William S. *Spirit of the New England Tribes: Indian History and Folklore, 1620–1984*. Hanover NH: University Press of New England, 1986.

Simms, Jeptha R. *History of Schoharie County, and Border Wars of New York*. Albany: Munsell & Tanner, 1845.

Skinner, Israel. *A History of the Revolutionary War between Great Britain and the United States in Verse*. Binghamton NY: Collier and Caroll, 1829.

Skousen, Royal, ed. *The Book of Mormon: The Earliest Text*. New Haven: Yale University Press, 2009.

Sleeper-Smith, Susan, Juliana Barr, Jean M. O'Brien, Nancy Shoemaker, and Scott Manning Stevens, eds. *Why You Can't Teach United States History without American Indians*. Chapel Hill: University of North Carolina Press, 2015.

Slotkin, Richard. *Gunfighter Nation: The Myth of the Frontier in Twentieth-Century America*. Norman: University of Oklahoma Press, 1992.

——. *Regeneration through Violence: The Mythology of the American Frontier, 1600–1860*. Middletown CT: Wesleyan University Press, 1973. Reprinted Norman: University of Oklahoma Press, 2000.

Smith, Erminnie. *Myths of the Iroquois*. Extract from the Second Report of the Bureau of Ethnology. Washington DC: Smithsonian Institute, 1888.

Smith, Ethan. *View of the Hebrews*. Poultney VT: Smith & Shute, 1832.

Smith, Joseph. *A Book of Commandments, for the Government of the Church of Christ*. Zion MO: W. W. Phelps, 1833, 1906.

———. *The Doctrine and Covenants of the Church of Jesus Christ of Latter-Day Saints*. Salt Lake City: Church of Jesus Christ of Latter-day Saints, 1921.

Smith, Richard. *A Tour of Four Great Rivers: The Hudson, Mohawk, Susquehanna, and Delaware in 1769*. Edited by Francis W. Halsey. Port Washington NY: Charles Scribner's Sons, 1906.

Smith, William. *The History of the Province of New-York, from the First Discovery to the Year 1732*. Philadelphia: Mathew Carey, 1792.

Smy, William M. *An Annotated Nominal Roll of Butler's Rangers, 1777–1784, with Documentary Sources*. St. Catharine's, Ontario, Friends of the Loyalist Collection at Brock University, 2004.

Snow, Dean R. *The Iroquois*. Oxford: Blackwell, 1994.

———. "Migration in Prehistory: The Northern Iroquoian Case." In *Archaeology of the Iroquois: Selected Readings and Research Sources*, edited by Jordan E. Kerber, 6–30. Syracuse NY: Syracuse University Press, 2007.

———. *Mohawk Valley Archaeology: The Sites*. Occasional Papers in Anthropology, no. 3. University Park: Matson Museum of Anthropology, Pennsylvania State University, 1995.

———. "More on Migration in Prehistory: Accommodating New Evidence in the Northern Iroquoian Case." In *Archaeology of the Iroquois: Selected Readings and Research Sources*, edited by Jordan E. Kerber, 41–47. Syracuse NY: Syracuse University Press, 2007.

Snow, Dean R., Charles T. Gehring, and William A. Starna, eds. *In Mohawk Country: Early Narratives about a Native People*. Syracuse NY: Syracuse University Press, 1996.

Sorg, David J. "Lost Tribes of the Susquehanna." *Pennsylvania Archaeologist* 74, no. 2 (2004): 63–72.

Spafford, Horatio Gates. *A Gazetteer of the State of New York*. Albany: H. C. Southwick, 1813.

Speck, Frank G. "Siouan Tribes of the Carolinas as Known from Catawba, Tutelo, and Documentary Sources." *American Anthropologist* 37, no. 2, pt. 1 (April-June 1935): 201–25.

Squier, Ephraim G. *Antiquities of the State of New York: Being the Results of Extensive Original Surveys and Explorations*. Buffalo: George H. Derby, 1851.

Stanford, Donald E. "The Giant Bones of Claverack, New York, 1705." *New York History* 40, no. 1 (January 1959): 47–61.

Stansbury, Philip. *A Pedestrian Tour of Two Thousand Three Hundred Miles, in North America. To the Lakes,–The Canadas–And the New England States, Performed in the Autumn of 1821.* New York: J. D. Myers & W. Smith, 1822.

Starna, William A. "Aboriginal Title and Traditional Iroquois Land Use: An Anthropological Perspective." In *Iroquois Land Claims*, edited by Starna and Christopher Vecsey, 31–48. Syracuse NY: Syracuse University Press, 1988.

Starna, William A., George R. Hamell, and William L. Butts. "Northern Iroquoian Horticulture and Insect Infestation: A Cause for Village Removal." *Ethnohistory* 31, no. 3 (Summer 1984): 197–207.

Steiner, Abraham G. "Account of Some Old Indian Works, on Huron River, with a Plan of Them, Taken the 28th of May, 1789, by Abraham Steiner." *Columbian Magazine* 3, no. 9 (September 1789): 543–44.

Stone, William L. *The Life and Times of Red Jacket, or Sa-Go-Ye-wat-Ha; Being the Sequel to the History of the Six Nations.* New York: Wiley and Putnam, 1841.

———. *The Life of Joseph Brant—Thayendanegea: Including the Border Wars of the American Revolution, and Sketches of the Indian Campaigns of Generals Hamar, St. Clair, and Wayne.* Vol. 1. New York: Alexander V. Blake, 1838.

———. *The Poetry and History of Wyoming: Containing Campbell's Gertrude, and the History of Wyoming, from Its Discovery to the Beginning of the Present Century.* 2nd ed. New York: Mark H. Newman, 1844.

Stothers, David M., and Timothy J. Abel. "Early Woodland Prehistory (1000–1 BC) in the Western Lake Erie Drainage Basin." In *Transitions: Archaic and Early Woodland Research in the Ohio Country*, edited by Martha P. Otto and Brian G. Remond, 79–116. Athens: Ohio University Press, 2008.

Sturtevant, William C. "Early Iroquois Realist Painting and Identity Marking." In *Three Centuries of Woodlands Indian Art*, edited by J. C. H. King and Christian F. Feest, 129–43. Vienna: ZKF, 2007.

Sweet, James H. "The Iberian Roots of American Racist Thought." *William and Mary Quarterly* 3rd ser., 54, no. 1 (January 1997): 143–66.

Sweet, John Wood. *Bodies Politic: Negotiating Race in the American North, 1730–1830.* Baltimore: Johns Hopkins University Press, 2003. Reprinted Philadelphia: University of Pennsylvania Press, 2006.

Swetland, Luke. *A Very Remarkable Narrative of Luke Swetland.* Hartford: self-published, 1780.

Taylor, Alan. *American Colonies: The Settling of North America.* New York: Penguin, 2001.

———. *The Divided Ground: Indians, Settlers, and the Northern Borderlands of the American Revolution.* New York: Knopf, 2006.

———. "The Early Republic's Supernatural Economy: Treasure Seeking in the American Northeast, 1780–1830." *American Quarterly* 38, no. 1 (Spring 1986): 6–34.

———. "The Great Change Begins: Settling the Forest of Central New York." *New York History* 75, no. 3 (July 1995): 265–90.

———. *William Cooper's Town: Power and Persuasion on the Frontier of the Early American Republic.* New York: Vintage, 1995.

Taylors, George Rogers. *The Transportation Revolution, 1815–1860.* New York: Reinhart, 1951.

Thomas, Cyrus. *Report on the Mound Explorations of the Bureau of Ethnology.* Washington DC: Government Printing Office, 1894.

Thompson, John H., ed. *The Geography of New York State.* Syracuse NY: Syracuse University Press, 1966.

Thompson, Robert G., et al. "Phytolith Evidence for Twentieth-Century B.P. Maize in Northern Iroquoia." *Northeast Anthropology* 68 (Fall 2004): 25–40.

Thwaites, Reuben Gold, ed. *The Jesuit Relations and Allied Documents*, vol. 51. Cleveland: Burrows Brothers, 1899.

Tiro, Karim M. *The People of the Standing Stone: The Oneida Nation from the Revolution through the Era of Removal.* Amherst: University of Massachusetts Press, 2011.

———. "'We Wish to Do You Good': The Quaker Mission to the Oneida Nation, 1790–1840." *Journal of the Early Republic* 26, no. 3 (Fall 2006): 353–76.

Tooker, Elisabeth. "Demise of the Susquehannocks: A Seventeenth-Century Mystery." *Pennsylvania Archaeologist* 54, no. 3–4 (1984): 1–10.

———. "Women in Iroquois Society." In *Extending the Rafters: Interdisciplinary Approaches to Iroquoian Studies*, ed. Michael K. Foster, Jack Campisi, and Marianne Mithun, 109–23.

Trigger, Bruce G., ed. *Northeast*, vol. 15 of *Handbook of North American Indians.* Washington DC: Smithsonian Institution, 1978.

Turner, Orsamus. *History of the Pioneer Settlement of Phelps & Gorham's Purchase.* Rochester NY: William Alling, 1852.

———. *Pioneer History of the Holland Purchase of Western New York.* Buffalo NY: Jewett Thomas, 1849.

University of the State of New York, Divisions of Archives and History. *The Sullivan-Clinton Campaign in 1779: Chronology and Selected Documents.* Albany: University of the State of New York, 1929.

Vecsey, Christopher. "The Story and Structure of the Iroquois Confederacy." *Journal of the American Academy of Religion* 54 (1986): 79–106.

Vogel, Dan. *Indian Origins of the Book of Mormon: Religious Solutions from Columbus to Joseph Smith.* Salt Lake City: Signature, 1986.

———. "The Locations of Joseph Smith's Early Treasure Quests." *Dialogue: A Journal of Mormon Thought* 27, no. 3 (1994): 197–231.

———, ed. *Early Mormon Documents.* 5 vols. Salt Lake City: Signature Books, 1996–2003.

Wallace, Anthony F. C. *The Death and Rebirth of the Seneca.* New York: Knopf, 1970.

———. "The Dekanawideth Myth Analyzed as the Record of a Revitalization Movement." *Ethnohistory* 5, no. 2 (Spring 1958): 118–30.

———. *Jefferson and the Indians: The Tragic Fate of the First Americans.* Cambridge MA: Belknap Press of Harvard University, 1999.

Wallace, Anthony, and Deborah Holler. "Reviving the Peace Queen: Revelations from Lewis Henry Morgan's Field Notes on the Tonawanda Seneca." *Histories of Anthropology Annual* 5 (2009): 90–109.

Wallace, Anthony, and William Reyburn. "Crossing the Ice: A Migration Legend of the Tuscarora Indians." *International Journal of American Linguistics* 17, no. 1 (January 1951): 42–47.

Walton, William. *A Narrative of the Captivity and Sufferings of Benjamin Gilbert and His Family: Who Were Surprised by the Indians and Taken from Their Farms, on the Frontiers of Pennsylvania, in the Spring of 1780.* Philadelphia: Joseph Crukshank, 1784.

Warrick, Gary. *A Population History of the Huron-Petun, AD 500–1650.* New York: Cambridge University Press, 2008.

Watson, Elkanah. *Men and Times of the Revolution; or, Memoirs of Elkanah Watson.* Edited by Winslow C. Watson. New York: Dana, 1856.

Watts, Isaac. *Psalms Carefully Suited to the Christian Worship in the United States of America. Being an Improvement of the Old Version of the Psalms of David.* New York: White, Gallaher, and White, 1831.

Weber, David J. *The Spanish Frontier in North America.* New Haven CT: Yale University Press, 1993.

Webster, Noah. "Antiquity." *American Magazine* 1, no. 1 (December 1787): 15–19.

———. "Antiquity. Letter II." *American Magazine* 1, no. 2 (January 1788): 87–93.

———. "Antiquity. Letter III." *American Magazine* 1, no. 3 (February 1788): 146–56.

Weiser, Conrad. "Narrative of a Journey, Made in the Year 1737, by Conrad Weiser, Indian Agent and Provincial Interpreter, from Tulpehocken in the Province of Pennsylvania to Onondaga, the Head Quarters of the Allied Six Nations, in the Province of New York," Translated by H. H. Muhlenberg. *Pennsylvania Historical Society Collections* 1 (1853): 6–33.

West, Elliot. *The Contested Plains: Indians, Goldseekers, and the Rush to Colorado.* Lawrence: University Press of Kansas, 1998.

White, Marian E. "Ethnic Identification and Iroquois Groups in Western New York and Ontario." *Ethnohistory* 18, no. 1 (Winter 1971): 19–38.

———. *Iroquois Culture History in the Niagara Frontier Area of New York State.* Anthropological Papers, no. 16. Ann Arbor: University of Michigan, 1961.

———. "Neutral and Wenro." In *Northeast*, vol. 15 of *Handbook of North American Indians*, edited by Bruce G. Trigger, 407–11. Washington DC: Smithsonian Institution, 1978.

White, Marian E., William E. Engelbrecht, and Elisabeth Tooker. "Cayuga." In *Northeast*, vol. 15 of *Handbook of North American Indians*, edited by Bruce G. Trigger, 500–504. Washington DC: Smithsonian Institution, 1978.

White, Richard. *The Middle Ground: Indians, Empires, and Republics in the Great Lakes Region, 1650–1815.* New York: Cambridge University Press, 1991.

Whyte, Thomas R. "Proto-Iroquoian Divergence in the Late Archaic-Early Woodland Period Transition of the Appalachian Highlands." *Southeastern Archaeology* 26, no. 1 (Summer 2007): 134–44.

Wilford, Francis. "An Essay on the Sacred Isles in the West." In *Asiatic Researches; or, Transactions of the Society Instituted in Bengal, for inquiring into the History and Antiquities, the Arts, Sciences, and Literature of Asia,* vol. 8. London: Vernor, Hood, and Sharpe, 1808.

Willard, Emma. *History of the United States, or Republic of America.* New York: White, Gallaher and White, 1828.

Williamson, Hugh. *Observations on the Climate in Different Parts of America.* New York: T. & J. Swords, 1811.

Wilson, Bruce. "The Struggle for Wealth and Power at Fort Niagara, 1775–1783." *Ontario History* 68, no. 3 (September 1976): 137–54.

Winchell, James M., ed. *An Arrangement of the Psalms, Hymns, and Spiritual Songs of Rev. Isaac Watts, D.D.* Boston: Lincoln & Edmands, 1821.

Winterbotham, William. *An Historical, Geographical, Commercial, and Philosophical View of the United States of America, and the European Settlements in America and the West Indies.* Vol. 3. New York: Tiebout and O'Brien, 1796.

Winterer, Caroline. *The Culture of Classicism: Ancient Greece and Rome in American Intellectual Life, 1780–1910.* Baltimore: Johns Hopkins University Press, 2002.

Witgen, Michael. *An Infinity of Nations: How the Native World Shaped Early North America.* Philadelphia: University of Pennsylvania Press, 2012.

Wonderley, Anthony. *At the Font of the Marvelous: Exploring Oral Narrative and Mythic Imagery of the Iroquois and Their Neighbors.* Syracuse: Syracuse University Press, 2009.

———. "The Iroquois Creation Story over Time." *Northeast Anthropology* 62 (Fall 2001): 1–16.

———. *Oneida Iroquois Folklore, Myth, and History.* Syracuse NY: Syracuse University Press, 2004.

Wood, Gordon S. *Empire of Liberty: A History of the Early Republic, 1789–1815.* New York: Oxford University Press, 2009.

Woodbury, Hanni. *Onondaga-English / English-Onondaga Dictionary.* Toronto: University of Toronto Press, 2003.

Worcester, Samuel. *Christian Psalmody in Four Parts; Comprising Dr. Watt's Psalms Abridged; Dr. Watt's Hymns Abridged; Select Hymns from Other Authors; and Select Harmony: Together with Directions for Musical Expression.* Boston: Samuel T. Armstrong, 1815.

Wright, James V. *The Ontario Iroquois Tradition. National Museum of Canada Bulletin* no. 210 (1966).

Wyckoff, William. *The Developer's Frontier: The Making of the Western New York Landscape.* New Haven CT: Yale University Press, 1988.

Young, Alfred F. *The Shoemaker and the Tea Party: Memory and the American Revolution.* Boston: Beacon, 1999.

Zeisberger, David. *Zeisberger's Indian Dictionary: English, German, Iroquois—The Onondaga, and Algonquian—The Delaware.* Edited by Eben Norton Horsford. Cambridge MA: John Wilson and Son, 1887.

| Index

Page numbers in italics indicate illustrations

Adam-ondi-Ahman, 183

Adams, John Quincy, 64, 105

Adams, Samuel, 196, 197

"Address on the Iroquois," 63

Adena culture, 166

Adirondack Mountains, 4, 51, 57

Adlum, John, 77, 197

African Americans, 62

Africans, 41, 149, 173

agriculture: of American settlers, 12, 47–49, 52–53, 63, 67, 68, 74; evidence of early practice, 172; of Haudenosaunee, 52, 63, 69–71, 151; history of in North America, 10, 37–39, 62; of Nephites, 173; New York's potential for, 114, 155; of Southeastern societies, 121; as stage of social development, 64, 69, 70

Akwesasne (St. Regis) Reservation, 51

Albany Centinel, 75–76

Albany Chronicle, 118, 151

Albany NY, 4, 6, 113, 114

alcohol, 42, 52, 81, 108, 174

Alden, Ichabod, 93

Algonquian-speaking peoples, 23–25, 31, 35–36

Allegany Reservation, 69, 190

Allegheny Plateau, 4

Allegheny River, 5, 50, 51

Allen, W. A., 195

Allen, Zimri, 165

Alligewi, 36–37, 149–50

American Academy of the Arts, 118

American Antiquarian Society, 144

American Antiquities and Discoveries of the West (Priest), 150

American Magazine, 120

The American Nations (Rafinesque), 148–49

American Philosophical Society, 59

American Revolution: appropriation of Indian culture after, 77, 78, 108, 193, 194; Cusick family during, 129; effect on landscape, 11–12, 47, 49, 67, 75, 76, 132; effect on Tuscaroras, 140; European settlement after, 19, 45, 123; Haudenosaunee farming during, 38, 48; Haudenosaunee influence during, 7; histories of, 85, 90, 96; James Clinton's role in, 116; John Harper's role in, 98; landmarks associated with, 79, 80, 81; military service during, 82; Montour family during, 84; poisoning of Indians during, 107; religion after, 174–75; war hero from, 55

Ancient History or Annals of Kentucky (Rafinesque), 144, 145

Angel, B. F., 107

animals, 49, 63–64, 68, 74. *See also* bears; mountain lions; wolves

Anishinaabe Indians, 32, 150

Annals of Tryon County (Campbell), 93

Appalachian Mountains, 11, 43, 47, 49, 145

Apple Town. *See* Kendaia

apple trees, 38, 52

archaeology: on American ancestry, 142; of C. S. Rafinesque, 148–49; in Iroquoia, Ohio, and Kentucky, 119; Joseph Smith's interest in, 158; Mormonism rooted in, 157; on Mound Builders, 120, 166; of Native American landscape, 163, 165. *See also* artifacts; earthworks

artifacts, 103–4, 120, 132, 157, 162–67. *See also* archaeology

Asia, 62, 124, 142, 143, 144, 149, 150

Asiatic Researches, 145

Asiatic Society of Bengal, 145

Assyria, 159, 168

Atchineankigh, 25

Atlanteans, Atlantes, 144, 149, 152, 159

Atotarho, 25, 26, 135

Atotarho VIII, 138
Atotarho IX, 138
Auburn NY, 118, 166
Aztec, 143

Babylon, 171
Barton, William, 50, 84
Bartram, John, 22, 38–39
Batavia NY, 54, 57
Bayard, Stephen, 113
Bean, Willard, 186–87
beans, 37, 38, 44, 49, 205n35
Beardsley, Levi, 54
bears, 53, 54, 55, 56. *See also* animals
Beatty, Erkuries, 23, 38
Beauchamp, William, 41
Belknap, Jeremy, 4, 69, 79, 122
Bering Land Bridge, 124, 128
Bering Sea, 147
Bible: comparison to Book of Mormon, 168,
     169, 170, 174; of David Cusick, 131–32; inter-
     pretations of, 14, 169, 185; as key to salvation,
     160; skin color in, 173; as source about ancient
     America, 144; in Welsh, 122
Big Bone Lick, 9–10, 14, 41–42, 60, 67
Big Neck. *See* Soh-nou-re-wah (Big Neck)
Big Tree Reservation, 51
Big Tree Village, 106, 110
Binghamton NY, 195
Biographical Memoir of Daniel Boone (Flint), 104
blacks. *See* African Americans; Africans
Blacksnake, Governor (Chainbreaker), 50, 91–
     92, 212n29, 213n41
Bloody Rock, 77, 90, 91, 109
Blue Throat (Talaguadeak), 88
Boewe, Charles, 148
Boggs, Lilburn, 184
Bolton, Mason, 87
Book of Mormon: battle accounts in, 158; cita-
     tions of, 222n27; city building in, 181; content
     of, 168; ending of, 172; history in, 177; ideas
     about ideal human characteristics in, 173; on
     Lamanites' role in religion, 180; place-names
     in, 171, 222n35; publication of, 157, 168; pub-
     lic reception of, 176; on redemption from sin,
     160, 175; rival peoples in, 170; source for, 14,
     167; story of Lehi in, 169; translation of, 164
Boone, Daniel, 81, 82, 104, 105
Boone, Hawkins, 81, 82, 92, 94–97, 105
Boston Tea Party, 85, 108, 194
Brackenridge, Henry Marie, 191

Brant, Joseph: in Canada, 133; captives taken
     by, 80, 98; education of, 98, 130; on Haudeno-
     saunee empire, 34; on Haudenosaunee war-
     fare, 27–28; history project of, 132; reputation
     of, 87–88, 90–91; role in Revolutionary War,
     85, 87, 88, 99, 211n23; support of British, 48;
     translation of Bible, 131
Brewer, James. *See* Quawwa
British Isles, 145. *See also* England
Broadhead, David, 50
Brodhead, Daniel, 84
Brulé, Etienne, 29
Buddhism, 143
Buffalo Creek, 28, 51, 69, 70, 129, 188, 190
Buffalo Creek Reservation, 160, 206n7
Buffalo NY, 53, 123, 188
Bullock, William, 135
Bumppo, Nathaniel "Natty" (Hawkeye), 15, 83
Burned-Over District, 156, 177
Burns, John, 148
Burrows, John, 23
Bushman, Richard, 176
Butler, John, 85–87, 89, 90, 93, 97, 99, 100, 101
Butler, Walter, 93, 94
Butler, Zebulon, 86, 87
Butternuts NY, 55
Buyers, John, 97, 213n39

Cahokia: Americans' destruction of, 151, 191; earth-
     works at, 119, 129, 181, 182; history of, 13, 29, 192;
     Mormons near, 180. *See also* Mound Builders
Caldwell County MO, 183
Calhoun, John C., 188
camels, 164–65
Camillus NY, 118
Cammerhoff, John Frederick, 21, 28, 33, 43, 44
Campbell, Jane, 94
Campbell, Samuel, 93, 94
Campbell, Thomas, 87–88
Campbell, William W., 93, 94
Canada, 20, 24, 51, 70, 72, 84, 132–33, 190
Canadarago Lake, 58
Canadasegy. *See* Kanadesaga
Canajoharie, 21
Canandaigua Lake, 20–21, 33, 137
Canandaigua NY, 138–39, 161, 170
Canawagus Reservation, 51
Caneadea Reservation, 51
Canisteo River, 75
Cannagargo, 31
Cannon, Matthew and Eleanor, 94

Carantouan, 29

Carey, Eleazer, 88, 90

Carey, Samuel, 88–89

Carleton, Guy, 85

Carthage IL, 185

Carver, Jonathan, 126

Cataraqui, 24

Catawba Indians, 33

Catharine's Town, 84, 100

Cattaraugus Reservation, 51, 190

Cayuga County, 131

Cayuga Indians, 3, 22, 28, 29, 33, 48, 137

Cayuga Lake, 3, 22, 58

Cayuse Indians, 9

Champlain, Samuel de, 29, 139

Chase, Sally, 162

Chase, Willard, 163

Chemung, 60, 99, 101, 208n29

Chemung River, 60, 75, 81, 99

Chenussio. *See* Genesee Castle

Cheroenhaka. *See* Nottoway peoples

Cherokee Indians, 31, 126, 146, 180

Cherokee Phoenix, 146

Cherry Valley Gazette, 72

Cherry Valley NY, 93–94

Chesapeake Bay, 5, 29

Chester NY, 61

China, 149, 157

Chippewa language. *See* Algonquian-speaking peoples

Christ, 170

Christianity: attempts to convert Indians to, 130, 131, 173; Eleazar Williams' observations about, 189; Indians' lack of understanding of, 133, 160; influence on Cusick family, 135, 136; millennialist view of, 156; Mormon version of, 14, 161, 168–70, 174–76, 180–83, 187

The Chronicles of Eri (O'Connor), 159

Chukchi, 124

Church of Jesus Christ of Latter-day Saints. *See* Mormons

Civil War, 130

Clark, Asahel, 118

Clark, George Rogers, 129

Clark, John B., 184

Clark, William, 174

Clifford, John D., 141, 143–45

climate, 61–62

Clinton, DeWitt: on agricultural production, 63; in American Philosophical Society, 60;

on ancient civilization, 13, 115–16, 122–24, 126, 129, 151, 159, 171, 172, 181, 216n17; and artifact collection, 103–4, 166; awareness of David Cusick's book, 141; background of, 116, 117; bones found by, 165; death of, 141; and Erie Canal, 73, 220n4; on mastodon extinction, 60, 61; opinion about Indians, 63, 71, 109–10, 114, 124–26, 128, 129, 143, 152, 175; at Painted Rocks, 79; praise of Georges Cuvier, 59; reputation of, 118; travels through Iroquoia, 118–19, 138; view of history, 126–29, 144

Clinton, George, 116–17, 141

Clinton, James, 11, 50, 89, 92, 98–100, 116, 151, 156

Coconeunquo, 89

Code of Handsome Lake, 70

Cohocton River, 75

Colden, Cadwallader, 6, 124, 133

"Colonies Planted; or Nations Blest and Punished" (Watts). *See* "Hymn for New England" (Watts)

Columbia College (University), 60, 116

Columbia Magazine, 60

Columbus, Christopher, 119, 136, 138, 146, 166, 173

Comanche Indians, 6

Conestoga Indians, 29. *See also* Susquehannock Indians

Connecticut, 55, 67, 98

Continental army, 50, 76. *See also* U.S. Army

Continental Congress, 116

Cooper, James Fenimore, 14–15, 83, 91, 142, 193–94

Cooper, William, 53, 71

Cooperstown NY, 53, 55, 57, 162

corn, 37, 38, 44, 49, 123, 205n35

Cornplanter: agriculture by, 69, 71; half-brother of, 70; at Hogback Hill, 99; and Painted Post legend, 196, 197; post-Revolution home of, 106; response to accusations of violence, 77; role in Revolutionary War, 85; runner of, 20

Cortland County, 55, 56

Couchsachraga, 57

Council houses, 23

Council of Fire of the League, 24, 26, 135

The Country of the Six Nations, 8

Covenant Chain, 5

Covenhoven, Robert, 92, 97

Coventry, Alexander, 52

Cowdery, Oliver, 167, 170, 180

Cree Indians, 126

Cumorah, 172

Cusick, Cornelius, 130

Cusick, David: background of, 129–30; citation by other writers, 152; creation myth of, 205n37; on formation of League, 30; on giant mosquito myth, 40; history of America, 13, 116, 129, 134–36, 148, 149, 218n48; home of, 135; illness of, 134, 151; interest in writing history, 132; on Mound Builders, 181; obituary of, 151; reception of book by, 141, 146, 150, 151; sale of books, 135; on significance of Onondaga village, 26; on Stone Giant myth, 35, 36, 165; use of oral histories, 139; on warfare within Five Nations, 140; writing skills of, 133–34

Cusick, Dennis, 129, 135

Cusick, James, 129–31

Cusick, Nicholas (Kaghnatsho), 129, 131, 133

Cuvier, Georges, 59

Danites, 184

Dansville NY, 78

Dartmouth College, 132

Daviess County MO, 183, 184

Davis, Stephen "Old Rodsman," 165–66

Declaration of Independence, 47, 73, 109

Dekanawidah. See Tekannawitagh

Delaware Indians: at Chemung, 101; at Hogback Hill, 99; holy man of, 42; place-names of, 204n34; reading of war paintings, 33; stories about giants, 36–37; Susquehannock with, 29. See also Lenni Lenape Indians

Dennie, Louis, 122

Dennison, Nathan, 86, 91, 93

Derickson, Mary, 81, 95, 96

de Soto, Hernando, 121

Detroit, 32

"The Devil and Tom Walker" (Irving), 163

DeWitt, Mary, 116

De Witt, Simeon, 60, 106, 118, 127, 128

disease, 28, 29, 30, 69, 140

Divers Lake, 39, 40

Divers Voyages Touching the Discoverie of America (Hakluyt), 121

Djo-geh-onh. See Little People

Doeg Indians, 122, 216n18

Drake, Benjamin, 56, 57, 64

Duck Creek Reservation, 189

Duncan, John M., 131

Dunham, Martin, 195

Durfee, Stephen, 52

Dutch, 4, 29, 31, 53

earthworks: built by Nephites, 171; at Cahokia, 181, 182; C. S. Rafinesque's research on, 144; David Cusick's research on, 134, 138; in Great Lakes region, 37, 204n34; in Haudenosaunee villages, 27; in New York, 115, 166; at Niagara Escarpment, 126; theories about builders of, 118–20, 122, 123. See also archaeology

Eastern Woodlands: "apes" in, 136; British policy toward Natives of, 43; colonialism in, 31; Haudenosaunee domination of, 34, 114; history of occupants of, 133; Natives' survival in, 42; supernatural beliefs in, 35, 152; terrain of, 20; war monuments in, 33

East India Tea Company, 108

Easton PA, 105

Eliot, John, 169

Elizabeth, Queen, 121

Ellicott, Joseph, 53

Elliot, Joseph, 89, 90, 91, 212n28

Elmira NY, 105

England: Edward Pollard in, 101; execution of Captain Kidd, 163; Haudenosaunee relations with, 5–6, 12, 20, 31, 32, 44; land claimed by, 1–2, 4, 6; maps created by cartographers from, 9, 34; Native allies of, 48, 76, 81, 85–87, 94–97, 107; Native attacks on settlers from, 43; poisoning of Indians, 107, 110, 213n59; regulation of settlement, 11; after Seven Years' War, 5, 47; threat to Haudenosaunee survival, 42. See also British Isles

Enlightenment, 64, 105, 118, 161

Enos, book of, 173

Episcopal Church, 189

Erie Canal, 73, 115, 117, 118, 135, 155, 188, 219n1, 220n4

Erie Indians, 23, 27, 28, 68, 138, 139, 140, 203n24

Erwin, Arthur, 105

Erwin, Charles H., 196

Erwin, Francis, 106

Erwin, Samuel, 105–6

European Magazine, 202n19

Europeans: agricultural imports of, 38; ancient ancestors of, 142, 144, 149; artifacts of, 166; as builders of earthworks, 115, 121, 122; effect on Haudenosaunee society, 28–30, 125; expansion into Native lands, 43; Great Spirit's creation of, 42; historical knowledge of, 34–35; interpretations of landmarks, 10, 13, 123; learned societies of, 118; maps by, 1; and Native history, 148, 152; warfare style of, 98

Evans, Lewis, 5, 7, 9, 10, 20

extinction: of animals, 41, 49; attitudes toward, 59, 61, 123; of mastodon, 58, 59; threat of Native, 43, 49, 68, 71, 130, 131

Farmer's Brother. *See* Honayawas

Far West, 183, 184

Fayette NY, 179

Ferguson, Adam, 64

Finger Lakes, 7, 57, 118

Finney, Charles Grandison, 156

fire-dragons, 39, 40

fishing, 49, 52, 63, 68

Five Nations: history of, 134–35, 137, 139; land claimed by, 34; name for Algonquin language, 24; peace promoted by, 24, 26; population in 1630, 68; Tuscaroras' joining of, 30–31; warfare of, 28, 139, 140. *See also* Haudenosaunee

Flint, 17, 134, 136

flint, 40. *See also* stones

Flint, Timothy, 104

Florula Ludoviciana (Rafinesque), 142–43

forest land: benefits of clearing, 62; clearing of animals from, 57, 63; haunted by Montours, 96; in Iroquoia, 21, 43–44; meaningful places in, 34, 39; migrations to, 37; Natives' survival on, 71, 73; as site of American heroism, 104, 105, 108; transformation of, 49, 53, 57–58, 63, 64, 67, 68, 151, 152

Fort Alden, 93

Fort Freeland: description of battle at, 94–97, 101, 213n39; description of structure, 81; John Montour's death and wounding at, 101, 102; and Painted Post legend, 77, 81, 82, 98, 105

Fort Kauquatkay, 139

Fort Kawnesats, 139

Fort Muncy, 92, 95, 97

Fort Niagara: John Butler's report to, 87; Natives' retreat to, 76, 101; news of John Montour's injury at, 101; poisoning of Indians at, 107, 213n59; prisoners at, 80, 82, 89, 94, 95, 98, 102; trader at, 84; Walter Butler's report to, 93

Fort Pitt, 84

Fort Schuyler, 117

Fort Wilkes-Barre, 86

Fort Wintermoot, 86, 88

Fourth of July, 73, 184

Fox Indians, 31

France: Eleazar Williams as dauphin of, 189; as enemy of Haudenosaunee, 124; invasion of

Iroquoia, 31–32, 50, 114, 204n28; land claimed by, 2, 7; threat to British-Haudenosaunee alliance, 20; trader from, 122; travelers in, 113; war with British, 47

Freeland, Jacob, 81

Frémont, John C., 186

French and Indian War. *See* Seven Years' War

French Catharine's Town, 84

Frey, Henry, 17, 18

furs, 29, 52, 81, 140

Gahontoto, 28

Gallatin MO, 184

Ganargua, 52

Gannogarae, 31

Ganounata, 32

Gardeau Reservation, 51

Gaschwechtioni, 17–19

Gazetteer of the State of New York (Spafford), 60, 103

Genesee Castle, 22, 50, 52

Genesee River, 22, 50–51, 106, 111, 138, 139

Genesee Turnpike, 51–52

Genesee Valley: account of Wyoming battle from resident of, 88; animal eradication in, 57; colonial settlement of, 48, 52; Continental army's attacks in, 50; fortifications near, 27; Haudenosaunee homeland in, 21; pre-Revolution occupation of, 76; Seneca land in, 190

Geneva NY, 52, 55–56

George, King of England, 47

George III, King of England, 109

Gertrude of Wyoming (Campbell), 87

Gientachne, 33

Gilbert, Benjamin, 102

Gilbert, Elizabeth, 102

Gilbert, Rebecca, 102, 103

Gilbert family, 89, 102

Glimmerglass. *See* Otsego Lake

Golden City, 136, 137, 146, 149

Gorham, Nathaniel, 50, 51

Goring, Francis, 101

Goshen, Orange County, 61

Grand Council, 133

Grand River, 51, 183

Grand River Reservation, 70

Grand Settlement, 32

Grave Creek, 165

Grave Creek Mound, 166, 221n23

Gray, Andrew, 133

Great Basin, 186

Great Chain of Being, 59

Great Hill People. *See* Seneca Indians

Great Island: giant animals on, 41; history of, 116, 134, 136, 146, 152; inhabitants of, 17–19, 25, 40–43, 63; revival of, 35; supernatural world of, 58. *See also* Iroquoia

Great Lakes: commerce on, 73, 115; contrast with Great Salt Lake region, 186; Haudenosaunee warfare with peoples of, 31, 32; inhabitants of area around, 36–37, 43, 136; Native lands in region of, 5, 6

Great League of the Five Nations, 25, 30

"Great Runaway," 86

Great Salt Lake, 186

Great Spirit, 41, 42, 74, 160, 169, 174

Great White Land, 145–46

Greeks, 124, 125, 128

Green Bay wɪ, 189–90

Green Mountains, 4, 162

Hahotschaunquas, 21, 28, 29, 33, 34, 43–44

Hakluyt, Richard, 121

Hall, Francis, 103, 106, 108

Ham, Curse of, 173

Hamilton Oneida Academy, 130

Hand, Edward, 99

Handsome Lake, 70, 71, 108, 194

Harmony ᴘᴀ, 163, 167

Harper, Alexander, 98

Harper, John, 80–81, 83, 98, 101

Harpersfield ɴʏ, 80

Harris, Martin, 163, 167, 176

Harrison ɪɴ, 158

Hartley, Thomas, 92, 93

Haudenosaunee: attempts to adapt, 69, 70, 74; captives taken by, 27; defense against Continental army, 50; dispossession of land, 48, 50–51, 76, 117; effect of Revolutionary War on, 48; Euro-Americans' beliefs about, 8, 63, 69, 98, 100, 124–26, 128, 134, 136, 151–53, 156; and extinction of mastodon, 60, 67; at Fourth of July celebration, 73; on hilltops, 4; historical knowledge of, 26–27; history of, 17–19, 31, 33, 34, 36, 37, 39–40, 44, 133–35, 140, 149, 177; homelands of, 1, 4–7, 11, 15, 19, 21–23, 30, 31, 34, 41, 43–44, 114, 116, 118, 137, 180, 190, 194; housing of, 22–23; identity of, 22, 24, 30, 44, 50; landmarks of, 10, 12, 51–52, 75–76, 78, 103, 110, 166; languages of, 30, 31, 146; matrilocality of, 22; meaning of name, 3; members of, 3, 30,

203n24; migration of, 36–37, 144; origins of, 30, 34, 134, 136, 137, 143, 150; and Painted Post legend, 83; political influence of, 6–7; relations with others, 23, 28; religion of, 70, 108; removal of, 187–91; representations of, 193, 195–96; reservations of, 51, 68, 106, 206n7; role in Revolutionary War, 7, 85, 94, 95, 101; sins of, 159–60; subsistence patterns of, 38, 69, 71; supernatural beliefs of, 34–35, 38–41, 58, 71, 74, 135, 165, 204n33; trails of, 19, 51–52, 201n6; villages of, 20–23, 27, 38, 44, 156; violence of, 25, 26, 28–29, 32–34, 77, 92, 124, 136, 139, 140. *See also* Five Nations

Hayouwaghtengh. *See* Hiawatha

Hebrew language, 150, 169

Heckewelder, John, 33, 36–37, 149

Hepburn, Colonel, 97

Herodotus, 124

Hiawatha, 25–26, 140, 218n48

Hill Cumorah, 167, 170–71, 174, 183, 186, 187, 222n35

Hindus, 143, 144, 145, 150

History of the Five Nations (Colden), 133

The History of the Five Nations of Canada, Which are Dependent on the Province of New York in America (Colden), 6

The History of the Province of New-York (Smith), 125

History of the United States (Willard), 85, 87

Hog-back, battle of the, 81, 98, 99

Holder of the Heavens, 17, 30, 35, 38, 40–41, 134, 136, 137

Holland Land Company, 51, 52, 188, 189

Holland Land Purchase, 51, 53

Honayawas, 123

Hooker, John H., 56

Hopewell culture, 120, 123, 182

Hopkins, Gerald, 70

Hopkins, Samuel Miles, 73

Hosack, David, 60

Hudson Bay, 125

Hudson River, 4, 14, 58, 68, 137, 204n33

Humphreys, David, 55

Hunter, Samuel, 97

hunting: in Adirondack Mountains, 57–58; Haudenosaunee land for, 31, 32, 140; by Haudenosaunee men, 49, 52; Native Americans' history of, 63; of predatory animals, 54–57; as stage of social development, 64, 68, 70, 105; subsistence patterns of, 38, 69, 71

Huron Indians. *See* Wyandot Indians

Huron River, 37
"Hymn for New England" (Watts), 67, 209n39

Ice Age, 41
Illini Indians, 29, 31, 129
Illinois, 184–85
Illinois River, 182
Improved Order of Red Men (IORM), 193–96
Independence MO, 180
India, 144, 145
Indian territory, 180
Ingersoll, Peter, 164
Inglis, James H., 187
Ireland, 149, 159
Iroquoia: agriculture in, 37–38, 47–48, 49, 63;
    Americans' destruction and alteration of,
    11–12, 31, 48–50, 52–53, 67–69, 74, 76, 83, 92,
    103, 113, 114, 116–18, 151, 191, 195–97; ancient
    treasure and artifacts in, 163–66; boundar-
    ies of, 6; captive in, 100; Christianity in, 183;
    description of, 4; Erie Canal travelers in, 135;
    European presence in, 18–19, 43–44; giants
    in, 35, 204n33; histories of occupants of, 25,
    30–31, 115–16, 119, 121–23, 128, 129, 134–35, 140,
    152, 176–77; maps of, 2, 5, 7, 8, 9; meaningful
    places in, 7–9, 13, 19, 24–28, 32–35, 39, 44, 138,
    187, 192, 196–97, 210n8; Mormons in, 14, 157,
    161, 176; mosquitoes in, 41; naturalists' explo-
    ration of, 59; peace in, 26; place-names in, 98;
    during Revolutionary War, 11, 99; transporta-
    tion in, 19–20; "vanishing Indian" stories in,
    79, 109, 110; villages in, 20–23. See also Great
    Island; Haudenosaunee, homelands of; New
    York State
Iroquoian language, 23–24, 30, 31, 146, 199n4
"The Iroquois" (Clinton), 109–10
Iroquois Six Nations. See Haudenosaunee
Irving, Washington, 163
Israel, 159, 168–69, 171
Ithaca Journal, 56
Ithaca NY, 56, 118

Jackson, Andrew, 104–5, 180, 188
Jackson County MO, 180, 181
Jefferson, Thomas, 47, 60, 62, 120, 141
Jenkins's Fort, 86, 90
Jennings, Francis, 4
Jerusalem, 168, 169, 171, 175
Jesuit missionaries, 40, 174
Jewish influence, 150–51, 169, 174
Jiconsaseh. See Yagowanea, Queen

Johnson, Guy, 7, 8, 19, 22
Johnson, William, 42
Jones, Horatio, 107
Jones, William, 145
Junius Township, 131

Kaaterskill Falls, 15
Kabarda, 124
Kabardinski, 124
Kahkwas. See Kakouagoga
Kah-yah-tak-ne-t'-ke-tah'-keh, 41
Kaiutwahku. See Cornplanter
Kakouagoga, 203n24
Kanadesaga, 22, 23, 32, 50, 52, 100
Kanastoretar, 114
Kanchilak family, 88
Kanonwalohale. See Oneida Castle
Kansas Territory, 190–91
Kanyu?keha:ka. See Mohawk Indians
Kauhanauka, 138, 139, 140, 152
Kauqautau, 108
Kauquatkay, 139
Kaw-na-taw-te-ruh, 137
Kayohkno'nq?. See Cayuga Indians
Kendaia, 100, 103
Kennebec Indians, 72
Kentucky, 41, 104, 119, 142, 143, 144, 147, 216n18
Kiadote ("King" of Onondaga), 114
Kienuka, 139, 218n48. See also Kauhanauka
King, John, 55
King, Rufus, 60
King, William, 123
Kings College. See Columbia College
    (University)
Kingston, Ontario, 24
Kirkland, Samuel: accounts of Seneca wars,
    122; crossing of Oneida Lake in thunder-
    storm, 35; on curse of Indians, 173; educa-
    tion of Indians, 130, 132; missionary work
    of, 189; on Native migrations, 37; support of
    Americans in Revolutionary War, 48; travels
    through Iroquoia, 21, 27, 38, 39, 138, 202n19
Kirtland OH, 179, 183
Knaphus, Torleif S., 187
Knox, John, 81, 83, 98
Krishna, 145, 146
Kuskehsawkich. See Oswego Falls

Lafayette, Marquis de, 129
Lake Champlain, 4
Lake Erie, 6, 51, 53, 118, 139

Lake George, 4, 40

Lake Huron, 6

Lake Ontario, 4, 6, 51, 57, 113, 118, 126

Lake Otsego, 93

Lakota Indians, 6

Laman, 168–70

Lamanites: in Book of Mormon, 180; characteristics of, 173–75; Joseph Smith's evidence of, 182; as Native Americans, 172, 173; New Jerusalem near, 180; redemption of, 176; rejection of Christianity, 171; remains of, 182–83; warfare of, 157, 171, 176

land, 42–44. *See also* Haudenosaunee, homelands of

Lapham, Fayette, 163

The Last of the Mohicans (Cooper), 14–15, 83

Lebanon CT, 98

Lebanon NH, 158

Leclerc, Georges-Louis, Comte de Buffon, 62

Lehi, 167, 168

Lenni Lenape Indians: as American ancestors, 143, 144; history of, 147, 149, 150, 176; place-names of, 204n34; stories about giants, 36–37; wooden tablet from, 148. *See also* Delaware Indians

Lewis, Meriwether, 174

Lewiston NY, 119, 126, 134

Licking County OH, 131

Lincklaen, John, 53

Literary and Philosophical Society of New-York, 59, 118, 142, 159

Little Beard, 88

Little People, 40

livestock, 49, 54, 55, 64, 70

Livingston, Henry, 115, 121, 122, 128

Longhouse religion, 70, 194

longhouses, 22–24, 49, 125, 138

Lord Dunmore's War, 79

Lossing, Benson John, 91

lover's leaps, 76

Lyceum at the New York Institution, 61

Lyceum of Natural History, 142

Lycoming County PA, 92–93

Lycoming Creek, 97

Lyman, William, 91, 110–11

Maclay, William, 97

Madoc, Prince of Wales, 121

Mahican Indians, 4, 68–69

Mahoning Creek, 102

Malay people, 142

Mammoth Cave, 142

mammoths, 59, 60–61, 87–88, 119. *See also* mastodons

Manchester Township NY, 158, 167, 170

Mandan Indians, 174

manifest destiny, 72

Map of the British and French Dominions in North America, 1–3, 2

Map of the Country of the Six Nations, 19

Map of the Middle British Colonies in North America, 5

Map of the State of New York (De Witt), 106, 127

Marbois, François, 68

Marcellus Township, 53

Marmaton River, 190

Massachusetts, 50

Massachusetts Bay Colony, 57

mastodons: colonists' fascination with, 58, 60–61; extinction of, 49, 60, 61, 67, 74; museum exhibit of, 58–59; Natives' imagining of, 123; presence in Iroquoia, 119, 204n33; remains of, 9–10, 41, 42, 61; research on, 142. *See also* mammoths

Mather, Cotton, 125

Mather, Increase, 174

Maude, John, 53, 55

Maxwell, Thomas, 105–6

May, James, 109, 212n28

McDonnell, John, 81, 82, 95, 97, 99, 213n39

McMaster, Guy Humphrey, 80, 82, 83, 94–95, 98, 103, 109

Meginness, J. F., 92, 95–96, 105, 213n39

Meherrin peoples, 31

A Memoir on the Antiquities of the Western Parts of the State of New York (Clinton), 159

men, 38, 63, 69, 71

Menominee Indians, 189

Mesoamerica, 37

Metamora, 193

Methodists, 161

Mexico, 149

Middle East, 159, 173

Miller, Sylvanus, 59, 61

Mingo Indians, 33

Mink, 17

Missionary Society, 131

Mississauga Indians, 6, 33, 138, 140

Mississippian culture, 181

Mississippi River: British land claims on, 6; earthworks near, 13, 120, 123, 181, 182; equator in valley of, 61; Haudenosaunee at, 30, 34, 149; Indian territory near, 180, 191; migrations across, 36–37, 147

Missouri, 180, 181, 183, 184, 185, 191

Mitchell, John, 1–3, 2, 5, 6, 7, 10–11, 34

Mitchill, Samuel Latham, 60, 61, 142, 144

Mohawk and Wood Creek, 4

Mohawk Indians: agriculture by, 70–71; as Haudenosaunee, 3; homeland of, 137; leadership of, 24, 48, 130; relations with others, 138; representations of, 108, 194; role in Revolutionary War, 87; supernatural beliefs of, 40; translation of Bible, 131; villages of, 21, 23, 26, 32

Mohawk River, 4, 7, 21, 26, 50, 76, 79, 93, 114

Mohawk Valley, 72

Monk's Mound, 181

Monongahela River, 5

Monroe, James, 188

"Monster Brant" (Campbell), 87

Montezuma NY, 73

Montgomery County, 131

Montour, Andrew, 83, 84, 211n17

Montour, Catharine: commemoration of, 109; identity of, 84, 211n17; reputation of, 85, 88, 89, 90, 92, 94, 95

Montour, Esther: commemoration of, 109; identity of, 84, 88; reputation of, 85, 89, 90, 91; sources of information about, 212n28; vengeance against, 92, 93

Montour, Isabel, 83, 211n17

Montour, John: anecdotes about, 111; commemoration of, 109, 110; family of, 211n17; history of, 84, 192–93, 197; and Painted Post legend, 77, 80, 82, 83, 96, 103, 105, 106, 109, 225n22; physical appearance of, 106–8, 110; reported death of, 97, 98, 102, 213n41; role in Revolutionary War, 85, 88, 90, 94, 95; as witch, 107

Montour, John (son of Andrew), 84

Montour, Margaret, 84, 211n17

Montour, Molly, 84

Montour, Roland: captives taken by, 102; commemoration of, 109; death of, 103; at Hogback Hill, 99; identity of, 84, 210n15, 211n17; role in Revolutionary War, 85, 88, 89, 90, 94, 101

Montour Falls NY, 84

Montreal, 4

Moravia, 17, 20, 32, 33, 43–44

Morgan, Lewis Henry, 140, 218n48

Mormon (general), 171

Mormon Hill. See Hill Cumorah

Mormons: conversion of Indians, 173; history of, 14, 160, 176, 177; hostility toward, 184–88; migration from New York State, 179; migration to American West, 186, 191; origins of, 157, 220n4; search for Zion, 180, 183–84

Mormon War, 185

Moroni, 161, 171, 172, 174, 176, 187

Moroni (city), 172

Morris, Gouverneur, 60

Morrison, John, 54

Morse, Jedidiah, 4, 69

Moscow NY, 110

mosquitoes, 40–41

Mound Builders, 13, 115, 120, 122, 129, 136, 149, 152, 165, 166, 181, 197. See also Cahokia; Naples 8 mound

Moundsville WV, 165

mountain lions, 49, 54, 57, 58. See also animals

Mountain Ridge, 35

Muskingum OH, 120

Nanabozho, 150

Nanabush, 147, 150

Naples 8 mound, 182. See also Mound Builders

Native Americans: attempts to "civilize," 70; attitudes toward, 56, 71–72, 76, 81, 86, 90–91, 108–10, 175; as builders of earthworks, 115–16, 120, 122, 123, 129, 136, 152; colonists on landscape of, 11–12, 15, 20, 49, 76, 191–92; creation by Great Spirit, 41; C. S. Rafinesque's historical work about, 147; as destroyers of civilization, 13, 14, 128, 149, 150, 152, 157, 165, 177; education of, 130; effect of white Americans' on, 69; and extinction of mastodon, 60; guns owned by, 29; Hernando de Soto's contact with, 121; history of, 18, 29–30, 116, 126, 132, 148, 149, 192, 197; identities of, 22, 28, 30; as Lamanites, 172, 173, 174; as Lost Tribe of Israel, 169; maps of settlements of, 2–3, 10–11; migration histories of, 37, 62–63, 124, 219n62; Mormons' ideas about, 180, 181, 182; poisoning of, 107, 213n59; religion of, 174; removals of, 68, 180, 187–91; representations of, 192–95; role in Revolutionary War, 77, 96–97; as "savages," 62, 63, 67–68, 71, 87–89, 92, 93, 109, 124, 125, 159, 165, 173, 175; threat of extinction of, 42, 72–74; warfare of, 63, 98, 174; Welsh ancestry of, 121–22

Nauvoo IL, 185
Naywaunaukauraunah, 139
Neolin, 42, 43
Nephi, 168–72
Nephites: altars of, 183; as children of Lama-
   nites, 175; conquering of, 157, 171, 172, 176;
   genealogy of, 175; Joseph Smith's evidence
   of, 164, 182; language used by, 167; story of,
   168, 170–74
Neutral Indians, 23, 27, 68, 139, 203n24, 218n48
New England, 67
Newfield NY, 56
New France, 4, 5, 6, 83, 174
New Jerusalem, 14, 180, 181
New Military Tract, 51, 113, 128, 131
New Netherland, 29
"New Town." See Kanadesaga
Newtown, battle of, 98–103
New York City, 4, 73, 115, 116, 117, 142, 143, 155
New York colony, 6
New-York Historical Society, 104, 109, 118, 119,
   126, 142
New York Institution, Lyceum at, 61
New York Land Office, 128
New York Magazine, 115, 121–22, 123
New-York Missionary Society, 129, 133
New York state: agricultural productivity in,
   72, 73; ancient history of, 115, 126–28, 132, 151,
   159, 164, 175, 177; bounties on animals, 54–
   55; canal routes in, 113; colonial settlement
   in, 48, 52, 64; development of, 117, 118, 131,
   155, 219n1; DeWitt Clinton's political career
   in, 117; flint source in, 40; Haudenosaunee
   land in, 3, 5, 12, 50–51, 110, 117, 191, 194; Haudenosaunee trail across, 52; historical sources
   about, 78; hymns in, 175; Indian removals in,
   188–89; Joseph Smith's family in, 157; landholdings of, 51, 117, 206n7; landscape of, 14–
   15, 63, 69; land speculation in, 81, 113–14;
   maps of, 60; mastodon remains in, 61; Montour family in, 83; Mormons in, 179, 182, 186–
   87; mounds in, 13, 158; mountain lions in, 57,
   58; population of, 68, 69; Revolutionary War
   in, 85; Second Great Awakening in, 156; Six
   Nations' foundation in, 30–31; treasure hunting in, 165; witches in, 108. See also Iroquoia
New York Tammany Society, 193, 194
New York Times, 192, 196, 225n22
Niagara County, 118
Niagara Escarpment, 126

Niagara Falls, 35, 135, 141
Niagara NY, 51
Niagara River, 135, 138, 218n48
Nichols, Roswell, 164
Noah (biblical figure), 173. See also Nanabush
North America: climate of, 62; endorheic
   watersheds in, 186; Haudenosaunee role in
   shaping, 7, 10, 18, 126, 195; history of, 34, 35,
   132, 135, 142–44, 149, 152, 158, 177; Lost Tribes
   of Israel in, 169; maps of, 1–3, 7, 19; mastodons
   in, 59; Mormon history of, 14, 185; war for
   control of, 47
Northampton County PA, 102
North Carolina, 30, 31, 137, 140
North Elkhorn Creek, 144
Northumberland PA, 82, 97
Norton, John (Teyoninhokarawen), 24–26, 30,
   32, 70, 131–33, 204n28, 205n37
Norwich VT, 158
Notes on the State of Virginia (Jefferson), 120
Notowa'ka. See Seneca Indians
Nottoway peoples, 31

Oakfield NY, 27
Observations on the Climate in Different Parts of
   America (Williamson), 62
O'Connor, Roger, 159
Odawa Indians, 31
Odgen, David A., 188
Odgen Land Company, 188, 189, 190, 194
Oestreicher, David, 219n62, 221n23
The Official History of the Improved Order of Red
   Men, 194, 195
Ohio: ancient history of, 115, 119, 149; earth-
   works in, 37, 120, 121, 123, 204n34; Mormons
   in, 179, 181; Native lands in, 5–6, 5
Ohio Company, 7
Ohio River, 5, 9, 13, 41, 144
Ohio River Country, 7
Oil Spring Reservation, 51, 190
Ojibwe (Chippewa) Indians, 31, 33
Old Smoke, 99, 100, 102–3
Onandagus, 183
Ondatshaigh (creek), 25
Oneida (village), 69
"Oneida Carrying Place," 4
Oneida Castle, 4, 21, 137
Oneida Creek, 21
Oneida Indians: Christian converts among,
   173; corn myth of, 38; fortifications of,
   122, 134; as Haudenosaunee, 3; removal of,

189–90; after Revolutionary War, 12; role in Revolutionary War, 48; sale of land, 50, 98, 117; supernatural beliefs of, 35; territory of, 69, 137, 140; threat of extinction of, 68; villages of, 21, 32

Oneida Lake, 4, 21–22, 35, 51

Oneida Reservation, 51

Onnahee, 20, 21, 33, 52–53

Onondaga (village): as center of longhouse, 24; destruction of, 50; keeper of the Council Fire at, 135; land speculators at, 114; location and description of, 7, 21–22, 53; mythological tales set in, 35, 40; peace tree at, 137–38; violent history of, 25, 26, 32

Onondaga Escarpment, 39

Onondaga Indians: adoptions by, 89; corn myth of, 38; as Haudenosaunee, 3; homeland of, 137; knowledge of places in Iroquoia, 26; name of, 3–4; origin story of, 17; relations with others, 24, 25, 42, 137–38; role in Revolutionary War, 48; Susquehannock with, 29; and Tuscaroras, 30, 31

Onondaga Lake, 24, 25

Onondaga Reservation, 51, 53, 190

Onoquaga, 22–23, 26, 88, 98

Onotaʔkekaʔ. See Onondaga Indians

Ontario, 6, 190

Onyotaʼaːka. See Oneida Indians

oral traditions: Book of Mormon compared to, 175; difficulties of tracing, 28, 78, 147; as historical sources, 143; about history of American frontier, 104; about life in Iroquoia, 44, 134; about migration, 37; about Peace Queen, 139; about poisoning of Indians, 107; on Wyoming Massacre, 91

Oswego, 24, 25

Oswego Creek, 30

Oswego Falls, 30, 137

Oswego River, 30

Otochtschiaco, 33

Otochtschiaco creek, 33

Otsego County, 54

Otsego Herald, 55, 57, 58, 60–61, 72

Otsego Lake, 4–5, 15

Owasco Lake, 118

Painted Post: Benjamin Patterson at, 83; captives led past, 98; deaths commemorated by, 100, 103, 109; dedication of, 195; history of, 75–76, 96, 104–5, 114, 192–94, 196; interpretations of, 12, 77, 79–80, 98, 104, 108

Painted Post region, 81

Palatine NY, 114

Palmyra NY, 52, 158, 161–62, 165, 167, 168, 186

Palmyra Register, 158, 159

Panama, 125, 222n35

Paris NY, 130

Parker, Arthur, 210n8

Parker, Caroline, 140

Parker, Eli S., 140

Patchin, Freegift, 79–80, 98, 103

Patterson, Benjamin: on battle of Fort Freeland, 94–95; death of, 107; on John Montour's wound, 97; and Painted Post legend, 80–83, 96, 98, 101, 105; revenge against Esther Montour, 92, 93

Patterson, Robert, 82

Peace House, 138

Peace of Paris, 48, 50, 51, 107

Peace Queen. *See* Yagowanea, Queen

Peale, Charles Wilson, 58–60

Peale, Rembrandt, 58–60

Pennant, Thomas, 124

Pennsylvania: animal encounters in, 57; Benjamin Patterson in, 81, 82; captives taken in, 102; Hawkins Boone's legacy in, 105; landmarks in and near, 28, 77, 109; missionaries from, 18; Montour family in, 83, 103, 109; protection from Indian attacks in, 81; reservations near, 51; Revolutionary War in, 85, 86, 92, 94, 98; Robert Covenhoven in, 92

Penn Township, 102

Petun Indians, 23, 27, 68

Phelps, Oliver, 50, 51

Phelps and Gorham's Purchase, 51

Philadelphia PA, 59, 117, 141

Pickering, Timothy, 70, 194

Pierson, Simon, 64–67

Pineries. *See* Kaw-na-taw-te-ruh

Pioneer History of the Holland Land Purchase of Western New York (Turner), 64, 65–66

Pioneers, 186

Pittsburgh PA, 5, 69

place-names, 9, 25, 128, 171, 204n34

Pocahontas, 193

Pollard, Edward, 84, 101

polygenism, 41

Pomeroy, George, 55–56

Pontiac's Rebellion, 43

Poultney VT, 169

Poverty Point LA, 119

Powhatan, 193

Pownall, Thomas, 57

Pratt, Orson, 186

Presbyterian missionaries, 21

Priest, Josiah, 150

Proclamation of 1763, 11, 43, 47, 200n12

Puritans, 125, 169, 174, 175

Putnam, Israel, 55

Quakers, 69–71, 189, 190

Quawwa, 107, 108

Quebec, 85

Queen Esther's Rock. *See* Bloody Rock

Rafinesque, C. S.: background of, 141–42;
   on Mound Builders, 181; opinion of David
   Cusick's book, 141, 146–47; research and writing of, 145–46, 148, 150, 152, 159, 176, 219n62

Randolph VT, 157

Rangers, 85–87, 89, 94, 99

Raymond, Peter, 131

Red Jacket, 106, 159–60, 189

Red Sea, 168

Richelieu River, 4

Rigdon, Sidney, 184

River Sidon, 171

Robin, Claude Cesar, 143

Rochefoucauld, Duke de la, 69

Rochester NY, 156, 165

rock painting, 79

Rocky Mountains, 72, 185, 186

Rogers, William, 89

Roman Iroquois, 125, 152

"Romans of the Western World," 114, 116, 126,
   128, 152

Rome, 126, 128, 144

Rome NY, 11, 118

Rose Meadow, 44

Royalton VT, 158

Russia, 124

"The Sacred Isles of the West" (Wilford), 145

Salmon Creek, 24

Saturday Evening Post, 146

Sayenqueraghta. *See* Old Smoke

Schoharie Creek, 26

Schoolcraft, Henry Rowe, 221n23

Scipio NY, 118

Scovell, Seymour, 158

Scythia, 124

Scythians, 124, 159

Second Coming, 169, 180

Second Great Awakening, 14, 156, 179

"Seneca Guns," 58

Seneca Indians: agriculture by, 38, 69; on builders of fortifications, 122–23, 132; communication by, 20; Continental army's attacks on,
   50; fortifications of, 27; as Haudenosaunee, 3;
   land of, 51, 137, 188–90; leadership of, 103; map
   of settlements of, 7; migration history of, 37;
   as missionaries' guide through Iroquoia, 21,
   32; name of, 3–4; and Painted Post legend, 77,
   196, 197; on poisoning of Indians, 107; positive attributes of, 110; relations with others, 138, 139, 140, 194; reservations of, 51; role
   in Revolutionary War, 48, 77, 86, 93, 99, 101;
   sins of, 159–60; supernatural beliefs of, 39,
   40; trade with settlers, 81; villages of, 22, 23,
   27, 31, 138, 202n19; witch hunting by, 107–8; at
   Wyoming battle, 91

Seneca Lake, 22, 32, 50–52, 58, 84, 100, 113, 115

Sermon on the Mount, 170

serpents, 58

Seven Years' War, 1–2, 5, 7, 10, 42, 47, 79, 85

Sexton, John L., 193

Sexton, Pliny T., 187

Shamokin PA, 94

Sharon VT, 158

Sharp Shins, 20

Shawnee Indians, 33, 42, 56, 60

sheep. *See* livestock

Sheshecunnunk, 92

Siberia, 59, 61, 144

Sidney NY, 134

"The Significance of the Frontier in American
   History" (Turner), 105

Six Nations. *See* Haudenosaunee

Sketches of Ancient History of the Six Nations
   (Cusick), 13, 36, 116, 133, 135, 136, 138, 146

Skinner, Israel, 90

Sky Holder. *See* Holder of the Heavens

Sky Woman, 17

Sky World, 17, 38–39, 44

Smith, Emma, 167

Smith, Ethan, 169

Smith, Hyrum, 185

Smith, Joseph, Jr.: birth of, 158; death of, 185;
   and Erie Canal, 220n4; on fate of Lamanites,
   173; golden plates found by, 14, 157, 161–62,
   167, 182, 183, 187; hired to help find Spanish treasure, 163; in Illinois, 185; interest in

Mound Builders, 181; migration from New York State, 179; Moroni's foretelling of, 176; opinions about, 164; religious questioning by, 160–61; on social development, 64; surrender in Far West, 184; version of Midwest history, 183; visions of, 160
Smith, Joseph, Sr., 157, 163–65
Smith, Joseph F., 186
Smith, Lucy Mack, 157, 162, 167
Smith, William, 125
Snake Island, 147
Snake people, 144
Society of Friends. See Quakers
Society of Red Men, 193
Soh-nou-re-wah (Big Neck), 134
Sons of Liberty, 194
Sorihowane, Governor, 139
South America, 72, 145, 169
South Bainbridge NY, 163
Spafford, Horatio Gates, 103
Spain, 121, 163, 164
Sperry, James, 54
Spirit Lake. See Divers Lake
Spring Hill, 183
squash, 37, 39, 44, 49
Squawky Hill Reservation, 51
Stiles, Ezra, 120
St. Lawrence County, 210n8
St. Lawrence River, 4, 24
St. Louis MO, 13, 119, 180
Stone, William Leete, 85, 88
Stone Giants, 35, 36, 165, 204n33
stones: landmarks consisting of, 78, 115, 165; as Native artifacts, 166–67; significance to Oneida, 4; at site of mosquito killing, 41; used for Book of Mormon translation, 167; use of seer, 162–65, 167–68. See also flint
Stowell, Josiah, 163
Stuttering John. See Montour, John
Sullivan, John: battle report by, 100; invasion of Iroquoia, 11, 50, 92, 98–99, 102, 116, 156; soldiers under, 89, 100, 151
Susquehanna River: flow of, 4–5; fortifications near, 134; Hiawatha at, 25; Indian incursion at, 80; meaningful places on, 28; military forces near, 50, 97; occupants near, 22–23, 29, 94, 137; roads near, 81; Samuel Carey's attempt to cross, 88; seer stones from, 162
Susquehannock Indians, 23, 29, 30, 68
S'wetam, 145

Swetland, Luke, 100
Syracuse NY, 73

Tadodaho. See Atotraho
Taggart, 80, 82, 83, 210n15
Taggart, Arthur, 82, 210n15
Taggart, Mary, 82
Talegans, 144, 146, 149, 150
Talleyrand (French diplomat), 81
Tartars, 124, 132, 142, 144
Tecumseh, 56
Tegatainedaghgwe, 27, 28
Tehotitachse, 28, 29, 30
Tekândie, 35
Tekannawitagh, 26, 218n48
Teyoninhokarawen. See Norton, John (Teyoninhokarawen)
Thaoughweanjawegen. See Harper, John
Thatotarho. See Atotarho
Tioga, 50, 92, 98
Tioga Point, 28, 34
Tioga River, 60, 75, 80
Tiononderoge (Fort Hunter), 21
tobacco, 39, 40
Tompkins County, 56
Tonawanda, 190
Tonawanda Creek, 27, 39, 138
Tonawanda Reservation, 51
Tories, 80, 109
Totiakton, 31
Tower Hill, 183
Trail of Tears, 180
Transylvania University, 143, 145
trapping. See furs; hunting
treasure hunting. See artifacts
Treaty of Big Tree, 51
Treaty of Buffalo Creek, 190, 206n7
Treaty of Canandaigua, 194
Treaty of Fort Herkimer (1785), 50, 117
Treaty of Fort Schuyler (1788), 50
Treaty of Fort Stanwix (1768), 11, 47
Treaty of Paris. See Peace of Paris
tree of peace, 137–38
Tryon County NY, 76
Tula land, 147, 150
Turnbridge VT, 158
Turner, Frederick Jackson, 105
Turner, Orsamus, 48, 64, 65–66, 151–52, 158
Turtle, 17, 134, 136, 150, 152
turtles, 147

Tuscarora Indians: agriculture by, 70; as Haudenosaunee, 3, 30–31; history of, 13, 26, 140, 146, 218n48; on history of Iroquoia, 133; homeland of, 137, 140; language of, 31; migration of, 219n62; reservation of, 51, 138; after Revolutionary War, 12; role in Revolutionary War, 48, 129; Welsh-speaking Indians with, 122

Tuscarora Reservation, 129, 131, 134, 138, 141, 190

Tutelos, 43

Umatilla Indians, 9

Uncas, 194

Unitarians, 177

United Brethren, 131

United States: DeWitt Clinton's campaign for president of, 117; earthworks throughout, 120, 121; eradication of wolves in, 55; population of, 48–49

Urim and Thummin, 167

U.S. Army, 69. See also Continental army

U.S. Congress, 72, 188

U.S. Constitution, 59

U.S. government, 48, 51, 70, 206n7

U.S. House of Representatives, 188

U.S. Senate, 190

Utah, 186, 191

Ute Indians, 186

Utica NY, 73, 118

Van Buren, Martin, 180, 190

Van Cortlandt, Philip, 113

Van Rensselaer, Jeremiah, 113, 114

Van Schaick, Goose, 49, 129

Vedas, 145

Vermont, 162, 167, 169

View of the Hebrews (Smith), 169, 174

Virginia, 7, 31

Walla Walla Indians, 9

Walum Olum (Rafinesque), 147–48, 150, 176, 221n23

wampum beads, 26, 103, 132

Ward, Dr., 148

War of 1812, 56, 189, 193

Washington, George, 68, 70, 84, 100, 113, 194

Watch-tower, 162

Watson, Elkanah, 113, 114, 115

Watt, Mr., 96

Watts, Isaac, 67, 68

Watts, James, 82

Webster, Noah, 120–21, 163, 216n17

Welsh, 122, 166, 216n18

Wenro Indians, 23, 27, 68, 139, 203n24, 218n48

West, American, 141, 142, 175, 185, 188, 191

Western Inland Lock Navigation Company, 113

wheat, 49, 53, 70

Wheelock, Eleazar, 98

Wheelock, John, 132

White Dog Sacrifice, 160

White Isles, 145, 148

whites: behavior during Revolutionary War, 77; creation of, 41; C. S. Rafinesque's history about, 147–48; education and conversion of Indians, 130, 131; expansion into Native lands, 44–45, 70, 72, 74–76, 104, 110, 113–14, 123, 151, 177; Great Spirit's dissatisfaction with, 42–43; as heroes of American frontier, 104, 109; interpretations of landmarks, 78–79, 152; Native Americans appearing as, 122; population in New York, 68–69; Red Jacket's warning to, 160; understanding of American history, 133; understanding of extinction, 49

Whitmer, David and John, 166–67

Wilford, Francis, 145, 148

Willard, Emma, 85, 87

Williams, Eleazar, 189

Williamson, Hugh, 59–60, 62, 63

Wisconsin, 189, 190

wolves, 49, 53–58, 70. See also animals

women, 38, 49, 63, 69, 71, 89, 95, 108

Wright, Lyman, 183

Wyandot Indians, 23, 27, 33, 39, 139

Wyckoff, William, 53

Wygant, John, 106

Wyoming Valley: battle in, 85–89, 91–93, 211n23, 212n29; captives taken in, 100; John Montour's death in, 102; landmark in, 77; memorial to victims in, 109, 212n28

Yagowanea, Queen, 138–39, 140, 218n48

Yale University, 120

Young, Alfred, 85

Young, Brigham, 186

Zarahemla, 171, 172, 222n35

Zeisberger, David, 17–19, 21, 33, 44

Zelph (Lamanite), 183

Zelph Mound, 183

Zion, 14, 180, 183–85

Zion's Camp, 181–82, 184

In the Borderlands and Transcultural Studies series

*The Storied Landscape of Iroquoia: History, Conquest, and Memory
in the Native Northeast*
by Chad L. Anderson

*How the West Was Drawn: Mapping, Indians, and the Construction of
the Tran-Mississippi West*
by David Bernstein

*Chiricahua and Janos: Communities of Violence in the Southwestern Borderlands,
1680–1880*
by Lance R. Blyth

*The Borderland of Fear: Vincennes, Prophetstown, and the Invasion of
the Miami Homeland*
by Patrick Bottiger

Captives: How Stolen People Changed the World
by Catherine M. Cameron

The Allure of Blackness among Mixed Race Americans, 1862-1916
by Ingrid Dineen-Wimberly

*Intermarriage from Central Europe to Central Asia: Mixed Families in
the Age of Extremes*
edited and introduced by Adrienne Edgar and Benjamin Frommer

Words Like Birds: Sakha Language Discourses and Practices in the City
by Jenanne Ferguson

Transnational Crossroads: Remapping the Americas and the Pacific
edited by Camilla Fojas and Rudy P. Guevarra Jr.

Conquering Sickness: Race, Health, and Colonization in the Texas Borderlands
by Mark Allan Goldberg

Globalizing Borderlands Studies in Europe and North America
edited and with an introduction by John W. I. Lee and Michael North

Illicit Love: Interracial Sex and Marriage in the United States and Australia
by Ann McGrath

Shades of Gray: Writing the New American Multiracialism
by Molly Littlewood McKibbin

The Limits of Liberty: Mobility and the Making of the Eastern U.S.-Mexico Border
by James David Nichols

Native Diasporas: Indigenous Identities and Settler Colonialism in the Americas
edited by Gregory D. Smithers and Brooke N. Newman

Shape Shifters: Journeys across Terrains of Race and Identity
edited by Lily Anne Y. Welty Tamai, Ingrid Dineen-Wimberly,
and Paul Spickard

*The Southern Exodus to Mexico: Migration across the Borderlands after
the American Civil War*
by Todd W. Wahlstrom

To order or obtain more information on these or other University of Nebraska Press
titles, visit nebraskapress.unl.edu.